What Witches Do

What Witches Do

A Modern Coven Revealed

Stewart Farrar

ROBERT HALE

For
Alex, Maxine and Maya

Blessed be

First published in Great Britain in 1971

This edition published in 2021 by Robert Hale, an imprint of
The Crowood Press Ltd, Ramsbury, Marlborough Wiltshire SN8 2HR

enquiries@crowood.com

www.crowood.com

British Library Cataloguing-in-Publication Data
A catalogue record for this book is available from the British Library.

ISBN 978 0 7198 3153 9

Printed and bound in India by Replika Press Pvt Ltd

Contents

'The experience of the archetype is frequently guarded as the closest personal secret, because it is felt to strike into the very core of one's being. . . .(These experiences) demand to be individually shaped in and by each man's life and work. They are images sprung from the life, the joys and sorrows, of our ancestors; and to life they seek to return, not in experience only, but in deed. Because of their opposition to the conscious mind they cannot be translated straight into our world; hence a way must be found that can mediate between conscious and unconscious reality.'

Carl G. Jung,
The Personal and Collective Unconscious

Preface to Third Edition

I wrote this book during my first year as an initiated witch. It was published early in 1971, just after Janet Owen and I had set up our own coven. To my surprise, and natural gratification, the book came to be regarded as a standard work. Long after its British, American and Spanish editions were out of print, second-hand copies were fetching three or four times the published price. I still get letters about it from all over the world.

I do not say this to boast. What happened, I think, was that in the present expansion of the witchcraft movement (which shows no signs of slackening off), *What Witches Do* filled a gap. It combined an overall survey of the basic beliefs and practices of modern witches, with a new witch's reactions to the process of learning those beliefs and practices. And it seems that new and old witches alike – not to mention non-witches who merely wanted to inform themselves on the subject – have continued to find it useful.

Now, thanks to publishers in Britain and America, I have been given the opportunity to have it reprinted, and I hope that the same categories of reader will still find that it fills a gap.

Janet and I (now long married) have been running a coven for twenty years – till 1976 in London, and since then here in Ireland. Other covens have hived off from ours in the normal process of growth, in both countries. So we have thought very carefully about whether, in the light of our experience, this new edition of *What Witches Do* should be a rewrite, or a reprint with a preface.

We came to the conclusion that there was very little in the text that we would wish to alter, or even comment on, and that these few points could be easily disposed of in a preface. Moreover, any tampering with the text itself might spoil the quality which many readers have told us is part of its appeal – the fact that it records the reactions of a new witch entering and studying an unfamiliar field; reactions which tend to dim memories over the years, but which can help the reader to identify with the writer if their original freshness is not interfered with.

So apart from this Preface, the present text is the original one. So are the line illustrations – with the sole exception of Fig. 7(c) on page 75, the sigil of the Third Degree, which was wrong and has been corrected.

Fig. 7(b) shows the inverted pentagram, which is the accepted European sigil for the Second Degree. American Wiccan practice, however, is to display it upright, since the inverted pentagram is widely used by American Satanists, and witches over there naturally do not wish their own symbolism to be misunderstood. So in the American edition of this book, it is shown upright.

On the book in general, many people in the Wiccan movement will probably be expecting me, with hindsight, to disparage that *enfant terrible* of British witchcraft, our original teacher, the late Alex Sanders. I have no intention of doing so because it would be both unjust and ungrateful. Alex and Maxine separated soon after we left them to found our coven, and we did not see him after 1971, though we corresponded with him occasionally. He died in Sussex on 30 April 1988. We can only judge him as we knew him. He was an excellent teacher, and a genuine clairvoyant and healer. He introduced us and hundreds of others to Wicca, and it was up to us what we made of it. He did some reprehensible things, as a joker in the pack will; but many of them were only reprehensible to critics without a sense of humour.

However, to put the record straight, I must point out a couple of his failings. First, he had romanticized his own past to the point where I think he believed in the fantasy himself. His story that he copied his Book of Shadows from his grandmother's simply cannot be true; Alex's Book of Shadows is the Gardnerian one, as it was finalized by Gerald Gardner and Doreen Valiente together in the 1950's, long after Alex was a grown man. How Alex got hold of it, and somewhat inaccurately copied it (or copied an inaccurate version), remains a mystery; but having acquired it, he used it to found his own coven and the Alexandrian movement. (He had failed to be accepted into at least one Gardnerian coven which we know of.) So my statement on page 25 that 'I have never seen a Gardnerian Book of Shadows' was innocently mistaken.

The other failing was his tendency to use other people's material in his teaching – often verbatim – without acknowledging its source. For example, I found out later that the mental exercises given on pages 51–52, and the Control Book exercise on pages 52–53, were lifted, with slight editing, from the late Franz Bardon's *Initiation into Hermetics*. Again, the Charge (Appendix 2) and the Witches' Rune (page 13) were the joint work of Gerald Gardner and Doreen Valiente (see our book

Eight Sabbats for Witches for the background to this). Having reproduced them, I must apologize for the unconscious plagiarism. (Once, Alex spent several evenings dictating to us the entire text of a booklet by Eliphas Levi, without ever mentioning that it was not his own; fortunately I never committed that one to print.) I do not think Alex meant any harm by all of this. When I found out, too late, about the Bardon material and challenged him about it, he replied quite casually: 'These teachers meant their work to be used by other teachers' and left it at that.

I would no longer rank Sanders above Gardner, or alongside Levi or Crowley, as I did on page 167. But for a few turbulent years, he fulfilled a real function in the movement; he set our feet on a path which we have never regretted and performed the same function for many others, so we remember him with affection.

Maxine said to us recently: 'I am sometimes asked – was Alex a genuinely powerful magician, or a charlatan? My answer has to be – both.' And that just about sums him up ... Showman and magician to the last, he even managed to die on May Eve!

Maxine continued her work, less flamboyantly than Alex but more consistently, after their parting, and we still see her as often as possible when we visit England. She is, and always will be, a natural and very gifted High Priestess, and I am proud to have been initiated by her.

It is no criticism of Alex or Maxine to note here that one or two practices, which in 1970 I took to be general to Wicca, I have learned were in fact purely Alexandrian. The God-name 'Karnayna', for example, is everywhere else 'Cernunnos' – the historical Gaullish form. The Sanders' habit of combining the second and third degree initiations (page 56) and of sometimes partnering the initiate in a third degree rite with a first degree witch who is not yet taking his or her third degree (page 74) are certainly not general, and we ourselves would never do either of them, except in very exceptional circumstances. But every coven is entitled to follow its own judgement.

Three one-word errors in the Alexandrian Book of Shadows have been corrected in this edition. First on page 77, last line, and on page 170, line 2, the word 'Controller' has been corrected to 'Consoler'. The last word on page 79, line 39, has been corrected from 'Some' to 'None'. And on page 172, line 20, 'door of youth' has been corrected to 'land of youth'. These were doubtless all copying errors, either by Alex or earlier in the chain.

I would disagree, now, with Alex's sweeping views on the nature of time (page 41), and I am not happy with his attitude to psychic abortion (pages 126–7); but these are matters of opinion to which he was entitled.

One statement has been overtaken by events; the Gardner witchcraft museum on the Isle of Man (page 6) no longer exists. The High Priestess to whom Gardner left it, Monique Wilson, sold the collection to American commercial interests – an act for which the Craft never forgave her.

And one maxim – 'Only a witch can make a witch' (page 9) – has I feel been made obsolete by developments. Interest in witchcraft, and in the neo-pagan movement in general, has been growing faster than existing covens can handle it. Many people are adopting Wicca and similar paths as a sincere way of life, whether or not they can find an established group to initiate them. So self-initiated groups are springing up and thriving, and who shall deny them? For such people, two suggested guides are Doreen Valiente's *Witchcraft for Tomorrow* (Robert Hale Ltd., London, and St. Martin's Press, New York, 1978), which she wrote on the principle that 'You have a right to be a pagan if you want to', and Janet's and my *The Witches' Way* (Hale, London, 1984, and Phoenix Publishing, Custer, WA, 1988), which takes the same attitude.

These are few enough qualifications, I think, to a twenty-year-old book. And having made them, I qualify Martin Luther's statement and say: 'Here I stand; I can do no other; so help me Goddess.'

STEWART FARRAR
Kells
Ireland
Samhain 1990

Introduction

Late in 1969, my Editor sent me to the press preview of a film called *Legend of the Witches*. Our paper does not review films, but 'King of the Witches' Alex Sanders and his wife Maxine—who had given technical advice on the film and also appeared in it—were to be present. Alex was just beginning to get into the news, and the Editor felt 'there might be a story'.

After the screening, free Scotch in hand, I maneuvered my way through the crowd around the Sanders. Alex was a slim, balding man in his early forties, wearing dark glasses, answering questions in a soft Northern voice and giving a quick, genuinely humorous smile every now and then. Maxine, taller than Alex and twenty years younger, a striking figure with long blonde hair and a diaphanous white gown, looked a very believable witch. I awaited my moment and asked if *Reveille* could have an interview some time in the next week or two. Alex agreed courteously, said a few kind things about the paper, and gave me his address in Notting Hill Gate.

Before the interview I did my homework by reading Alex's biography, *King of the Witches* by June Johns, which had been published the month before. I found it an absorbing account of an extraordinary man. He had been initiated as a witch by his grandmother when he was seven years old, after he had accidently interrupted one of her solitary rituals. Neither Alex nor the family had any idea she was a witch, and it could have been a traumatic experience for the boy, bursting through the door to find the old lady stark naked among her strange weapons and paraphernalia; but she gave him no time to brood. She had the clothes off him, initiated him on the spot, and told him that he was now a witch too and that various dreadful things would happen if he betrayed the secret.

Fortunately for his mental health, Alex not only loved his grandmother but was himself a psychic 'natural', so he took to her training like a duck to water. For long after her death, he tried vainly to contact other witches while he continued his study of all the material he could lay his hands on. Then there was a long, materially profitable, but spiritually disastrous period of devotion to Black Magic, from which he finally extricated himself with a drastic process of self-purification.

Renewed and revitalized, he started building up his contacts, this time with more success. He met, initiated, and married Maxine Morris, another 'natural'. (By the grades through which his grandmother had taken him, he was fully entitled to initiate others according to the rules of Wicca—the witches' name for their Craft—but strictly speaking, only women; for initiation must be man-to-woman or woman-to-man.) Together, Alex and Maxine created what came to be called the Alexandrian movement: they initiated witches who in due course 'hived off' to found their own covens, from which others hived off in turn, till today Alex has no idea how many Alexandrians there are, but they are certainly the fastest-growing section of the Craft.

Homework done, I visited the Sanders (three of them now, with two-year-old Maya) at their basement flat in Clanricarde Gardens, London W.2.

I found Alex infinitely more impressive without his dark glasses. (I and others have tried to persuade him to stop wearing the things for public appearances, and I am glad to say he seems to have taken our advice.) He has an unmistakable air of authority and knowledge, and his eyes are compelling, some would say disturbing. But this aura does not cross the border into melodrama; it is saved by his puckish sense of humour, which breaks through at the most unlikely moments.

We talked for two or three hours, and he proved to be not merely visually impressive, but also extremely well-read, with a coherent and articulate philosophy.

He gave me early evidence of his powers. After he had been talking about clairvoyance and precognition, I asked him to tell me something about myself. He told me several things which could have been merely shrewd, and then said: 'In the next month or two you're going to make about £500 or £600 from a freelance assignment—something to do with law or the police.'

I could think of nothing likely at the time; but a few weeks later, out of the blue, I was asked to write an episode for the Thames Television series *Special Branch*. The fee was £550.

4

To my delight he invited me to watch an initiation the following Saturday. I realized later that he did so only because he had satisfied himself that I intended to write an impartial and not a 'knocking' piece.

The initiation struck me as dignified and moving, and the coven members as a naturally varied group who were anything but cranks. I wrote a two-part feature in *Reveille*, which seemed to go down well both with our readers and with Alex and his friends. For weeks afterwards I was getting letters asking for Alex's address. (The Editor cast a careful eye over them to make sure that none were from schoolgirls. He need not have worried; Alex is equally careful, and will not initiate anyone under eighteen.)

After the articles had appeared, Alex told me that the publishers of *King of the Witches*, Peter Davies, would like a second book as a complement to it; not a biography this time, but one dealing with the present situation—what modern witches do and beleive, and why. Would I be interested in writing it?

I would—and here it is.

I set to work, at first merely as a sympathetic observer, talking with Alex, attending his Tuesday and Thursday training classes, grilling the coven members in the local pub, and building up a library of books on witchcraft, magic, and the occult movement generally (the astonishing range and intellectual respectability of which I had, in my ignorance, not suspected until I started reading).

I soon realized that if my own book was to have any value, all this was not enough. I had to be inside.

This was a difficult decision. I had been brought up a Christian, had rebelled via Marxism and atheism, and for many years past I had settled down into what I defined as 'interested agnosticism'. Now, after a few weeks of study, I had to admit that Wicca appealed to me; that it seemed to meet my individual spiritual needs, while not presenting the stumbling blocks that had prevented my return to the Church. Above all, it seemed to offer a technique for tapping those areas of the human psyche of whose existence I was perfectly well aware, but which I had thought to be inaccessible except to a psychically lucky few.

On the other hand, if I asked to be initiated, would I merely be rationalizing a writer's ingrained curiosity?

I took the problem to Alex, with the intuitive sense that he would know (and the certainty that he would tell me) if my motives were self-deceptive.

Enough to say that Maxine initiated me into the coven on 21 February 1970—which happened, satisfactorily, to be the night of the full moon; and that I have not regretted it since.

So I would like it to be clear that I write as a witch; but that I am,

I hope, close enough to the days when I had no contact with Wicca to be able to appreciate the doubts, misapprehensions, and baulking-points of those other 'interested agnostics' to whom the book is principally addressed.

I would also like to emphasize that I write with malice towards none; for unfortunately Wicca is divided, sometimes bitterly, into more than one school of thought.

Ignoring black covens, which all of them condemn, there are four sects: Hereditary, Traditional, Gardnerian, and Alexandrian.

The Hereditary witches are those, of course, who have kept the Craft alive in a direct family line. The theory is that these lines descend unbroken from the Old Religion itself; how true this is only the families know, if indeed they do know. Alex himself is hereditary in the sense that the grandmother who initiated him was a witch before he was born, but how many generations before her followed the Craft she never told him. Alex knows of five hereditary witch families scattered about the country, but they have no dealings with him.

Quite what it is that the Traditionals do (except that apparently they wear robes for their rites) I cannot say. They keep themselves to themselves, and I have never to my knowledge met one; and since nothing goes into this book that I have not experienced, or been told at first hand, or read from a source that seems to me reliable, I must regretfully leave the Traditionals at that. If one of them reads this and cares to enlighten me, I shall be delighted.

The Gardnerians stem from Dr. Gerald B. Gardner, who was initiated by a hereditary witch called Daffo in the New Forest, led a revival movement in the 1940's and 1950's, wrote several books on the subject, founded a witchcraft museum in the Isle of Man which still flourishes, and died in 1961. Gardner was attacked by the 'old' witches for the same offence as that with which Gardnerians now charge Alex—courting publicity, which the 'old' witches shunned like the plague.

The Alexandrians are those whose initiation was received, either directly or at first, second or nth remove, from Alex or Maxine Sanders.

This question of publicity is a tricky one. Alex's view is that it clears away the fog of misunderstanding, and that at least the tip of the iceberg should be plainly and accurately visible to all and sundry if they want to see it. 'He that hath ears to hear, let him hear' is his motto; he claims that in any case only those who are ready to understand will understand. 'You could tell it all and still give nothing away,' he once said to me—a deliberate exaggeration, because there are many things Alex would not reveal except to an initiate of the appropriate grade, but I knew what he meant. The bald facts are largely available in print to those with diligence

6

and the appropriate library ticket; but much more can only be directly experienced and taught face-to-face. That is the meaning of initiation; not that it is the traditional way, or the most secret way, but that in the end it is the only way.

Three brief quotes might help here, the first from *The Tarot of the Bohemians* by the nineteenth-century French occult writer Papus:

But those who think that occult science should not be revealed must not be too angry with us . . . It is one characteristic of the study of true occult science that it may be freely explained to all men. Like the parables, so dear to the ancients, it appears to many as only the expression of the flight of a bold imagination: we need, therefore, never be afraid of speaking too openly; the Word will only reach those who should be touched thereby.

The second from a book by a more recent writer, Mervyn Llewellyn's *Initiation and Magic:*

That real knowledge in the hands of brash and ignorant man, to be used by his personal self, is dangerous, is one of the reasons why it has ever been guarded by being cloaked in the garments of symbology, allegory, parable and mythology. However at the present day, with the unconscious powers [by which Llewellyn means the unawakened majority] having more means of propaganda to aid them . . . more knowledge is being disseminated than before, in order that those who are capable may be able to take advantage of it and speed their evolution.

The third quotation is a very revealing one from Gerald Gardner himself, in his book *Witchcraft Today:*

I think we must say goodbye to the witch. The cult is doomed, I am afraid, partly because of modern conditions, housing shortage, the smallness of modern families, and chiefly by education. The modern child is not interested. He knows witches are all bunk—and there is the great fear. I have heard it said: 'I'd simply love to bring Diana in, she would adore it and she has the powers, I know; but suppose in some unguarded moment she let it out at school that I was a witch? They would bully and badger her, and the County Council or somebody would come round and take her away from me and send her to an approved school. They do such awful things by these new laws nowadays . . .' Diana will grow up and have love affairs, is not interested, or is interested but gets married and her husband is not interested, and so the coven dies out or consists of old and dying people. The other reason is that science has displaced her; good weather reports, good health services, outdoor games, bathing, nudism, the cinema and television have largely replaced what the witch had to give. Free thought or spiritualism, according to your inclinations, have taken away the fear of Hell that she prevented, though nothing yet has replaced her greatest gifts: peace, joy and content.

Gardnerians and Alexandrians alike would insist that Gardner's fears have proved groundless; Wicca is growing as never before. But his words, on the one hand, prove the need for healthy publicity (if only for 'Diana's' sake), and, on the other, support Alex's main criticism of certain of Gardner's followers (for more on this point, see p. 44) that they have allowed themselves to become 'cozy' and middle-aged, and are unwilling or unable to encourage and train young people. 'Diana' would be perfectly at home in an Alexandrian coven (and doubtless, to be fair, in many Gardnerian covens too).

At first I thought it was the publicity question, aggravated by Alex's sense of humour and undoubted gift for showmanship, that was the main bone of contention between Alex and his Wiccan critics. That and his title 'King of the Witches'—which is easily dealt with, because the title was given to him unasked by a gathering of sixteen of his own covens, and he never claims to be king of anything but his own witches.

But gradually I came to realize that his critics' real objection was deeper: namely, that Alex does not put witchcraft in a watertight compartment, but sees it as part of the occult movement as a whole. 'Sanders isn't a witch, he's a magician,' I have been told; in fact he is a witch *and* a magician. For him, the first three of the traditional ten degrees of occult initiation are (or can be, among several equally legitimate paths) those of witchcraft. Even his critics allow that he is a very powerful magician; but he remains a witch too, and a very knowledgeable and effective one.

Personally—and with due diffidence, being comparatively new to Wicca—I cannot understand this objection. Learning from Alex and Maxine, with their broader horizons than some witches would approve, I have found that this broader background puts purely Wiccan lore into perspective, making it easier to understand and appreciate its real worth. I do not see how the spectrum can be chopped up.

However, let each choose his own horizons. It is distressing to a newcomer to see witches attacking each other over their differences instead of honouring each other for the Craft they share. One wonders sometimes if certain witches have learned anything from the Christians who burned their predecessors and one another with equal fervour, and who, even as I write, are murdering each other in Northern Ireland.

So if this book offends any witch, I ask his pardon. And if he takes exception to any detail in it, I ask him to consider whether that detail is really as important as the whole picture.

When in doubt, I have accepted Alex's guidance on what should be revealed and what should be left unsaid, but since I too have taken the Oath of Initiation, I cannot shelve my own responsibility if anyone feels I have overstepped the mark. I have tried to set up signposts for those who want to understand Wicca, and I have tried to do so wisely.

Speaking of responsibility, I have written this book and must answer for its shortcomings. But 'if there be any virture, if there be any praise', I should point out that without Alex's help, information, and instruction, and many hours of his undivided time, it would not have been possible at all. From that point of view, it is as much his book (not to mention Maxine's) as mine.

Finally, a warning to non-witches who may be tempted to try out the procedures described in this book: if you are interested in anything more than the simple concentration excercises given in Chapter 4 (which are safe and even beneficial for anyone) you would be well advised to seek out a coven, or a responsible occult teacher, and work under guidance. Otherwise you may get dangerously out of your depth, and I assure you I am not over-dramatizing. And do not imagine that by getting a few friends together and trying to act out the rituals, you will have made yourselves into witches. Only a witch can make a witch—not because Wicca is a closed shop, but because, like mountaineering, it can only be safely learned from someone who knows a good deal more about it than you do, and who was trained himself in the same way. So if you want to be a witch, find yourself an existing coven, of whatever sect, because even the most rigid sectarians would agree that any coven, providing it is not black, is better than do-it-yourself.

Explanations over—let us light the candles and cast the Circle.

1.

Initiation

In the living-room of a London flat, a man stands naked* and blindfolded. His wrists are bound together behind his back with red cord, which is looped round his neck and holds his arms up to form a triangle. A white cord is tied round his right ankle.

He bought the cord himself this morning—three yards each of white, red and blue rayon upholstery cord—sellotaped the ends against fraying ('No knots yet,' he was warned). The only other things he was told to bring with him were a bottle of red wine and a black-handled knife. He had some difficulty in finding a knife which satisfied him; he knew that it must sit comfortably in his own hand, and that in due course he would have to engrave symbols on the hilt. With the idea of choosing an appropriate antique, he spent an hour in the Portobello Road market, only to discover that knifes with smooth black engraveable handles were surprisingly rare (except for Nazi daggers, which he refused to consider). He settled finally on a shapely bowie-knife from an ordinary cutler's shop. It had a brown hardwood handle, so he sprayed it with black gloss enamel.

It is just as well today is a Saturday, because the coven gave him little warning. One thing he has learned already about these people: there is an element of spontaneity, not to say capriciousness, in their arrangements. They admit to it, saying that some elasticity is needed to take best advantage of 'the power'.

---

*Editor's Note: Nudity is quite uncommon in North American traditions; most witches in the United States and Canada wear robes.

He has talked at length with the High Priest and High Priestess; as a guest (self-conscious and clothed, on a chair outside the Circle) he has watched an initiation; he has waited over a month since he asked to be initiated himself. Yesterday the High Priestess rang him up and told him to be here tonight with his knife, his cords, and his wine.

He wonders if would-be initiates in the old days, too, were kept waiting and then summoned abruptly. He suspects that they were.

The thought of the 'old days' brings another: that, naked and blind, hearing nothing but the tread of bare feet and the clink of ritual objects being arranged, smelling nothing but incense and the sweat of his own tension—he might *be* in the old days. He is fully conscious, but every stimulus reaching him is undated. This could be a sixteenth-century room full of sixteenth-century witches preparing to make him one of themselves. For some reason the fancy disturbs him, and he reaches for factual reassurance, persuading himself, for instance, that he can feel his blindfold to be twentieth-century Terylene. . .

Momentarily, although he does not move, he panics. What does he really know of these people, before whom he has allowed himself to be made helpless? What are they really going to do? Perhaps that other initiation he watched was a blind; perhaps they have something nameless in store for him; perhaps . . . He takes a grip of himself, knowing this fancy to be as groundless as the first one. It passes, but leaves in its wake a heightened sense of the meaning of the ritual. The 'ordeals' he is about to face are symbolic but not empty; they stand for an inner process, like the conquest of that unforeseen tremor of atavistic unreason.

To give his mind a specific task, he attempts to recreate what he cannot see, from his memory of that other man's initiation.

He is standing at the north-east edge of a nine-foot circle (Fig. 3, p. 45). At each of the cardinal points, a candle burns in a brass candlestick on the floor. On a small altar at the north of the Circle are a number of objects, which he tries to list in his mind. A white-handled knife. A wand. A scourge made with very unsadistic embroidery silk. A 'pentacle' or metal disc inscribed with various symbols. A censer of burning incense. Salt. A small bowl of water with a sprinkler. A metal chalice into which his red wine has been poured. White, red and blue cords like the ones he bought himself. A reel of red cotton. Most important of all from his point of view, his own black-handled knife, which from tonight will be his 'athame', his principal tool and the symbol of his membership of the Craft.

On the floor before the altar, he remembers a sword with a flat cruciform brass hilt, and a well-worn manuscript book of rituals—the hereditary Book of Shadows, which he will have to

11

copy out for himself in the days to come . . .

He finds himself calmed by the exercise of remembering. The coven themselves: except for the High Priest and High Priestess, they are waiting outside the Circle, as naked as he—but for the ankhs (those strange crosses with the looped upper arm) worn on silver chains by some of them, and the amber and jet necklaces of one or two of the women. When he was present before, as a guest outside the Circle, a few of the women had been robed. Although 'ye shall be naked in your rites' is a rule of the Goddess, he understands that its application to particular occasions is regarded as a matter of personal choice, if only out of consideration of the monthly female rhythm. Whether it was because of that, or because then he was a stranger and now he is a postulant, he does not know; but the entire coven is naked tonight. Except for the High Priest, who wears the red robe of his office.

Sudden silence jerks him away from his private Kim's Game. The movements, the murmuring, the occassional suppressed laugh, have ceased. He tenses himself, knowing that something is about to happen. The measured tread of one pair of feet tells him that the Circle is being ritually cast, the High Priestess is prescribing it with the point of the sword, leaving a 'gateway' in the north-east through which the postulant will be led.

The High Priestess speaks: 'O thou Circle, be thou a meeting place of love, and joy, and truth; a shield against all wickedness and evil; a rampart of protections that shall preserve and contain the power which we shall raise within thee. Wherefore do I bless thee and consecrate thee, in the name of Karnayna and Aradia.'

Now that the words are being spoken, the blindfolded postulate feels less blind, and his tension eases a little.

He hears the sword being laid down, and the footsteps starting again. A spray of cold water down his front makes him jump; he should have remembered that the sprinkling of the Circle came next.

His nose tells him that the censer is being carried around the Circle, and he gropes in his memory for the next step. A whiff of a different smoke reminds him; a burning candle is going round it its turn. Blade, water, incense, fire; the Circle is ready.

Now, one by one, the coven brush past him, through the 'gateway' into the Circle; each man being kissed by the High Priestess, and each woman by the High Priest, on the threshold. Man-to-woman, woman-to-man; the law of every ritual of the Craft.

Just to his left, the High Priestess's voice again; 'Ye Lords of the Watchtowers of the East, I do summon, stir, and call you up, to witness the rites and to guard the Circle.' Feet and voice move, repeating the invocation to south, west, and north.

Now the High Priest murmuring; he cannot catch the words, and his memory fails him. Straining his ears, he makes out the phrase 'that shall kneel at the sacred altar', and realizes that the High Priest is giving the High Priestess the Fivefold Kiss, which she in turn will be giving to the postulant himself later on. The spirit of the Moon Goddess is being called down into the body of the High Priestess, who will personify her for the rest of the ceremony.

He hears the whole coven start to move, stepping clockwise hand-in-hand (man-to-woman, woman-to-man again) as they chant the Witches' Rune:

Darksome night and shining moon,
East, then south, then west, then north,
Hearken to the witches' rune;
Here I come to call thee forth.
Earth and water, air and fire,
Wand and pentacle and sword,
Work ye unto my desire,
Hearken ye unto my word.
Cords and censer, scourge and knife,
Powers of the witch's blade—
Waken all ye unto life,
Come ye as the charm is made.
Queen of heaven,
Queen of hell,
Horned hunter of the night.
Lend your power unto my spell
And work my will by magic rite.
By all the power of land and sea,
By all the might of moon and sun,
As I do will, so mote it be;
Chant the spell, and be it done.
Eko, Eko, Azarak,
Eko, Eko, Zamilak,
Eko, Eko, Karnayna,
Eko, Eko, Aradia.

Three times the 'Eko, Eko' chorus is repeated, *diminuendo* and *accelerando*. Then the High Priest addresses him directly for the first time: 'Listen to the words of the Great Mother, who was of old also called among men Artemis, Astarte, Athene, Dione, Melusine, Aphrodite, Cerridwen, Dana, Arianrhod, Isis, Bride, and by many other names . . .'

The High Priestess takes up the Charge: 'Whenever ye have need of anything, once in the month, and better it be when the

13

moon is full, then shall ye assemble in some secret place and adore the spirit of me, who am Queen of all witches . . .'

She has a musical voice, young and mature at the same time, and he does not find it hard to identify her with the many-named Goddess for whom she stands. He finds himself listening to the music rather than the sense—and yet the sense seems to reach him: 'I am the beauty of the green earth, and the white moon among the stars, and the mystery of the waters . . . From me all things proceed, and unto me all things must return . . . Let there be beauty and strength, power and compasssion, honour and humility, mirth and reverence within you . . .'

So the Charge unrolls; but its end strikes the deepest chord of all, because he knows instinctively that it is true: 'And thou, who thinkest to seek for me, know thy seeking and yearning shall avail thee not unless thou know the mystery: that if that which thou seekest thou findest not within thee, thou wilt never find it without thee. For behold, I have been with thee from the beginning; and I am that which is attained at the end of desire.'

A pause, and the High Priest speaks, from the centre of the Circle. The postulate hears the words but cannot understand them: 'Kether, Malkuth, ve Geburah, ve Gedulah, le olham. Bagabi laca bachabi . . .' He stops trying to follow it, and his ears catch the High Priestess picking up the sword. He braces himself slightly as the point touches his heart.

She challenges him: 'O thou who standest on the threshold between the pleasant world of men and the terrible domain of the dread lords of the outer spaces, hast thou the courage to make the assay?'

Glad to be able to speak at last, he answers: 'I have.'

'For I say verily, it were better to rush on my blade and perish, than to make the attempt with fear in thy heart . . . Say after me: "I have two perfect words—perfect love and perfect trust." '

'I have two perfect words—perfect love and perfect trust.'

She removes the sword. 'All who have are doubly welcome. And I give thee a third to bring thee into the Circle.' So she kisses him on the lips, and leads him in, turning him to face east.

'Take heed, ye Lords of the East, that John is properly prepared to be made a priest and a witch of the Goddess.'

He has been standing still too long, and he stumbles a little as she leads him to the south, west and north to repeat the call. Then, suddenly, he finds himself in the middle of the Circle, being spun round and round, pushed from side to side, surrounded by nothing but thrusting hands and laughter. He is helpless and off balance, blind and tottering, but held up by the ring of bodies, and laughing himself with the sheer relief of movement.

After a while the hands steady him, and a bell is struck eleven times. The High Priestess speaks again; this time her voice comes to him from below.

'In other religions the postulant kneels, while the priest towers above him; but in the art magical we are taught to be humble, so we kneel to welcome them, and we say: Blessed be thy feet, that have brought thee in these ways . . .'

He feels her lips touch first his right foot, then his left . . .

'Blessed be thy knees that shall kneel at the sacred altar . . .'

Right knee, left knee . . .

'Blessed be thy phallus, without which we should not be . . .'

Just above the pubic hair . . .

'Blessed be thy breast, formed in strength . . .'

Right breast, left breast . . .

'Blessed be thy lips, that shall utter the sacred names.'

And finally she kisses his mouth. He has received the Fivefold Kiss, from the wording of which the witches' greeting of 'Blessed be' is derived.

'Before thou art sworn,' she asks, 'art though willing to pass the test and be purified?'

'I am.'

He feels fingers touching his head, and other fingers at his heels; for a moment he is puzzled, and then he remembers—his 'measure' is being taken in red thread.

'In the old days,' the High Priestess tells him, 'at the same time as the measure was taken, hair and nail clippings would have been taken from you too, and put with your measure into a secret place. Then if your tried to leave the coven, the coven would use them to bring you back, and you would never break away. But because you came into our Circle with two perfect words, perfect love and perfect trust, we give you your measure back.'

He feels the thread, doubled several times, being tied round his left arm. Then the cord which binds his right ankle is secured to his left as well, and he is helped to kneel, with his head bowed well down towards his knees.

A bell rings, three times, and he feels the flick of the silk whip across his back—one, two, three. The bell, the whip, the bell, the whip—he loses count of the exact number of 'lashes', but he knows that each group of strokes has a ritual meaning which will be explained to him in due course. The thought crosses his mind that he wishes the scourge were just a little more real—not, he hopes, because he has masochistic leanings, but through a dim feeling that a status worth having should be learned the hard way. But then, he reminds himself, the way of study and practice will be hard enough, so perhaps the wish is really for a short cut . . .

The High Priestess's voice breaks in on his self-analysis, and he realizes that the scourging is over.

'Thou has bravely passed the test. Art thou ready to swear that thou wilt always be true to the Art, and ever ready to protect, help and defend thy brothers and sisters of the Wicca, even though it should cost thee thy life?'

He wonders how it could ever come to that, but remembering all too many twentieth-century witch-hunts of other kinds, he finds he can answer 'I am' without either absurdity or insincerity.

'Then say after me . . .'

He repeats the oath, phrase by phrase: 'I, John, in the presence of the Mighty Ones, do of my own free will and accord most solemnly swear that I will ever keep secret, and never reveal, the secrets of the Art, except it be to a proper person, properly prepared within a Circle such as I am now in. All this I swear by my hopes of a future life, mindful that my measure has been taken; and may my weapons turn against me if I break this my sacred oath.'

The hands which helped him to kneel now raise him. The cords are untied, the blindfold removed; he blinks in the candlelight. The High Priestess smiles at him.

She has a phial of oil in her left hand, and with the little finger of her right she dabs oil on his right breast, left breast, abdomen, and right breast again, to mark an inverted triangle. 'I consecrate thee with oil . . .'

She dips her little finger in the chalice of red wine and repeats the four touches. 'I consecrate thee with wine . . .'

Now she kisses the same spots, and says, 'I consecrate thee with my lips, priest and witch.'

From this moment he is, indeed, a witch. He had been waiting for these words, and they bring a tingle of excitement, an actual prickling sensation that passes briefly over his skin. From somewhere in memory, a warning emerges: 'If you take but one step in this path, you must arrive inevitably at the end; this path is beyond Life, and Death.'

A warning or a promise? He has taken the step, and is content to see where the path leads.

It is time for the presentation of the tools. The High Priest is kneeling at the altar, ready to hand them up to the High Priestess one by one, for her to give to the new witch. The Maiden moves to the initiate's other side; she is the High Priestess's deputy, without as yet the impressive dignity of her senior, but definitely with the promise of it. One thing they have in common–the youth which the Law of Wicca demands of a High Priestess (and thus, by implication, of her Maiden).

The High Priestess speaks. 'I now present thee with the working tools of a witch. They are also the magical weapons. First, the magic sword. With this, as with the athame, thou canst form all magic circles, dominate, subdue and punish all rebellious spirits and demons, and even persuade angels and good spirits. With this in your hand, you are the ruler of the Circle.'

She hands him the sword, with a kiss. Once he has formally accepted it, he hands it to the Maiden—again with a kiss—to be laid on one side.

'Next I present thee with the athame. This is the true witch's weapon, and has all the powers of the magic sword.'

It is a moment which he has been secretly worrying about, for while all the other tools belong to the coven and are already consecrated, the black-handled athame is his own, still new and unblessed. And within the Craft, tools can only be consecrated in one way.

The Maiden moves to face him.

'Feet to feet, body to body, lip to lip,' the High Priestess orders. He and the Maiden hold the sharp bowie-knife carefully between them, point downwards. The Maiden places it flat against her skin, between her breasts, and he embraces her, the knife trapped by their two bodies.

She is a shapely girl, almost as tall as he; a Highland Scot, having that unique femininity which goes with soft accents, hard landscapes, and the title 'lass'. In fact, everything which would normally stimulate him.

He had obliquely questioned the High Priest about such a possible embarrassment, and the High Priest had replied cheerfully, 'Oh, you mean erections. They sometimes happen, especially with new youngsters. We don't take any notice, or else we make some joke in passing. They soon get over it.'

All very well, but nobody wants it to happen to *him*. Especially as he has talked with and likes the girl, and knows she is happily engaged to another witch. So he has remained apprehensive about this blessing.

To his surprise, what saves him is not willpower, but a sudden sense of the meaning of the rite; a feeling that as he and the Maiden hold each other, length against length, they form a polarised completeness which does indeed bless what lies within it. The moment is certainly sexual, even erotic; but he finds it holy. Its focus is not the loins, but the imprisoned blade. Desire is bypassed.

What is it that makes a witch? Perhaps basically, a sense of wonder.

He holds the athame as they step apart again, and passes it to the Maiden with the thought that whenever he uses it, her essence will lie beyond it. It is, truly, no longer a mere knife, but an athame . . . The Maiden lays it at his feet.

17

'Next I present the white-handled knife. Its use is to form all instruments used in the Art. It can only be used in a magic Circle . .

'Next I present the wand. Its use is to call up and control certain angels and genii, to whom it would not be meet to use the sword or athame . . .

'Next I present the pentacle. This is for the purpose of calling up the appropriate spirits, the appropriate spirits for an initiation being the God and the Goddess . . .

'Next I present the censer of incense. This is used to encourage and welcome good spirits and to banish evil spirits . . .

'Next I present the scourge. This is a sign of power and domination. It is also used to cause purification and enlightenment, for it is written, "To learn you must suffer and be purified." Art thou willing to suffer to learn?'

'I am.'

'Next, and lastly, I present the cords. They are of use to bind the sigils of the Art, and also the material basis; and they are necessary in the Oath.

'And now I salute thee in the name of Karnayna and Aradia, newly made priest and witch.'

The High Priestess kisses him and leads him by the arm to face the east, with the coven behind them. Making the sign of the five-pointed star in the air with her athame, she declaims: 'Ye Lord of the Watchtowers of the East, we bring before you John, newly made priest and witch. And ere ye depart to your pleasant and lovely realm, we say: hail and farewell. Hail and farewell.'

The same to the south and west, but to the north the call is longer. 'Ye Lords of the Watchtowers of the North; Boreas, thou guardian of the Northern portals; thou powerful God, thou gentle Goddess; we bring before you John, a duly consecrated priest, witch and hidden child of the Goddess. And ere ye depart to your pleasant and lovely realm, we say: hail and farewell. Hail and Farewell.

There is a sense of calm withdrawal, of the Circle fading. The initiation is over, but there is a small celebration still to come. The High Priest kneels before the High Priestess, kissing her feet and her knees. He is handed the chalice of red wine, and he holds it up to the High Priestess. She takes the athame between her palms and dips the point into the wine.

'As the athame is to the male,' says the High Priest, 'so the cup is to the female; and conjoined, they bring blessedness.'

The High Priestess drinks, and the wine and a dish of biscuits are handed round, woman-to-man and man-to-woman, each time with a kiss.

The Maiden asks him pleasantly, 'Well, how do you feel?'

He thinks about it for a moment.

'A little tense, but good,' he decides.

2.

The Roots of Modern Wicca

The roots of the *spirit* of Wicca are the fundamental nature and needs of the human psyche in its relation to the universe. The roots of the *form* of Wicca are many and various.

A great deal of misunderstanding and irrelevant criticism has arisen from confusing these two. The witchcraft movement as it exists today is a revival movement, and only a tiny handful of its members ('if any', some critics would add) can claim hereditary witch blood. Even of this handful, I doubt if any can say with certainty that their line descends unbroken from the heyday of the Old Religion. If they can, that is a fascinating historical curiosity— but it does not really affect the issue.

The revival of interest in occultism which arose during the nineteenth-century, and in 'pure' witchcraft which followed during the twentieth, spawned theorists, leaders and organizers like any other revival. Even if some of them had the spark of greatness, they were human and fallible. So critics have been able to point out that Eliphas Levi, or Aleister Crowley, or MacGregor Mathers, or A. E. Waite, or Margaret Murray, or Dion Fortune, or Gerald Gardner (or, come to that, Alex Sanders) got this or that wrong, or was naively credulous on some points, or had certain personal failings. From these undeniable facts the critics have triumphantly inferred that the whole structure is unsound, fraudulent, or at best a self-delusion.

The critics are missing the point.

When a new baby is born, one goes out and buys clothes for it. The design of those clothes is partly determined by cultural traditions stretching back to the first cave-woman who wrapped her child in an animal skin, and partly by today's conditions, materials and techniques. As the baby grows, one provides it with new clothes (still determined by the same two factors) in step with its development. But the clothes are not the baby.

Today's Wicca is a lusty child, growing fast and exercising its lungs. It was not found under a gooseberry bush, but had real parents which are reflected in its genetic make-up. It wears today's clothes, suitable for catching buses in, but the older needs of the hunter or the horseman can still be traced in their cut. Some of the family stories it has been told may have embroidered history a little, as family stories do; but that does not mean its ancestors were fictional, or that they are not still alive and kicking in its chromosomes.

To get down to cases: modern Wicca has had to build its own structure out of the materials available. These materials come from two main sources (though they overlap and always have done). First, witchcraft proper, the fertility-based philosophy of the old countryside. This was largely unwritten, nebulous, sometimes degenerate thanks to the ravages of Church persecution and the creeping fog of the Industrial Revolution; but if nineteenth-century science scorned it, twentieth-century science has done much to redress the balance by equipping the folklorist, the archaeologist and the psychic researcher with a clearer perspective and more accurate techniques.

The second source is the occult tradition. This has been continuous from time immemorial, it has a vast literature, and in one form or another its various orders and fraternities have never ceased to operate; passing on the tradition and its secrets from teacher to pupil by their own brand of Apostolic Succession.

Some modern witches would put all the emphasis on the first source, maintaining that the occult stream, while allied, is separate and should be kept so; though even they may be more influenced by it than they admit. Others acknowledge and draw on both.

What matters is not this or that detail of the form, but the spirit, and whether it works. No coven which has found a given ritual effective is going to abandon it just because a scholar proves it was invented by Eliphas Levi on the basis of misunderstood Hebrew. Nor is it going to throw away its Book of Shadows because a passage in it demonstrably derives from Charles Leland's researches among North Italian witches which he published as *Aradia, the Gospel of the Witches (see also* note 4, p. 30). After all Levi, if he was 10 per cent erratic, was learned and 90 per cent brilliant; and Leland, a folklorist of world repute, had no doubt that some of his Italian families had a witch ancestry stretching back 'to mediaeval, Roman, or it may be Etruscan times' (ibid., preface). So even when parts of the sources in current use are recent, the sources of those sources may be immeasurably ancient.

The basic theory of witchcraft and occultism is universal and constant, but the details of its practical application are the result of trial and error in many traditions, whether arrived at thousands of years ago or yesterday. That which is found to work is retained and passed on, and improvements to it which are found to work even better are adopted.

Another point might be considered, which I think any occultist would endorse. An effective ritual raises psychic power, and not all of that power is absorbed in the work to which it is put on any one occasion. Some of it accumulates. The thousandth performance of a successful ritual has behind it something of the accumulated power of the earlier 999. Tradition is not merely familiarity, it is momentum. So even if all the rituals of the Wiccan revival were new (which they certainly are not), those of them which have proved themselves in practice to be soundly based would by now have acquired a psychic momentum, and become valid parts of a living Craft. Every ritual, every spell, every evocation, or incantation must have been 'invented' at some point in history, even if one accepts that it was divinely inspired or given to its human originator on the Inner Planes. Age may have enriched it, but in the first place it was sanctified by its own effectiveness and by nothing else.

The two deity personifications of witchcraft are the Horned God and the Mother Goddess.

The Horned God must be as old as man's ability to personify ideas; he is certainly as old as religious art. 'The earliest known representation of a deity,' says Margaret Murray in *The God of the Witches*, 'is in the Caverne des Trois Freres in Ariege, and dates to the late Palaeolithic period. The figure is that of a man clothed in the skin of a stag and wearing on his head the antlers of a stag.' The Horned God's relationship to the primeval hunter is clear though complex; revered totem animal, life-sustaining prey, guise assumed for ritual purposes by the shaman who was the custodian of the tribe's psychic power, sacred victim, Sacrificed God—a complexity which has surrounded him throughout pre-history and history, to Calvary and beyond. As later economic structures replaced tribal hunting, the horns progressed from being a part of the direct representation of an animal form to being a symbol of divinity, or of the divine inspiration. As such, they passed over into the rayed halo of Christian art.

The Mother Goddess was as inevitable a concept as the Horned God. To survive, man had first to be born and suckled, and then to reach maturity and find food for himself, his mate, and her young; all else was embellishment. So humanity shaped its idea of the dual aspect of the divinity or life-force that sustained it, in terms of human polarity. Misquoting Genesis (though only, I think, to show the other side of its coin): 'Man created God in his own image . . . male and female created he Him.' The active, fertilizing, energetic, pursuing principle he saw as the divine Male; the passive, fertile, gestating, nourishing principle as the divine Female. And if He (occasionally She too, as in the case of Isis) retained the horns of His earliest personification, this was because the first image formed of any concept has the greatest vitality and tends to become the archetype.

These two, the basic God and Goddess, have survived indestructibly, precisely because they represent man's natural, archetypal visualization of that ultimate reality which he can never apprehend directly. As society grew more complex, they were multiplied into pantheons, but at their core these were only sub-aspects of the two fundamental aspects, further personified for more subtle understanding of their nature. Later, the Church tried to banish the Goddess, but failed as countless Lady Chapels testify; and it was the worshippers, closer to the facts of life than the hierarchy, who forced her readmission.[1]

Sometimes the God has predominated, sometimes the Goddess; the emphasis has varied as society became matriarchal, patriarchal, hunting, herd-raising, agricultural, predatory or pacific. On occasion, when one concept or the other symbolized the vital needs of oppressor or oppressed (whether classes or nations), God and Goddess seem to have taken sides—with the Goddess usually for the underdog. For example, the Italian witches' allegiance, as recorded in Leland's *Aradia*, was wholeheartedly to the Goddess, their natural champion against the aggressively masculine faith of their persecutors.

Modern witches honour God and Goddess, while regarding the Goddess as their special patroness and teacher (though here, too, the emphasis varies between schools of thought). The nature and rationale of their beliefs are dealt with in the next chapter, but briefly, their attitude is that since the Ultimate is unknowable, personification is necessary as a channel for tapping its power; that a God-only personification is incomplete and unbalanced, so to reach out to the God alone evokes an incomplete response; that a God-and-Goddess duality is natural, balanced, and the nearest and most complete approach to the Ultimate that man can achieve in his present state; and that these two concepts, while man-visualized, are not man-created illusions, but real and responsive. If witches lean towards the Goddess, it is to redress the balance of contemporary civilization, which is heavily oriented towards the male prinicple (socially, theologically and psychically) and dangerously out of contact with its own roots.

And if they equip their God with horns, it is because the Horned God is the archetype of the polarised God, who cannot exist or be conceived of without his complement.

The gods of the old religion always become the devils of the the new. For a thousand years after Christianity first became a State religion in Byzantium, it coexisted with older beliefs—at least away from the centres of ecclesiastical power. Many, including priests, followed both. When William who became the Conqueror (and who was himself reputed to be the son of a witch) allowed Harold to leave for England, he made him swear loyalty on two altars, one Christian and one pagan, and this incident, recorded in the Bayeux Tapestry, must have seemed perfectly natural at the time. But when the Church felt powerful enough to impose its monopoly of belief—the milestone being Pope Innocent VIII's Bull of 1484, condemning witches as heretics—it could no longer allow the Horned God to be an alternative visualization of universal divinity; he had to be branded as Satan.

In the process, Satan's image was transformed just as much as the Horned God's. In the Old Testament, Satan appears as 'the adversary'; not a rebel against God's authority, but a sort of heavenly Public Prosecutor, licensed to draw attention to the debit side of a soul's record (much as the Promoter of the Faith or 'Devil's Advocate' does when the Pope is considering a proposed canonization) or to test man's spiritual stamina (as with Job). Not a very endearing function, but perfectly respectable, and in the New Testament there seems every reason to see the Temptation in the Wilderness in this light, and Jesus's abrupt answer as a condemnation of the offer rather than of the offerer, who was 'only doing his job'. The image of Satan as the Prince of Evil at war with God is mainly a post-Biblical creation, and his horns (once a symbol of divinity) an invention of heresy-hunting days. The process was simple and neat. First, equip Satan with horns. Then point to the Horned God of the Witches and say 'Look! The Devil incarnate— and he has the horns to prove it!' Public belief that witches worshipped the Devil was further reinforced by official witch-trial records. If the defendant spoke of his God, the recorder would substitute the word 'Devil' even in a 'verbatim' report.[2]

If at the height of the 'burning time'[3] some witches fell for this propaganda themselves, and felt that while they were being hounded to death in the name of the Christian God, the Devil (equally Christian in fact) was their only friend, we can hardly be surprised. But let us be clear about it. This was an aberration, a human reaction in a period of bigotry and terror. The Horned God is not the Devil, and never has been. If today 'Satanist' covens do exist, they are not witches but a sick fringe, delayed-action victims of a centuries-old Church propaganda in which even intelligent

Christians no longer believe.

Books on witchcraft have perhaps laid too much stress on the witch trials. In the first place, the vast majority of the victims where probably not witches in any sense, but innocent scapegoats, or the losers in some local feud, or targets of personal spite. That was the golden age of paranoia and hysteria, when all the power of Church and State was ready and eager to endorse the wildest psychopathic delusions. In the second place, the only record we have of them are the official ones, which are just about as impartial as Stalinist 'histories'.

The witch trials are of interest to the student of Wiccan roots in two ways. First, because they are the source of most of the popular images of witchcraft, which must be understood to be corrected. Second, because they helped to bring about a state of affairs which many romantics prefer to ignore but which should be honestly faced; the degeneracy of a substantial part of the Craft in those days. Battered by persecution, brainwashed by hostile propaganda, driven underground, much of the old Religion must have been in a bad way. Of the witch-trial victims who were in fact witches, quite a number must have been genuinely guilty of the malice with which they were charged; malice begets malice, and terror, terror.

Where the old worship survived relatively uncorrupted, it was because it succeeded in avoiding attention, and therefore left minimal traces. In its day-to-day application (herbalism, spells, clairvoyance), something of it did survive more or less openly as the lore of wise-men and wise-women in scattered villages. But how much of the pure stream of organized worship had continuous existence, we shall probably never know.

If such was the case in England, fortunately in Italy the pure stream was found and recorded before it was too late. Charles Godfrey Leland (1824-1903) made friends with Maddalena, a Tuscan witch, who passed on to him a great deal of the lore of her kind, culminating in 1897 in the text—part prose, part verse—which he published two years later as *Aradia, the Gospel of the Witches*. Though it shows evidence in places of the effect of mediaeval politics, its basic beliefs are clearly of much greater antiquity. Leland's researches became one of the three stimuli of the twentieth-century witchcraft revival.

The second stimulus was Dr. Margaret Murray and her three books *The Witch-Cult in Western Europe, The God of the Witches* and *The Divine King in England*. Dr. Murray's weakness was that she relied too heavily on the accuracy of the witch-trial reports; her great strength was that she was the first to look at them without a preconceived Christian bias. Though her work has been much criticized, she did lay the foundations of a proper

24

understanding of the Horned God and stripped him of his 'Devil' disguise. One result of her primary interest in the trials was that she dealt only with the God, for the judges ignored the Goddess, being preoccupied with their Satan-image of the God.[4]

The third stimulus was Gerald Gardner, to whom I have already referred. Of the three, Gardner was the only initiated and practising witch, and in his practice, he was certainly influenced by the other two.

I have never seen a Gardnerian Book of Shadows, but I gather it is substantially the same as that used by Alexandrian covens. It would be an interesting study, one day, to track down the source of as many as possible of the elements in the Book of Shadows (though, as I have said, acceptance or rejection of the tenets of Wicca is not dependent on establishing the age of the Book). But one item in it may be mentioned here: that section of the Charge[5] which reads: 'Whenever ye have need of any thing, once in the month, and better it be when the moon is full, then shall ye assemble in some secret place, and adore the spirit of me, who am Queen of all witches. There shall ye assemble, ye who are fain to learn all sorcery, yet have not won its deepest secrets; to these I will teach things that are as yet unkown. And ye shall be free from slavery; and as a sign that ye be really free, ye shall be naked in your rites . . .'

This is almost a direct translation of Aradia's words to her human pupils after she had taught them the secrets of witchcraft, in the version given to Leland by Maddalena on 1 January 1897.[6]

Whether, therefore, the whole of the Book of Shadows is post-1897 is anyone's guess. Mine is that, like the Bible, it is a patchwork of periods and sources, and that since it is copied and re-copied by hand, it includes amendments, additions, and stylistic alterations according to the taste of a succession of copiers,[7] which makes it that much more difficult to estimate periods from internal evidence. Parts of it I sense to be genuinely old: parts suggest modern interpolation. I am content to accept and use it as it stands—as a kind of stalagmite of tradition, on which the drops are still falling.

The occult stream cannot be entirely separated from the popular religious stream, because it is the esoteric lore behind the public worship. This relationship has been closest when a religion has been the fundamental philosophy and way of life of a whole community, as in Egypt. Another clear example, and perhaps the best documented for academic study, is the way in which the Cabala stands behind the Bible (*see* note 16, p. 117). When, on the other hand, a religion has been persecuted and its organization fragmented, the link has often been weakened, to the impoverishment of that religion.

Esoteric teaching has always been literate (indeed, in the earliest days of writing only the initiate-priests and their trained servants *were* literate) and has never been subjected to the thorough-going persecution which public religions have suffered. This does not mean it has never been officially attacked on particular sectors of its front at particular periods, but in general the trunk has remained unscathed in spite of the lopping of individual branches. (The real trunk, occultists would point out, is in any case unassailable because it functions not in the material plane but on the Inner Planes.) Apart from anything else, the literate and cosmopolitan sophisticate has always been less vulnerable in practice than the serf or peasant, however unjust this advantage may be in theory. The priest in his temple, the magician in his study, have always been safer than the witch in her cottage or the cult-worshipper in his glade.

The origins of esoteric teaching are lost in legendary pre-history. A firm occult tradition places them in Atlantis; not merely an inherited tradition, but one reinforced by psychic techniques of recalling past incarnations, and reading the Akashic Records (*see* p. 139).

One may or may not accept the validity of such techniques, or agree about their interpretation, but the picture that emerges is a coherent one and is interesting in its relation to the spread of cultures.

The tradition places Atlantis in the Atlantic Ocean in the remote past. Its civilization, always occult-based, went through a long development under the influence of successive cosmic-evolutionary Rays, reached a very high peak, turned in the end to black magic, and sank under the sea in a final cataclysm. During that development, however, three Emigrations took place.

The First Emigration, led by priests trained under the Power Ray, crossed northern Europe and Asia and turned south along the Pacific coast, contacting more primitive cultures as it went. This Emigration is the ancestor of jujuism, fanteeism, and the astral-based cults of primitive power magic, which became a contaminated and dangerous stream.

The Second Emigration, under the influence of the Wisdom Ray, came after the polar ice-cap had moved south; it crossed Central Europe to reach the Himalayas. From here its influence spread south down the river valleys of India. This inheritance, mental-based, is still pure where it is not tainted by contact with the First, and is the source of the great mind-mastering philosophies of the East.

The Third Emigration occurred under the influence of the Love Ray, and had its focus in the spiritual plane. It happened just

26

before the cataclysm, being in fact a final salvaging by the most devoted Atlanteans of the best of their culture. Crossing North Africa, they settled in Egypt. (Going the other way, some of the collegues settled in Central America—explaining the marked affinities between the civilizations which developed there and in Egypt.) From this Third Emigration blossomed the Egyptian, Tyrian, Greek, Hebrew, Christian and Moslem spiritual achievements.

The Magi of the Second Emigration came from a culture which had absorbed the achievements of the First period, so although their teaching was Wisdom-centered, it embraced the mastery of Power. Similarly, the Third Emigration teaching was based on the Love Ray, but included Wisdom and Power and operated on spiritual, mental and astral planes.

Whether one regards the Atlantis account as factual or symbolic, its supposed effects tally with the facts of cultural development.

With Egypt, we enter recorded history. The civilization of Egypt lasted for about two and a half thousand years, and ended with Alexander the Great's conquest in 333 B.C. Throughout that extraordinary span it was, barring occasional disturbances, one of the most stable civilizations the world has known, and its culture, government, and philosophy were wholly occult-based.[8] It was inspired and run by initiates, whose esoteric learning—clear, effective, and consistent—was the heart of a richly multifarious public worship; of an economy which (owing to its dependence on the Nile floods) leaned heavily on mathematical and astronomical science of extraordinary accuracy; and of a vivid and purposeful art which has never been surpassed within its particular idiom.

The debt of Western occultism—and indeed of Western religion—to Egypt is incalculable. Moses, the tap-root of Judaism, Christianity and Islam, was a Prince of Egypt, a high initiate who defeated the magicians of Egypt on their own ground, not because he was different in kind from them, but because he was a more powerful, more highly-developed, and purer magician than they were. He took more than his people across the Red Sea; he took the Egyptian spiritual inheritance as well.

Greek esotericism drew its inspiration from Egyptian; its mysteries were those of Isis. Gnosticism, the dualistic philosophy which played an important part in the development of early Christianity until the Church partly absorbed it and partly crushed it, had obvious affinities with both Egyptian and Cabalistic thought, particularly in the concept of rising through the planes, though it developed an ascetic horror of the lower planes which was foreign to the balanced outlook of Egypt and the Cabala. (Incidentally, Gnosticism had a strong Mother Goddess tradition.)

The key source-book for a study of Egyptian religion is the Book of the Dead, or, as the Egyptians themselves called it, the 'Chapters of Coming Forth by Day'. It is a collection of texts, hymns, litanies and rituals which are really far more concerned with the living soul than the dead body. In it can be found a great many of the concepts of modern occultism; for example, the various components or levels of the human individual—physical, astral, mental, spiritual, divine spark—which I discuss in the next chapter. And from it derive many of today's occult rituals.

This spectrum of levels, through which both the cosmos and man descend from Godhead to matter and rise back again—levels which constantly interact—is the basic concept of the Cabala, the Hebraic esoteric teaching. Its 'ground-plan' is the Tree of Life, which I describe in Chapter 9.

Direct knowledge of the Egyptian sources has had to wait until the recent and tremendous achievements of scientific Egyptology, with its excavations and its breaking of the hieroglyphic code. But interited knowledge and the Cabala both influenced the mediaeval and later 'grimoires' or books of magical practice. These are dealt with in Chapter 10.

They also influenced alchemy, which most people dismiss as pre-science, while conceding that in its pursuit of the will-o'-the-wisp of transmutation it laid almost by accident the foundations of modern chemistry. Whatever one's attitude to magic, this interpretation misses the crux of the matter: that the Great Work at which the alchemist aimed, by his own technique of rising through the planes, was only incidentally concerned with the transmutation of metals. Its central purpose was the transmutation of the alchemist himself.

All these springs contributed to the mainstream of the continuing occult fraternities (which were of varying degrees of purity or degeneracy) such as the Rosicrucians, the Freemasons, and others less public. Madame Blavatsky's Theosophical movement added an Eastern element which had been largely lost in Europe.

From these bases arose the great occult revival of the nineteenth-century, the culmination of which, in many ways, was the Order of the Golden Dawn.

The Hermetic Order of the Golden Dawn was founded in 1887 by members of the Societas Rosicruciana in Anglia, which itself had been founded by a group of Freemasons, some of them claiming continental Rosicrucian initiation, in 1865. It was responsible for much brilliance and a certain amount of nonsense; its effect on the Western occult tradition was widespread and long-lasting.[9] Its ten grades of initiation, its gathering and codifying of many traditional occult elements, set standards which for good or ill are the ones by which others are judged. Among its outstanding members were S. L. MacGregor Mathers, A. E. Waite, the poet W. B. Yeats, Dion Fortune and that unmanageable genius Aleister Crowley, whose impact split it apart at the seams. He went his own way to found his Astrum Argentinum order, and Dion Fortune to found her Fraternity of the Inner Light. Of these three bodies, only the last survives actively and publicly, though it has been so 'revised' that I doubt whether its late founder would recognize it.

Crowley combined brilliance and nonsense to an even higher degree than the Golden Dawn, the difference being that much of his nonsense was deliberate, for he had a wickedly provocative sense of humour. Most people have heard only of his sexual extravagances and his title of 'The Great Beast' but he was a scholar of unique stature in his field. *Magick in Theory and Practice, The Book of Thoth,* and *777* are indispensable text-books, and his Tables of Correspondences, in particular, are generally accepted as definitive.

Such are the roots of modern Wicca. It has been a highly condensed account, because it would take a small library to cover the subject in any depth.

Within Wicca, there is much variety of emphasis on the factors I have mentioned. But the strength of Wicca is its flexibility. Rigid dogma, conformism, and monolithic organization are foreign to its spirit. The basic unit of Wicca is not any particular sect, but the individual coven and the people who compose it. Each coven has its own way, its own character, its own emphasis—and its own contribution. The mine of tradition is so rich that each coven can work its own seam.

'There are nine and sixty ways of constructing tribal lays,' said Kipling, 'And—every—single—one—of—them—is—right.'

---

[1]And, incidentally, clung to their pantheon of sub-aspects, often practically unchanged, in the form of the saints. In *Witches: Investigating an Ancient Religion* T. C. Lethbridge shows the widespread correspondence between the saint-names of English parish churches and the pre-Christian deities of the same localities.

[2]Much as the London *Daily Express* substitutes 'Socialist Party' for 'Labour Party', even within direct quotes.

29

[3]The phrase, though sometimes heard among witches, is a modern romanticism. Witches in England were customarily hanged, not burned.

[4]Though much earlier, in the ninth century, the Council of Ancyra did issue a decree that 'Certeine wicked women following sathans prouocations, being seduced by the illusions of diuels, beleeve and professe, that in the night times they ride abroad with Diana, the goddesse of the Pagans, or else with Herodias, with an innumerable multitude . . .' (*Discoverie of Witchcraft* by Reginald Scot, London 1584). Leland identifies 'Herodias' with Aradia.

[5]Given in full in Appendix 2.

[6]In the orginal Italian:

Quando io saro partita da questo mondo,
Qualunque cosa che avrete bisogna,
Una volta al mese quando la luna
E piena . . .
Dovete venire in luogo deserto,
In una selva tutte insieme,
E adorare lo spirito potente
Di mia madre Diana, e chi vorra
Imparare la stregonerie,
Che non la sopra,
Mia madre le insegnera,
Tutte cose . . .
Sarete liberi dalla schiavitu!
E cosi diverrete tutti liberi!
Pero uomini e donne
Sarete tutti nudi, per fino . . .

[7]Maxine mistrusts this tendency. Standing over me as I copied my own, she warned me: 'Every dot and comma . . .'

[8]For an illuminating explanation of Egyptian philosophy as its best, read *Winged Pharaoh* by Joan Grant.

[9]The most comprehensive account of its teaching and rituals is *The Golden Dawn* by Israel Regardie, a work which originally appeared in 1937 in four volumes but is now published in two, even though the material has been revised and enlarged. A simpler book is *the Inner Teachings of the Golden Dawn* by R. G. Torrens.

3.

What Witches

Believe

Wicca is a religion. Witches claim that it is the oldest religion on earth, that it underlies all the others and is in no way incompatible with their essence. Alex and Maxine, for instance, have initiated Christian ministers of more than one denomination into the Craft.

Priests of the ancient world would have understood this attitude. Papus insists that 'every priest of an ancient creed was one of the Initiates; that is to say, he knew perfectly well that only one religion existed' and that its various public forms merely translated the basic truths according to local cultural and temperamental needs. A priest of one deity was therefore received with honour by his colleagues in the temple of any other. They would have laughed at modern sectarian struggles for supremacy, being 'unable to suppose that intelligent men could ignore the unity of all creeds in one fundamental religion'.

The follower of One God may find it hard to see how such a system could embrace both a faith like his and the polytheisms of Egypt, Greece and Rome, or how a twentieth-century Christian clergyman could enter a Wiccan circle and salute the Horned God and the Mother Goddess. Witches would answer that the divine principle is one and unknowable at our stage of development (or as the New English Bible puts it, 'My face you cannot see, for no mortal man may see me and live'—Exodus 33:20) but the principle may be split up into aspects for our comprehension. Every monotheism does this, except perhaps Islam and Unitarianism. Christians worship a Trinity, plus that unbanishable Mother Goddess in the Lady Chapel. Even the Hebrews originally worshipped a male-female duality, although the fact is obscured in

Biblical translation; 'Elohim' is a feminine noun with a masculine plural termination, and actually means 'God-and-Goddess'.

As Dion Fortune says in *The Mystical Qabalah,* 'a goddessless religion is half-way to atheism'.[1]

Witches differ from one another in the relative importance they attach to the Horned God and the Mother Goddess. The mediaeval and post-mediaeval trials gave perhaps undue prominence to the witches' worship of the Horned God, because, as we have seen, it was deliberate Church policy to identify him with Satan and to focus attack on him for propaganda purposes. On the other hand, the mystery cults have tended to centre (like the Catholic peasant's instinctive allegiance) upon the Goddess, from Isis through Cerridwen to Aradia. Anyone who has seen the murals in the Villa of Mysteries at Pompeii, and has also seen a modern witch initiation, knows that Wicca is in this direct tradition.

In fact, as we saw in Chapter 2, modern witchcraft is a reconvergence of two traditions; the basic fertility cults of tribe and village on the one hand, and the sophisticated occultism of the Egyptian temples, the Cabala, and the magical grimoires on the other. Some Wiccan purists would insist on a sharp division between the two, but I do not think this is any longer possible or desirable. They are in a continuous spectrum, each wavelength of which enriches the others. The modern witch can buy or borrow such classic magical authorities as Eliphas Levi, such recent Wiccan pioneers as Gerald Gardner, and such able popularizers as Richard Cavendish, C. A. Burland, and Eric Maple, in paperback; key writers like Dion Fortune, Aleister Crowley, A. E. Waite, S. L. MacGregor Mathers, and Israel Regardie, and translations of the Egyptian Book of the Dead, in hardback; and mediaeval grimoires such as the Key of Solomon and Abra-Melin from the specialist bookshops, with a little searching. When all else fails there is the British Museum Library or its equivalent in other countries. These sources were inaccessible to his illiterate forerunners, but there is no reason why he should cut himself off from them, and of course he does not. The embracing of the whole spectrum is not a distortion of the Wiccan tradition, but rather a natural expansion of it in a world of increasing literacy and affluence.

'It's a matter of spiritual progression,' Alex says. 'We're beginning to pick up what the ancients had in mind, to stand on their shoulders and perhaps see a little further. We had to go through the dark ages, and now we're're coming into our own right again.'

Like all other religions, Wicca regards the non-material as the ultimate reality. But unlike many, it accepts the entire range of being, from the unknowable divine principle to the grossest matter, as inseparable aspects of that reality. Here, too, it is a question of embracing the whole spectrum, and joyously (for Wicca is above all a joyous creed). The witch does not, like the Christian ascetic, regard matter and the flesh with horror as inherently sinful; nor, like the Christian Scientist, as an illusion to be overcome. The witch shares the Moslem's belief that 'the world is the cloak of Allah', and holds that neither could have existence or meaning without the other.

Pan, the best-known form of the Horned God, is a clear symbol of this integrated range of levels. Where his hooves touch the earth, he is all vigorous animal, and his beautifully proportioned body flows upwards to be crowned by the intelligent, music-making head.

The witch does not simplify reality into mind and matter like the agnostic, nor even into spirit, mind and matter like most religions. His spectrum is more finely subdivided.

At one end is the unknowable ultimate, the Ain Soph Aur or Limitless Light of the Cabalists, from which all stems (see p. 109).

Next, the spiritual plane: the God and Goddess, by whatever names they are known or in whatever aspects they are personified—what may be called the manifestations of the Ain Soph Aur in humanly comprehensible terms; the hierarchy of lesser spiritual beings; and the souls, or essential individualities, of men and women.

Next, the mental plane. From the human point of view, this means the accretion of traits and mental functions which gather round the soul in any given incarnation. Some divide this further, into the abstract and concrete mental planes.

Next, the astral plane. This is grosser than the mental but less tangible than the physical. It can be explored by astral projection (see Ch. 12), in which the mind learns the technique of separating the astral body from its grosser twin the physical body, and using it as a temporarily independent vehicle. This plane, too, is sometimes further divided into the higher astral, lower astral, and etheric.

Finally, the physical plane—the body of flesh and bone, the universe of solid, liquid and gas, the desk at which I am writing. But to the witch, my desk, and the world outside the window, have their links and inter-dependences with the other planes just as my body has, though at differing rhythms and response-sensitivities.

This brings us to two other basic concepts in the Wiccan view of the universe: polarity and analogy.

To the witch, everything is a web of balancing opposites—positive and negative, male and female, light and darkness. Without these counterpoises, the universe would collapse.[2] This outlook (which is basically that of the modern scientist) has given rise to

33

much misunderstanding, largely because of the terminology employed. Witches speak of the 'elements' of fire, air, earth and water, and of electrical and magnetic 'fluids', which leads some people to think that witches deny the past two or three centuries of scientific advance. They do nothing of the kind, and in fact many witches are highly knowledgeable professionals in various branches of modern science and technology. These 'elements' and 'fluids' are not to be understood in the crudely literal sense of the words, but as principles. Modern knowledge of atomic structure, wave mechanics, electro-magnetic theory and so on are not, to the witch, a demolition of these concepts, but an ever more sophisticated and subtle expression and vindication of them.

Incidentally, the polarities should not be over-simplified—for example, by arbitrarily identifying male with positive and light, and female with negative and dark—but should be conceived as an interlocking network whose overall equilibrium is maintained by constant flux. Occultists regard the male as positive (active) on the physical and mental planes, and negative (receptive) on the psychic and spiritual; and the female as the other way round. Even this is an over-simplification of a complex pattern of concepts.

Fig. I. The Hexagram.

Analogy is the Hermetic principle of 'as above, so below, but after another manner'. In other words, the Microcosm (the little world, man) is a miniature of the Macrocosm (the great world, the universe) and subject to the same laws of structure and activity. This is the meaning of the best known of all occult symbols, the hexagram or Seal of Solomon, with its two interlacing triangles. It is the rationale of all sympathetic magic, because the witch believes that not only are the Microcosm and Macrocosm analogous, they are also inter-resonant; that through consciously bringing them 'in tune' by ritual, by trance, or by any other suitable one of the Eight Paths that are symbolized in the rayed star on his athame (Fig. 2), he can make the Microcosm affect the Macrocosm, just as a singer, standing in a belfry and voicing the right note, can make a great bell hum in sympathy.

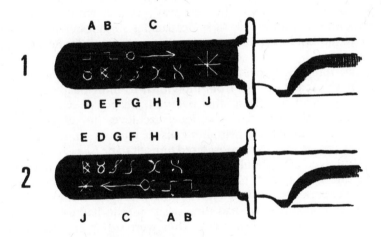

Fig. 2. Athame hilt symbols (1) as used by Alex Sanders, and (2) as given to him by a Gardnerian friend. The layout differs, but individual symbols are the same. (A) Kneeling man. (B) Kneeling woman. (C) Arrow of power. (D) The Horned God. (E) Disguised initial of Karnayna. (F) The Kiss. (G) The Scourge. (H) Waxing and waning moon. (I) Hebrew letter Aleph—initial of Aradia. (J) The Eight Paths to Magic.

The witch coven at work[3] is the singer in the belfry; it is the self-starter in the car, triggering off power greater than its own. And herein lies the key to the whole of Wiccan theory and practice.

Witchcraft is the raising and manipulation of psychic power.

Few thinking people would deny that the human psyche has vast areas that are at present untapped, dormant, and little understood. Such riddles as telepathy and precognition do not merely absorb the attention of fringe intellectuals. Budget-conscious universities investigate them and hard-headed men in the Pentagon and the Kremlin devote public funds and personnel to trying to bring them under usable control. Their existence is widely acknowledged, but whether the key to them lies in the individual, in a collective unconscious, or in a non-material plane that includes more than human forces and entities, remains a subject of debate. While the debate goes on, the witches' coven, as it has done from time immemorial, continues to work with them by methods that have been proved in practice.

There are many techniques for tapping psychic power; the witches' Magic Circle is only one of them. 'The outward expression of using the Circle dates from ancient times,' Alex points out, 'and this is the best way yet that we've found for exploiting the so-called "lost" capacities. It doesn't mean that we're old-fashioned, it just means that we haven't found a better way.'

One thing Alex does maintain; that while the range and power of these capacities vary from individual to individual, no one is without them. he claims that every single person who accepts initiation and works conscientiously achieves (for example) the power of clairvoyance within weeks or months, no matter how unpsychic he may have considered himself to be (*see* Ch. 8).

Moreover, every human being has psychic power which, even if it is unconscious and inexperienced, can be tapped by those with more experience, provided it is willingly offered. One evening, at Alex and Maxine's, we had three visitors who had asked if they could watch the Circle at work. They were sitting expectantly on the settee, sharing the pre-Circle chat, when Maxine suddenly invited them to join in.

'I want all the power I can raise to night,' she explained.

Surprised, the guests looked at each other, and nodded. They took off their clothes with the rest of us and did their best to follow the simple rites. It turned out to be a particularly successful evening's work, with which Maxine was well satisfied. Two of the three have since become witches.

The power raised within a Magic Circle is in itself neither good nor evil, neither moral nor immoral. It is simply the raw stuff of the universe, unlocked by the united will of the coven using the key of ritual; it amplifies, and is directed by, that united will. A hi-fi amplifier boosts a harsh or a pure note with equal efficiency, drawing on the impartial voltage of the mains for the purpose; the psychic amplifier of a coven within the Circle does the same.

The 'white' witch, however, maintains that 'black' working, while it may be intially successful, carries the seeds of its own retribution. Not only does power misused corrupt the user; it can also have a boomerang effect. it is a well-established occult principle that a psychic attack which comes up against a stronger defence rebounds threefold upon the attacker. Like the hi-fi amplifier again, feed-back can build into a scream of self-torment which overloads the whole circuit.

Although the power can be used for good or evil, it is not easy to use it for both, changing over at will. Dion Fortune in *Psychic Self-Defence* compares it to a flywheel, and writes:

If we have concentrated on a work of malediction and death in order to achieve an act of revenge, we cannot immediately reverse the spin of the soul and reconcentrate upon works of wisdom and redemption. We may liken the soul moving with the tide of evolution to a wheel spinning clockwise, or deosil; and a soul moving against the tide of evolution to a wheel spinning counter-clockwise or widdershins . . . The normal movement of the soul is deosil, forward with the current of evolution. We need to think many times before we undertake to reverse that spin even momentarily, in order to undertake a work of malediction and death. The old saying, 'There is the devil to pay,' is a true one. Indeed, it is questionable whether there is such a thing as momentary reversal of spin. Momentum has to be checked and worked up again before reversal of spin can take place.

This concept is reflected in the witches' name for black working—the Left-Hand Path. Beneficial working is the Right-Hand Path, and no one can go both ways at once.

An undesirable momentum can be built up intentionally, and that too may be hard to reverse. I remember a Circle on one occasion in which things began to go wrong. The acting High Priest (not Alex) was making mistakes in the ritual, perhaps through tiredness and imperfect concentration. There also happened to be a guest witch[4] from another coven taking part. The guest was certainly not malicious, but I suspect he was giving more thought to the three pretty young women of the coven than to the work at hand. Altogether, the feeling of unease was tangible. Maxine, who had delegated her High Priestess role to one of these youngsters, was watching from an armchair at the far end of the room.

The mistakes seemed to accumulate of their own accord, even after Maxine had given a warning. Finally she strode among us, stopped the rite, banished the Circle, voiced one or two pungent reprimands, and then, suddenly gentle, sent us all home.

'It's going to take me three or four hours to clear this room,' she said.

Chastened, we left her to it. The hour was past midnight, but she was far too Wicca-wise to leave the effects of such blundering to roll on unchecked.

One occasion on which Alex's help was sought was when a young pop group (all non-witches) performed, as entertainment, a magic rite about which they really knew nothing but the approximate form. Alex did what he could to keep the performance harmless, at least. But afterwards he had to bring one girl out of a deep trance, and to clear up what he called the 'psychic chaos' the group had succeeded in arousing.

The very organization of Wicca into covens, each under a High Priestess and High Priest, is not only for 'amplifier' purposes: it is also a recognition that psychic power is inflammable stuff to handle. 'You may not be a witch alone,' says the Law, and although this has several meanings,[5] one of them is certainly that when it comes to exercising psychic power there is safety in numbers, because the different personalities (and the male and female elements) balance, check and strengthen each other, and the leaders' knowledge and experience are an insurance against the power getting out of hand or being unwittingly (or wittingly) misdirected.

The storybook image of witchcraft as essentially malevolent was created by centuries of Christian brainwashing, but of course it was not entirely without foundation at the time. Apart from the fact that during what Alex calls the 'dark ages', sections of the Craft had unquestionably become degenerate, even the purer stream was also subject to the principle that persecuted minorities, being human, hit back at their persecutors with the weapons they are skilled in. *'Cet animal est méchant; quand on l'attaque, il se défend.'* And the Church had done its best to rob witches of their traditional white function. They had been the G.P.'s and spiritual advisers of the community, but in the Church's eyes, the priest was all the spiritual adviser a village needed, and bodily ailments were God's punishment for sin anyway, so who wanted a witch? It was hardly surprising that witches helped only those who trusted them, and occasionally vented their bitterness on the rest. Those were not gentle times.

Today there is no persecution, unless one includes the quickly forgotten outbursts of the *News of the World* and its kind, so there is no excuse for black working. Those who undertake it are consciously anti-social. 'Mainstream' witches, whether Alexandrian, Gardnerian, Traditional or Hereditary, regard black covens as anathema and ignore them, apart from helping their victims where the opportunity arise.

What do witches regard as 'good' and 'evil'? I asked Alex, who said: 'A thing is good for me until I feel it's not right for me. And the moment that I realize it's not right, then it's sinful to carry on with it. It is detrimental to me, whether physically, or mentally, or spiritually.'

Unlike some other religions, Wicca seems reluctant to lay down in codified detail what is 'sinful'. This reluctance is certainly not indifference to moral issues. I have found Alex and Maxine almost touchingly moral in their attitudes to malice, trouble-making, selfishness, insincerity, cruelty, disloyalty, hypocrisy, promiscuity and all the traditional sins. (Maxine's most scathing adjective is 'degenerate'.) It is, rather, a faith in man's instinctive awareness of what is good or evil, and a belief that Wicca develops that instinct.

'Wicca teaches power,' Alex told me, 'and free will to use it, once you understand *how* to use it. The training brings such a balanced outlook about power, that it gives you a sense of responsibility. So you very rarely use your power: only when you think it's absolutely necessary, and only when it's with the will of the other person.

'You're working on your physical, material level, but you're also pulling the highest aspects of yourself down into that level, and realizing them: spiritual realization in the physical manifestation.

'Aleister Crowley said, "Do what thou wilt shall be the whole of the Law,"—and that's the only thing that's ever quoted publicly. But the rest of it is "Love is the Law, love under will"—love in the general sense of living in the community.

'The moment you get this sense of the power of love, you think: I'd better not do this. It's all right for me, and it might be all right for the next person, if he's agreed to it, but it must be his will as well as mine. And this is power, it gives you a sense of responsibility.'

He added drily: 'But people aren't interested in this moral aspect of witchcraft. They're interested in sex—not in its natural sense, but in its blatant, exploited sense. If everybody who did a write-up on witches publicized the good side of what witches do, we'd be perfectly well accepted.'

Maxine put in: 'They just don't want to know.'

'I've got people off drugs,' Alex went on, 'off social security, made them reorganize their living, made them understand that you must have a certain amount of discipline for your own self—and Wicca is a discipline, because it teaches levels of consciousness, levels of being. When you try to explain this to journalists, there's nothing sensational in it. They'd rather hint at women's breasts and buttocks.'

If he sounded bitter, it was understandable. While I was drafting this chapter, he and Maxine went down to a regional T.V. studio, by invitation, for a live interview. Having the same baby-sitting problems as ordinary mortals, they took two-year-old Maya (a lovely child, bright as a button) with them. From the moment they arrived, they were treated as evil, as psychically leprous. They were alternately avoided and insulted. Perhaps the stupidest cut was when Maya was sitting quietly consuming a glass of mineral water, and someone was heard to mutter: 'Look at them—giving that child gin!'

For four hours they argued and discussed, cajoled and swore, and tried to ensure that the proposed interview would make some kind of sense. The struggle was successful, because in the end the interview went well, and they parted friends, at least with the key people. But Alex came home exhausted and angry, and postponed an important second-degree initiation for which we had all arrived at their flat prepared.

'I'd be a hypocrite to try it,' he apologized. 'I could sail through it, of course, but it wouldn't mean anything.' Then he laughed, and added, 'In my present state, you'd do better to form a Circle and protect yourselves against *me*.

Even high-grade witches are human, but if they are as they should be, they have the self-knowledge and sense of responsibility to act (or refrain from acting) accordingly. We arranged the evening's programme, and by the end of it Alex was himself again.

With Maya, Alex and Maxine face the same moral dilemma as any other parents whose views are generally regarded as 'odd'.

'People think the Craft is something dark and dirty and undesirable,' Alex told me. 'They would take great umbrage if they thought I was bringing a baby into our Craft, and for her sake I have to bow to this prejudice at the present time. I feel it's wrong that I can't say honestly and openly: "My child has to have a spiritual future, and I don't wish her really to be inside any other religion than my own, because I feel it is good for me, good for my wife, good for people around, therefore it must be good for my child."

'But we have to protect her, so Maxine took water and blessed it—the Bible says you can do these things "in my name"—and baptized her in the name of the Father, the Son and the Holy Ghost. We haven't quite decided yet, but she'll probably have a convent education. She will be in the Craft—this we know; but not for years yet. And with the amount of publicity Wicca is getting, maybe in twenty or twenty-five years she'll be able to have Wiccaning parties for her own babies, and announce it in the newspapers, and it will be perfectly acceptable. Meanwhile, we have to compromise, and this makes me slightly bitter. Maya is ours, and we give her all the love of a father and mother. Maybe a lot more than some so-called Christian parents.'

Knowing the Sanders family quite well, I can confirm that they do.

Wicca is a religion, and therefore bristles with philosophical and moral issues. Many of them are dealt with in other chapters, but one more should be touched on here: the question of reincarnation.

Witches and occultists in general believe in it, and many claim that with increasing psychic development comes awareness, dim or vivid, according to the individual, of those other lives. Alex admits to this awareness himself, but regards it as a personal thing and prefers to keep it so. The late Dion Fortune, who was not only perhaps the clearest and most intelligent of modern occult writers but also a distinguished professional psychoanalyst, regularly took patients' other lives into consideration during her diagnosis of psychic troubles, and had techniques for arriving at such information even when the patients were intially unconscious of it. *Psychic Self-Defence* gives several examples of this, and *Sane Occultism* discusses the techniques.

She asserts repeatedly that meaningful initiation into an occult order in one life has its effect in other reincarnations, and Alex says the same, believing that those who seek out Wicca are often returning to their own. 'Returning' is perhaps not quite the right word, because it implies a one-way stream of time, whereas in Alex's view time and space do not really exist. (Otherwise, for example, clairvoyant precognition would be no more than shrewd guesswork.)

'Time and space are concepts,' he says, 'to aid our understanding of the attributes and vibrations around us. All Things are there, they've already happened, and you're living it out. But there are so many pathways and passages and formations of this already-happening that you, in your own consciousness, can move in your own orbit, and can experience all these things in many different ways. You're a man in this life—you could be a woman in others. There's a general occult belief that your sex alternates from life to life. And your "next" life could be "earlier" in world history than this one. You're as close to ancient Egypt now as you will be in ten thousand years from now. We have this time concept; but a woman 105 years old, a baby six months old, and I in my forties—we're all as old as each other, because we've been coming here right from the first moment of creation.'

One last point should be made clear, on the question of morality. The witch's own conscience is and must be the final arbiter, and if it rebels against some suggestions from High Priest, High Priestess, or anyone else, he must follow his conscience.

For example: the Atlantean Emigration tradition which I outlined in the last chapter has occasionally been interpreted, particularly in nineteenth-century occult circles, in what are to me unacceptably racialist terms. (I hasten to add that Alex's coven has no such prejudices.) If anybody, no matter how impressive his Wiccan status, were to try to impose racialist attitudes on me, or to suggest treating any individual, of whatever origin, otherwise than as a human being in his own right, I would tell him bluntly what he could do with his suggestion. I might also point out that he could be a negress in his next incarnation.

Wicca does not lessen personal responsibility; it makes larger demands on it.

[1]She also offers a more accurate translation of Genesis 1:2—'And the spirit of the male and female conjoined principles moved upon the surface of the formless, and manifestation took place.'

[2]'Everything human is relative, because everything rests on an inner polarity: for everything is a phenomenon of energy. Energy necessarily depends on a preexisting polarity, without which there could be no energy. There must always be high and low, hot and cold, etc., so that the equilibrating process—which is energy—can take place.' (Carl G. Jung, *Collected Works*, 2nd Edition, Vol. 7, p. 75).

[3]This word 'work' is much used in witchcraft, and while I hope my whole book will have made its meaning clear, a brief definition may help at this point. Like the 'Great Work' of the alchemist, its central aim is the spiritual development and opening-out of the witch himself; healing and the clairvoyant helping of others are by-products. This is why 'black' working is in the end self-destructive—because the by-products frustrate what should be the central aim.

[4]Occasional courtesies apart, the general rule is that no witch may work in more than one coven. In persecution times, this was a security rule, similar to the practice of wartime Resistance cells. Today, it relates mainly to the fact that an effective coven is an organic whole with its own unique balance, which even a friendly stranger can distort. This may seem to conflict with the example given above of the three visitors, but the decision always depends on the High Priestess's judgement of the people concerned and the work to be done. And a trained witch tends to be more disturbing than an unititiated guest, even if both are well-intentioned, because his psychic personality is more clearly delineated. Also, being used to his own coven's way of working, he may become an involuntary 'back-seat driver'.

[5] Another is that solo male, or solo female, working is ipso facto incomplete. Yet another, from persecution days, is the warning that 'even if you say you're a witch alone, they won't believe you but will look for the coven'.

4.

Training of a Witch

A first-degree witch, newly initiated, may or may not be ignorant in the ways of Wicca. That depends on his personality and attitude, on how he came to the coven, and on the methods of the coven itself. At one extreme, he may be a cautious type who has read and studied for months, and been allowed to watch or take part in coven meetings, before deciding 'This is for me.' At the other extreme, he may have known it intuitively, on his first contact with the coven, and plunged straight in. Both types can make good witches, and an effective coven is a varied coven.

Covens' attitudes to recruiting differ, too. A few will initiate anyone who asks, as soon as he asks, with all the fervour of evangelists totting up the number of souls saved. Some others, slightly more logically, are lavish initiators on the principle that the unserious and the kick-seekers will drop out anyway, leaving the ones who are worth keeping. In other words, they see initiation as a filter rather than as a dedication.

I know one man who was offered initiation by a coven in Yorkshire whom he had never met, on the strength of an exchange of letters, the High Priest writing that 'we trust you completely'. My friend decided, reasonably, that if they were rash enough to trust him without seeing him, he was disinclined to trust them.

Traditionally, Wicca (like occult fraternities in general) has never actively sought recruits, but has stuck to the principle that those who were ready would find a way to it. Witches and occultists who argue bitterly about the 'secrecy or publicity' issue seem agreed on this. Even the ones, who, like Alex, believe that publicity can clear the air and counter misconceptions, are concerned merely to set up signposts for those who need them, and not tout for membership just for the sake of numbers. Alex feels, however, that this reluctance to recruit can go too far, to the extent of turning away good material. 'I try to overlook all the bickering between the sects,' he says, 'so if somebody asks to be put in touch with a coven in an area where there isn't one of my own, rather than disappoint him I give him the address of a Gardnerian witch. (Only of a publicly known one, of course. I don't want to be accused of giving anybody away.) And some of these High Priests and Priestesses ring me up and say, "We don't want these people—we've got a waiting list of three or four years." That's not wisdom. We don't want a religion of priests and priestesses—we want one of priests, priestesses and congregations: first-degree initiates, outsiders in to watch, outsiders who can come and talk. That's why my house is full of people, and other High Priests and Priestesses should be doing the same. But so many of them, in their late forties, have got a nice little thing going and they don't want the youngsters in to train. They've got nothing to teach . . . Put that in your book; it's about time it was said.

'I'm trying to establish, out of the people who get in touch with me, not just a coven of witches but a circle, of people of like mind, wanting to congregate together and practise the old rituals—for spiritual attainment in this life, not in another life. In that sense it can be said that I'm seeking converts. And out of them, I'm hoping I'll get one or two who will qualify for the priesthood in its highest sense, and who will take on the work. Male or female, married or single, I couldn't care less. I'm interested in young people—and in older ones too, to keep the balance.'

I have watched, with interest, Alex and Maxine's very flexible attitude to would-be witches. They follow no set formula, but judge each one as an individual, assessing both his own needs and potential, and his likely effect on the coven. Some applicants are initiated almost at once. Some are kept waiting, and of these, again, some only attend the classes, while others are admitted as guests to coven meetings. The system works: I have only seen one case where an error of judgement seemed to be made, and even from that the rest learned some useful lessons.

Alex and Maxine's coven is a training coven *par excellence,* and is probably unique in that respect, even among Alexandrians. I know, for instance, one Alexandrian coven which does no training at all. It meets regularly, it welcomes genuine recruits, and those recruits pick up the coven's few and simple basic rituals by example. The theory behind the rituals might just as well not exist. And yet that coven works well, and happily. It has, in particular, a fine record of healing to its credit. There is a place for the 'instinctive' coven, as well as for the intensive training ones. If every coven were a miniature university, precious little practical work would get done—and if every coven were purely instinctive, Wicca would stagnate.

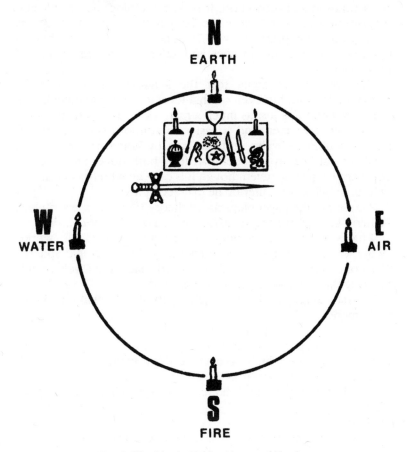

Fig. 3. The Magic Circle, Altar, and Tools.

One thing every witch must learn: how to cast a Magic Circle. The Circle has a double function: concentration and protection. It has been used in witchcraft, magic, and occult ceremonial down the ages. Its first cousins are the church, the mosque, and the synagogue, and its ancestors are Stonehenge, Avebury, and other such places in many lands.

In its concentration aspect, it symbolizes the relationship between Microcosm and Macrocosm. It is, at the same time, infinity and the focus within infinity. As a protection against hostile psychic entities and forces, it is the Akashic Egg, the consecrated sanctuary, the barrier set up by ritualized (and therefore amplified) will.

When it is a question of evoking and handling entities which might otherwise be too powerful to control, the Circle combines concentration and protection. It is both the block-and-tackle and the asbestos suit—and these are fair parallels, for with them, as with magic, the prime mover, is none other than the human operator, made both stronger and safer by the application of known laws.

The sceptic will argue that the Magic Circle is merely a psychological aid; but even on that level it is a valid and effective one. The church is just as much a man-made environment as the Circle, yet most men find it easier to attune themselves to the infinite within its walls, and the Law of Sanctuary expresses a fundamental human attitude. Man feels both holier and safer on consecrated ground, even though it is only he who has declared it sacred, by whatever criterion he may recognize.

Maxine put the psychological-aid theory to me in one sentence: 'When a kid sees the tea things laid, he knows it's teatime.'

Whatever explanation you accept, the Magic Circle works. 'Magic Circle' is a misnomer; it should really by 'Magic Sphere'. The concept is of a completely enclosed space, the Circle merely marking the place where it cuts the ground.

To cast a Magic Circle, the witch needs the following minimum equipment:

four candles in candlesticks
a sword or athame which has been duly consecrated
a pentacle,[1] also consecrated
a small bowl of water and the means of sprinkling it (a teaspoon will do)
some salt
a censer with incense (joss-sticks in a holder will do).

The Circle may be of any radius from two or three feet for solo working in a bed-sitter, to fifty feet or more for an outdoor festival combining several covens. For the normal work of a single coven indoors, the Circle is as large as the room will allow.[2]

Any witch, of any degree, may cast a Circle; witches often cast them alone for meditation or other private work. When two or more witches meet, and one of them is a woman, the Circle should be cast by her. When the coven meets, it is the job of the High Priestess.

The Circle is prepared by lighting the four candles, just outside the circumference, at the four cardinal compass points. Some witches hold that it does not matter if these are the actual north, east, south and west points, as long as it is agreed which is which. They place the 'north' candle (in front of which the altar must be[3]) at the point which best suits the layout of the room—or, for example, when the meeting is out of doors, it could be next to a rock which is suitable for an altar. Others feel more at ease if nominal and actual north are the same.

Fig. 4. The Pentacle. For the meanings of the symbols, see Figs. 2
and
7 (a)-(c).

Normally, all artificial lights are turned off, and the candles are the only illumination, apart from any fire which may be present for ritual purposes within the Circle—or for heating purposes outside it, for there is not occult virtue in goose-pimples.[4]

The incense is lit, and the censer placed together with all the other items just inside the circle in front of the north candle, either on an actual altar (usually a draped box) or an area of floor representing one.

Next, the witch consecrates the water. She places the bowl on top of the pentacle, puts the point of the athame in the water, and says: 'I exorcise thee, O creature of water, that thou cast out from thee all the impurities and uncleanliness of the spirits of the world of phantasm. In the names of Karnayna and Aradia.'[5]

She then moves the bowl aside, pours a little heap of salt on to the pentacle, and holds the point of the athame in it, saying: 'Blessings be upon this creature of salt.[6] Let all malignity and hindrance be cast forth hencefrom, and let all good enter herein. But ever mind, water purifies the body, but the scourge purifies the soul. Wherefore I bless thee, that thou mayest aid me, in the names of Karnayna and Aradia.'

She lifts the pentacle and pours the salt into the water. All is now ready for the actual casting of the Circle.

Starting at the north, she walks clockwise (deosil)[7] pointing the sword or athame down the circumference of the Circle, until she reaches the north again, saying as she does so: 'I conjure thee, O Circle of power, that thou beest a boundary between the world of men and the realms of the Mighty Ones, a guardian and protection that shall preserve and contain the power that I (we) shall raise within thee. Wherefore do I bless thee and consecrate thee.'[8] If anyone else (an initiate, or the rest of the coven) is to enter after the Circle is cast, she leaves a 'gate' in the north-east quarter by raising the athame up and over an imaginary doorway as she passes it. (In that case, once everybody is inside, the 'gate' must be closed and the Circle sealed by passing the athame, pointed downwards, over that arc of circumference.)

Now she sprinkles the consecrated water round the Circle (deosil from north to north again). Next she carries the burning censer round the Circle, and finally the fire in the form of a lighted candle, usually the north candle, which is afterwards replaced. Alternatively, there may be a pair of lit candles on the altar, and one of these may be used.

She picks up the athame, faces east, and holds the blade out in front of her, saying: 'Ye Lords of the Watchtowers of the East, I do summon, stir, and call you up, to witness my rites and to guard the Circle.'

As she speaks, she describes a five-pointed star in the air with the athame, starting at the top, down to bottom left, across to upper right, across to upper left, down to bottom right, up to the top, and down again to bottom left: six strokes in all. (This is the Invoking Pentagram in terms of the Earth element: for each element there is an Invoking and a Banishing Pentagram, with its own starting and finishing points and direction of tracing.) After she has described the pentagram, she points the athame at its centre, then kisses the blade and lays it against her heart. Facing

48

south, she now summons the Lords of the Watchtowers of the South in the same way; next those of the west, and finally those of the north.[9] The Circle and its protection are now complete.

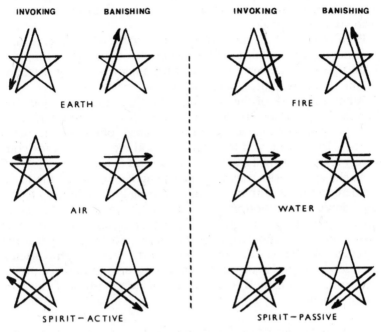

Fig. 5. Invoking and banishing pentagrams.

All these acts and phrases are, of course, merely the outer form. As with everything from celebrating the Mass to telling a woman that you love her, the form is meaningless (and may even be dangerous) without the appropriate mental, emotional and spiritual attitude. For example, when blessing the salt, it is pointless to say, 'Let all malignity and hindrance be cast forth hencefrom,' without a deliberate effort to do the same with your own thoughts. Or when casting the Circle, to call upon it to be a 'meeting place of love and truth' without banishing (or at least suspending) any feeling of resentment or deception you may have towards some other member of the coven in his everyday role.

Imagination should be consciously called upon to reinforce the ritual. While the five-pointed star is being traced into the air, Alex recommends you to visualize the point of the athame leaving a line of electric-blue light in its path. Again, for example, to the north he likes to visualize the pentagram as a window on to a cool, restful landscape of forests, lakes and grassy clearings.

If the High Priestess casts the Circle with the coven waiting outside it, she usually admits them after the carrying round of the fire. First she calls in the High Priest through the 'gate', kissing him at its threshold and spinning him to her right and behind her into the Circle. The rest are then beckoned one by one, the High Priest admitting each woman with a kiss, and the High Priestess each man, in the same way.

Each member, if he wishes, may then take part in the summoning of the Lords of the Watchtowers by duplicating the High Priestess's gestures with his own athame—having placed it on the altar in readiness, before the Circle was cast.[10]

When the work of the meeting is finished, the Circle must be banished. The High Priestess, with the coven behind her, faces east, pointing her athame, and says: 'Ye Lords of the Watchtowers of the East, I thank you for attending; and ere ye depart for your lovely realm, I say hail and farewell. hail and farewell.

As she speaks, she traces the Banishing Pentagram of the Earth element in the air with her athame, starting bottom left, up to the top, down to the bottom right, across to upper left, across to upper right, down to bottom left, and up again to the top. She kisses the blade and lays it on her heart. She then repeats the formula to the south, west and north (the coven placing themselves behind her to face each way in turn, and again copying her gestures with their own athames if they wish) and thus the Circle is banished.

Wicca teaches levels of consciousness; that, really is Wicca in a nutshell. In other words, it teaches the transfer of awareness, and action, to levels of reality (already discussed in Ch. 3) other than that on which they normally (and for most people, exclusively) function. Clairvoyance, trance, astral projection are all forms of this transfer, as are the incommunicable experiences of the mystics. They are all hard work, and have to be learned.

Alex, as I have already said, maintains that anyone can learn them, though of course the degree of success, and the number of levels which can be reached, depends on the individual. The ability to distinguish between illusory and genuine transfer of awareness to another level must also be learned: pathological hallucination is not the same thing as psychic vision. In making this distinction, common sense and a working knowledge of psychological mechanics are a great help, as is the advice of someone who is more experienced in the field than you are. There is also the elementary scientific criterion of checking results against known facts, a habit not to be despised as scepticism, because Wicca is a practical Craft. Dion Fortune in *Psychic Self-Defence* gives very useful guidance on this whole question of distinguishing the genuine from the pathological.

Learning levels of consciousness demands mind-control, so excercises to develop this come early in the training of a new witch. Alex recommends the setting aside of a few minutes every day for these, if possible morning and night, so that they become a habit. Here are three of the basic ones; each one should be mastered before the next is tried.

Exercise 1: Sit or lie comfortably, with your eyes closed, and watch your own train of thought, as though a part of your mind were a silent observer standing to one side. Latch on to one particular train of thought and pursue it attentively, allowing nothing irrelevant to that train to intrude. For example, if you find yourself thinking of a tree and decide on that subject, picture a tree, analyse it, visualize its metabolism, its development, its life-span, its seasonal rhythm, its relation to its surroundings, the 'habit' of its particular species, and instantly banish any 'non-tree' thought that starts to arise. At the same time, remain conscious throughout of yourself as observer of your own train of thought. Keep this up for five minutes on the first day, lengthening the exercise by one minute a day until you reach ten minutes.[11] If you find the exercise difficult, lengthen it more gradually. Above all, beware of falling asleep during the exercise. If there is a danger of it, stop and try again when you are less tired, or if you want to start again at once, go and rinse your face in cold water first. Some deep breathing before you begin will also help to prevent sleepiness. As you get more skilful with this exercise, you will also acquire the technique of slowing down your train of thought so that only a few concepts pass through your mind during the allotted time.

Incidentally, this exercise would do most people a lot of good, quite apart from any occult aim. It is simply a self-training in concentration, which would benefit anyone's job, hobbies or domestic life.

Exercise 2: This time hold on, not to a train of thougnt, but to a single thought or picture,; statically, allowing neither intrusion of other thoughts nor modification of the original thought. This is far more difficult to maintain, and only short periods will be possible at first, but again you should gradually increase the time until you can manage a full ten minutes.

Exercise 3: The most difficult of all—producing and maintaining an obviously vacant mind. It will not be possible at all until you have mastered Exercises 1 and 2, and even then you will only a manage a few seconds at first. Lie down very comfortably, relax your whole body, and close your eyes. After a few attempts you will find you can lengthen the time. You will have mastered this exercise when you can remain in this state of mind for ten minutes without either losing self-control or falling asleep. Thinking of absolutely nothing, while fully conscious, may sound impossible, but in fact it is quite possible, provided you build up to it through the earlier exercises.

It is a good idea to keep a diary of these exercises, entering your successes, failures, time achieved, disturbances, and any other relevant comments. 'The more attentive and honest you are with these tests,' Alex says, 'the easier it will be to be initiated into the inner mysteries when the time is ripe for you.'

The central aim of Wicca is the spiritual and psychic development of each individual witch, and for this, self-analysis and self-criticism are essential. Many occult systems ignore them, which Alex maintains is why they do not achieve good results.

Self-criticism does not have to mean self-abasement in public, or the 'mea maxima culpa' of the confessional, or Maoist breast-beating. Alex sees it as a private responsibility, and recommends the keeping of a 'Control Book' which should be for one's eyes alone. Into this book you should first enter what he calls 'all the bad side of your soul', mercilessly recording every deficiency or failure in your personality, and recalling past situations in order to put your attitude and behavior under the microscope. Every subtle variation of fault should be put down; you should return to the book day after day, re-thinking every item, adding, amending. 'The more you discover,' Alex says, 'the better for you. Nothing must remain hidden, nothing unrevealed, however great or insignificant your faults may be. Wash your soul perfectly clean, sweep all the dust out of it.'

Next, try to assign each fault to one of the four elements—fire, air, water and earth.[12] For instance, jealousy, hatred, vindictiveness and anger can be ascribed to the fire element; frivolity, self-presumption, boasting, squandering and gossiping to air; indifference, laziness, negligence, rudeness and instability to water; and lack of conscience, laziness (in another sense), melancholy and dullness to the element of earth. Any faults you find difficult to assign can be listed under 'Indifferent'; later on, with sharpened insight, you will probably be able to assign them to one of the elements. (*See also* pp. 138-40.)

Now spend a week subdividing your faults further into three groups: (1) serious major faults; (2) less serious, more occasional faults; and (3) minor and infrequent faults. This process can be more illuminating than you expect.

Having got so far with your faults, you now repeat the whole process with your good qualities. Assign such traits as activity, enthusiasm, determination, courage and daring to the fire element; diligence, joy, dexterity, intellectual gifts, kindness, lust (in the sense of joy of living) and optimism to air; modesty, abstinence, compassion, tranquility, tenderness and forgiveness to water; respect for others, endurance, thoroughness, sobriety, punctuality and responsibility to the earth element.

Subdivide these, too, into (1) major assets; (2) fairly consistent good qualities; and (3)minor virtues and occasional flashes.

You will now have what Alex calls two astral psycho-mirrors, one black and one white. 'You'll be able to recognize exactly which element is prevailing in your black and white mirror. This recognition is absolutely necessary to attain the magical equilibrium, and your further development depends on it.'[13]

Trying this 'know thyself' exercise for myself, I have found the most practical way is to use a small-format loose-leaf notebook, divided by ten thumb-index cards (to cover the four elements plus 'Indifferent' in both black and white). With one fault or virtue to a sheet, it makes classification and amendment much simpler. And if anyone tells me this is over-organized, I am prepared to enter 'obsessiveness' as a minor fault (under 'Earth', I think)!

Such mental and moral exercises might be accepted as sound by almost anyone, whatever his outlook; they are essential to Wicca, but by no means unique to it. But Wicca is specifically a magical Craft, and here of course the training enters more controversial ground.

I am not thinking of the reactions of out-and-out materialists to whom the whole thing is mumbo-jumbo. They will not be reading this book anyway, except as a pathological case-history. Nor of the more sympathetic attitude of sceptics who admit the usefulness, as devices for organizing one's mental efforts, of formulae which may not be literally 'true'; they at least will know what I am talking about. I am concerned with the problem of the new witch under training.

He accepts the basic outlook and principles, or he would not have joined. If he belongs to what I have called an 'instinctive' coven, where his training is confined to taking part and getting the feel of what goes on, his problem will be minimal. Either he will find himself increasingly in tune with the coven, and his powers developing accordingly, or he will not—in which case he will decide he is wasting his time, and will drop out. (From a 'white' coven, that is; if he has been foolish enough to involve himself in the Left-Hand Path, dropping out may not be so easy.)

If, however, he has joined an intensive-training coven such as Alex and Maxine's, with classes, dictated notes, and diagrams to copy, he will quickly have a lot of material given to him which is strange and which (to say the least) cannot be immediately proved. If he has any kind of a trained mind, whether at plumber or professor level, he will have learned to take no information on trust, and also to differentiate between objective demonstrable fact on the one hand and subjective opinion on the other. Occult knowledge is not like that. You have to absorb a great deal of it on trust before you can develop far enough to test it for yourself. If you are sincere and intelligent but are not a psychic 'natural' (and that description would, I think, fit most of Alex's initiates) you may worry a little about this method of advance.

It is an old problem, common to all occult fraternities, and wise teachers recognize it. No occult teacher worth his salt and water demands blind faith. If he does, he is better avoided. A sensible one says, as Alex does, 'These things have worked for me, or have been passed to me by other teachers who have satisfied me that they know what they are talking about. They are part of a very long tradition which countless people through the ages have found to work for them. So I suggest you accept them as working hypotheses for the time being, until you have developed far enough to find out whether they work for you, too.'

That seems to me to be a reasonable attitude, providing your teacher strikes you as being sincere and intelligent himself—and experienced. I must say that, in studying under Alex, I have found it to be a practical approach. Many times I have taken down notes which seemed meaningless or bizarre at the time, only to have them suddenly make sense weeks or months later, either by direct experience or by linking up with something else.

There are many paths to occult development, and no one of them suits every temperament. An individual can only discover his own path at his own speed. This, too, an experienced teacher recognizes, and he may often see the path more clearly, and sooner, than the student. I once heard Alex say to a witch of a few month's standing (a young man we all greatly liked, and a diligent student), 'I am not your teacher; I will help you all I can, but yours is such-and-such a path.' Then he sent him off with his (and certainly our) blessing. He still visits us sometimes, and is welcomed as a friend and as a witch, but his real occult work lies elsewhere, and it was Alex who spotted it. I wonder if all High Priests would have been as perceptive.

¹A disc of copper or silver, five or six inches across, marked as in Fig. 4.

²A more detailed circle—the standard one in medieval magic—is double, with an outer radius of nine feet and an inner of eight. Between the two, symbols and names of power are inscribed. *The Key of Solomon* describes the method.

³Though it may also be placed in the centre.

⁴It has been suggested that the traditional witch figure of British folklore, an arthritic crone, may have arisen not entirely from Church propaganda, but also from the realities of naked outdoor rites in our climate!

⁵Or whatever names the coven uses for the God and Goddess.

⁶The salt is blessed and not consecrated, because it is already pure by nature. Because of its preserving and sterilizing qualities, it is regarded as a kind of spiritual antiseptic. In the old days, its preciousness probably entered into the symbolism as well.

⁷A black Magic Circle is cast anti-clockwise or widdershins, as one would expect from devotees of the Left Hand Path.

⁸Like so much Wiccan ritual, this blessing is flexible in its wording, for as the Book of Shadows says, 'the exact words matter little if the intent be clear, and you raise the true power and sufficient thereof'. For instance, the words 'O thou circle, be thou a meeting place of love and truth' may be inserted, as in the example I gave in Chapter 1.

⁹This summoning, too, is flexible. For example, to the west may be added 'Lords of the realm of death and of initiation', and to the north, 'Boreas, thou gardian of the northern portal, open the gate that the powerful God and gentle Goddess may enter in'—a favourite of Alex's. These additions are merely verbalizations of what the individual witch visualizes, and as such are both legitimate and helpful.

¹⁰The athame is soley a ritual tool, and should therefore be deliberately blunted at edge and point—for obvious safety reasons in a crowded Circle. Purists who think otherwise must be extra careful in their gestures. The white-handled knife, however, is used for practical work in the shaping of other tools, and is not waved about in the vicinity of other people's bodies. Therefore it can and should be sharp.

¹¹A useful aid is a kitchen timer which 'pings' after a pre-set number of minutes. This avoids constantly glancing at your watch, which is itself an interruption of the train of thought.

¹²It cannot be too often emphasized that these 'elements' are not to be taken literally, nor as a reversion to a pre-scientific ignorance of the nature of the physical world. They are concepts, principles, applicable to many spheres of occult thinking. The way in which they are here applied to the moral sphere should give the reader a clue to their basic meaning.

¹³This concept of personal equlibrium is exactly expressed by Shakespeare in Mark Antony's epitaph on Brutus:

> His life was gentle, and the elements
> So mixed in him that Nature might stand up
> And say to all the world 'This was a man!'

5.

The Coven at Work

How often a coven meets is up to the coven. The year's eight festivals or sabbats (described in detail in Ch. 7) are the high spots of the calendar. For these, two or more covens may join forces. The ordinary meetings or esbats are traditionally held 'once in the month and better it be when the moon is full', but an active and enthusiastic coven is likely to meet more often. Alex and Maxine's coven meets almost every week, and uses the words 'meeting', 'Circle', or the name of the festival rather than esbat or sabbat, but some coven's preserve the old terms.

The work of an ordinary coven meeting may include initiations, either first degree (making a newcomer into a witch) or second and third (which are normally taken together; the second degree qualifies a witch as a High Priest or High Priestess, and the third celebrates the fact). It will almost certainly include healing work, for members of the coven or for non-witches who may or may not be present. It may include the tackling of personal problems (amatory, professional, domestic), again for witch or non-witch. It may include scrying, evocation, trance—either to help in healing or problem-solving, or as independent exercises for the development of individual witches and the coven as a whole.

Problems of fertility or its limitation, once a mainstay of a coven's activity, are seldom brought to witches in these days of (among other things) fewer horses, factory farming, better hygiene, and the Pill. Problems of psychic defence and counter-attack (another old mainstay) have softened, with the end of persecution and terror, into neutralizing the occasional case of personal malice. So the role of healing has expanded in proportion. I have more to say on this in Chapter 11.

After the Circle has been cast, every meeting starts with Drawing Down the Moon.[1] In fact the whole of the Circle casting ritual enters into this, but the heart of it is the calling the Goddess to descend into the body of the High Priestess, who then continues to personify the Goddess until the Circle is finally banished.

Instead of the High Priestess, the Maiden may be chosen for this role on any particular occasion. The Maiden is, in effect the Deputy High Priestess. In Alex and Maxine's coven, because of its emphasis on training, the Maiden may be any of the women witches, appointed for the evening to give her practice in the ritual. In the average coven, the office of maiden will probably be a permanent appointment—permanent, that is until the holder takes over as High Priestess or 'hives off' to form her own coven; a Maiden is usually appointed with one of these ends in view. When the Maiden is not acting as High Priestess, or personifying the Goddess, she assists the High Priestess as necessary.

For Drawing Down the Moon, the High Priestess stands in the north of the Circle, facing south and assumes the 'God position'— feet together and hands crossed on her breast. The High Priest gives her the Fivefold Kiss.

Then the High Priest kneels before her or the Maiden (whichever is to personfy the Goddess) and with the wand touches her right breast, left breast, and abdomen, and the same three points a second time, saying:

I invoke thee and call upon thee, O Mighty Mother of us all, bringer of all fruitfullness
By seed and root, by bud and stem,
By leaf and flower and fruit,
By life and love do we invoke thee to descend upon the body of thy servant and Priestess.

He and the other men kiss the High Priestess (or Maiden), and the women bow to her. She then traces the Pentagram in front of her, saying:

> Of the Mother darksome and divine
> Mine the scourge, and mine the kiss,
> The five-point star of love and bliss—
> Here I charge you in this sign.

She assumes the 'Goddess position'—feet astride and arms outstretched making a Pentagram of her own body—and recites the Charge.[2] The Drawing Down of the Moon is now complete.

Any initiations on the agenda usually come out. The second and third degree rite is dealt with in the next chapter. I have tried to show in Chapter 1 how the first-degree ceremony appears to an initiate, but a few comments on it from the coven's point of view might be helpful here.

Alex admits that he seldom enjoys an initiation. He is too conscious of the responsibility he is taking on, because a new witch is very much a responsibility, all potential and no experience. High Priest and High Priestess must watch him carefully and sympathetically till he finds his feet, to make sure that his weaknesses do not cause him to stumble and that his individual talents are correctly assessed and developed. To a lesser degree, of course, the whole coven shares this responsibility. They must not only make him feel welcome, but also actively help him to become an effective part of the organism.

Alex says that he can always tell if an initiation has 'taken' or not, and one does very quickly develop this sense. Having helped (and the whole coven does help) at several initiations since my own, I think I now know when one has been successful--that is, a genuine experience for the initiate, and a genuine sense of gathering-in for the coven—or when it has been a mere form. In the latter case, Alex and Maxine do not shake the initiate's confidence by telling him so. They know that, provided he is sincere, his true initiation will come about gradually as the weeks pass, and he will be none the worse for that gradualness in the long run.

It can work the other way, too. Some 'naturals' Alex regards as being truly initiated already by virtue of their own character and experience.[3] For them, the ceremony merely sets a ritual seal on something already achieved.

How much of the initiation rite is spoken by the High Priest, and how much by the High Priestess, is a matter for them. The High Priest, for example, may on occasion recite the whole of the Charge, substituting 'she' for 'I'—speaking, in effect, as a personification of the consort of the Goddess. But the challenging with the sword, the Fivefold Kiss, the anointing, and the presentation of the weapons, must always be done man-to-woman or woman-to-man, because only a woman can initiate a man, or vice versa. (Though tradition says that in an emergency, a woman may initiate her daughter or a man his son.) Apart from this, the only difference between initiating a man and initiating a woman is the wording of the Fivefold Kiss. For a woman, it is 'blessed be thy womb' instead of 'blessed be thy phallus', and 'thy breasts, formed in beauty' instead of 'thy breasts, formed in strength.'

The taking of the initiate's measure—cutting a piece of red

thread the exact length of his body—used to be an insurance, as the High Priest's words given in Chapter 1 explain. The coven kept the measure as a hostage against desertion or betrayal. Some covens may still do this, but Alex dislikes any custom which suggests intimidation. Witches who drift away are left to their own devices. Any who are actively disloyal may be banished—a rite equivalent to excommunication, which the offender may ask to have lifted after a year and a day have passed. (For some reason, Alex finds that a substantial proportion of ex-witches, whether drifters or banished, tend to become Buddhists.)

Alex's advice to initiates is either to burn their measures, or to hide them away where no one can get at them. Some put them in lockets for husbands, wives or lovers to keep, or wait till they form their own covens and then present them to their High Priest or High Priestess partners. 'Perfect love and perfect trust', indeed.

One other point should perhaps be emphasized, to avoid misunderstanding. The sharing of cakes and wine, which follows every invitation (and most meetings, in fact), is in no way a parody of the Christian Mass, whatever professional persecutors may have said. It is far older, as indeed were the roots of the agape or love-feast of the early Christians, which in due course converged with the rite established by the Last Supper. If at the height of the persecution it occasionally became such a parody, that was an understandable human reaction, but it is neither its original, nor its present, meaning.

One member of the coven may be appointed to keep the record—the equivalent of minutes—of the coven meetings. In our coven this is my particular job, presumably because I am a journalist. I keep rough notes in the Circle (wishing sometimes that my body had a marsupial pocket) and type them out at home. During healing and problem-tackling work, individual wishes are recorded (unless anybody wants to keep one of his private) for a later check on progress. Being a training coven, we note who played what part in the ritual, so that over the weeks everybody can have a chance to practise the various operations.

The record of our most recent meeting is perhaps fairly typical. It was an ordinary work night, with no initiations, and not a seasonal festival.

Wendy and Charles helped cast the Circle—consecrating the water, blessing the salt, and carrying round the sprinkler, the censer, and the flame.

After the Drawing Down of the Moon—by Alex and Maxine—the Witches' Rune (*see* p. 13) was chanted while we circled deosil, hand in hand, faster and faster. This is a standard method of 'raising the power', which may be defined as a heightened psychic togetherness, a pooling and a mutual amplification of psychic voltage, or in Jungian terms, a deliberate opening-up and reinforcing of the Collective Unconscious (but *see* note 1 on p. 102). It is conceived as being localized, and is therefore often called the Cone of Power, visualized as a cone rising within the sphere which is the true form of the Circle.

These visual concepts may be regarded as having objective psychic reality, or as psychological aids. For myself, I visualize the Circle as a sphere of pale Akashic violet, becoming more intense where it cuts the ground. At the cardinal points, I visualize the Invoking Pentagrams in their elemental hues, suspended in the air at no fixed distance—at the same time just beyond the sphere, and a million light years away—windows on the Macrocosm, so to speak. (Alex as his own pictures within those windows, but I have not yet clearly developed mine.) And once the Cone of Power has been raised, I see it as having its base just inside the Circle, and its apex just short of the 'roof' of the sphere. I conceive of sphere and Pentagrams as self-maintaining until they are ritually banished, but of the Cone of Power as needing our steady concentration to maintain and exploit it. I try to hold these visual concepts in my imagination throughout the meeting. Whether they are purely subjective, or an approximation to psychic fact, frankly I am not sure, but I am satisfied that by holding on to them, I am contributing to the group psyche in action (however inadequately as yet). Holding on to them, with so many things going on in the Circle which require my attention, is not easy, but it does become easier with each meeting. However one explains these phenomena, or visualizes their components, they unquestionably work.

But to return to our last meeting. The Witches' Rune ended, as always, with everybody sitting down in a ring facing inwards.[4] It was followed by a scrying session (*see* Ch. 8). Graham, who had never tried it before, was given the crystal. He sat in the west of our ring, facing east. "Think of the past as behind your back and the future as before your face,' Alex told him. Two tall candles where placed on the floor, one each side of the crystal in Graham's fingers and a foot or so away, so that it caught their light. Graham gazed into the crystal, while the rest of us shut our eyes and concentrated on the crystal to help him. What he saw we did not know yet; Alex told him to save it up for next time.

'And if you don't see anything at all, don't let it worry you,' he said. 'These things have to develop naturally.'

We kept it up for five minutes in silence. (Have you ever tried, with your eyes shut, to think of nothing but the mere physical fact of an egg-shaped crystal for five minutes? I don't know about the others, but I felt exhausted.)

Next, we all worked with the cords. In many covens, the members work individually with their own cords, holding and knotting them while they concentrate on their wishes. Alex prefers a group operation. The coven again sits in a ring facing inwards, each witch holding one end of a cord. The cords are half-hitched together in the centre, and radiate outwards like the spokes of a wheel, held taut by everyone pulling slightly. Each cord should have a man at one end and a woman at the other; tonight there happened to be more men than women, so two of the women held a cord in each hand.

Each of us had announced beforehand what he intended to work on (and I had duly noted it down). For example, Rusty needed a new bed-sitter, as did Charles. Wendy worked for her sister, who had been ill, and Janet for the healing of an old lady that she knew. Ken was to have his new white-handled knife consecrated later, and worked to reinforce that consecration. Alex worked to counteract a tendency towards intolerance which he had noted in himself in the past few days. Maxine ('I'll bring you all down to earth!') worked for more money, and for 'a private wish.' Ron for unspecified healing. I worked for the successful completion of this book, and for the easing of a friend's work burden.

When the cords were in place and taut, each of us concentrated on one of his wishes, and then tied a knot in his cord without allowing it to slacken. As he tied the knot, he applied all his will to the thought that the wish was already granted, held that thought for a while, and then moved on to the next wish and its knot. All the time he kept his eyes fixed on the centre of the 'wheel' of cords, as the focal point of the group's combined power. Throughout, he tried to be aware both of his own power reinforcing the others' wishes, and of theirs reinforcing his. I found it helpful, once I had dealt with my own wishes, to tie another couple of knots while I concentrated on the group effort as a whole.

The work over, we all retrieved our own cords, but in accordance with tradition, left the knots in them, not to be untied until just before the cords were needed again.

There were a good many objects to be consecrated on this particular night. Apart from Ken's white-handled knife, they were mostly items of personal jewellery, ankh pendants, and so on. Ron and Ken, both first-degree witches, worked at consecrating the various items on the Pentacle under third-degree Charles' guidance, and Rusty and Janet completed the blessings face-to-face in the traditional way.

Wine and cakes were as usual the last item on the agenda. Rusty knelt with the chalice while Wendy blessed the wine with her athame; then it was passed, with the cakes, man-to-woman and woman-to-man, each time with a kiss.

Finally, Janet banished the Circle, with Charles beside her ready to prompt if necessary (in fact it was not, though Janet was quite a new witch), while the rest of us ranged ourselves behind her and matched her gestures with our own athames.

Fig. 6. The Ankh.

The use of herbs has always been a part of witchcraft, and no modern doctor would deny that much of today's pharmacopoeia has its roots in what the witches discovered. Nor has orthodox medicine entirely shed its magical past, as any G.P. who has ever prescribed a placebo will confirm—even if he uses some other word than 'magic'.

Wiccan herbalism of course is not afraid of the word, nor does it see any contradiction in combining modern analysis of physical properties with the application of occult principles.

Maxine is a very knowledgeable herbalist. In general, herbs seem to be the traditional province of female witches. Here are two of her recipes.

First, a formula to strengthen weak eyesight:

Take equal amounts of camomile flowers and eyebright (*euphrasia officinalis*) and infuse them in boiling water. Strain the liquid off; take seven willow sticks, light them and plunge them into the liquid, which should then be filtered.

Soak pads of cotton-wool in the filtered liquid, and lay them on your eyes for ten minutes. (The magical factor in this is the introduction of the fire element.)

The second formula uses the same herbs, but it is more detailed in its preparation. It produces what witches call the Universal Condenser, a fluid that can be used medically as a lotion, or magically for rituals of evocation, or to improve clairvoyance or clairaudience. It is also sometimes called the Elixer of Life, though this is a name that has had many other meanings.

Take two level teaspoonfuls each of camomile flowers and eyebright and put them into a bowl. (Old recipes say a 'lead' vessel, which has puzzled many people, but it merely means lead-glazed, i.e., non-porous.) Bring two cupfuls of water to the boil on an open fire or gas (*not* electricity) and pour it over the herbs. Cover immediately, and allow to cool for fifteen minutes.

Filter through four layers of purified linen (four boiled handkerchiefs will do). The filtered liquid is the Universal Condenser.

Traditionally, the four layers represent the four elements, and the equal proportions of the herbs represent the balance, fundamental to occult science, of 'that which is above' with 'that which is below'—the Macrocosm and the Microcosm symbolized in the interlaced triangles of the Hexagram.

Any chemist will tell you that there is nothing harmful in this. Diluted in seven parts of warm water, it can be drunk for stomach-ache and is slightly laxative. Neat, it can be used for various aches and pains by applying it with cotton-wool every two hours. For more deep-seated pains, a soaked pad can be bandaged in place for a few hours. Ears can be treated by sleeping overnight with cotton-wool earplugs soaked in the Condenser.

This brings us to its magical applications, for the same earplug method is used to induce clairaudience. For clairvoyance, put soaked pads on your eyes and keep them on for twenty or twenty-five minutes.

'Don't try to look through your eyelids,' Maxine says. 'let the ordinary natural pictures run across your vision, and suddenly you'll find pictures coming through which are not your ordinary ones. You have to persist in this, though.'

Localized occult sensitivity, in the palms of the hands, for instance, or the soles of the feet, can be induced, so those who have tried it maintain, by applying the liquid to the part concerned.

The word 'Condenser' (or, more exactly, 'Fluid Condenser') refers to its use for concentrating the effect of the occult electrical and magnetical fluids in a particular place for a particular purpose. In certain rituals, metals are used in the same way, hence the apparently contradictory description 'Solid Fluid Condensers'.

In evocations, the sigil (seal or sign) of the entity to be evoked may be drawn on a piece of blotting paper before the ritual. The blotting paper is then soaked in the Universal Condenser for this same focusing effect. (A substitute for the traditional, and messy, mixture of blood and sperm.)

To return to the Universal Condenser's bodily uses, there is a very much stronger and rather unpleasant-tasting version, which is said to be a sure and safe abortive. Naturally the recipe for this is not bandied about, nor would I feel justified in giving it.

A first-degree witch must have his own white, red and blue cords of initiation; the significance of their colours is one of the things I must not publish. It is possible to work with the blue cord only, and in some covens they wear their blue cords round their waists ready for use. ('Horrible thing,' says Alex. 'Cuts a woman in half.')

By the time he is ready for the second degree, a witch is supposed to have grasped the meaning and magical application of the elements, so for this the cords are red (fire), yellow (earth), blue (air), and green (water). These can be used for appropriate working: for example, if you want to master the fire element in yourself, because you are too aggressive or destructive (or want to strengthen it because you lack drive), you work on the red cord. For problems of love or affection, which are of the feminine water element, green. For craftsmanship, or to counteract laziness, the yellow of earth. For enhanced joy of living, or to root out malicious gossip, the blue of air. And so on.[5]

When you understand the Akashic Principle, the all-pervading 'ether' in which psychic processes are regarded as taking place and their effects as being transmitted and stored, you can use a correspondingly purple cord.

The colour-code of cord magic is a rich and varied symbolism, so any colour may have different meanings in different contexts: red, for example, or blue, means one thing in initiation, something else in the elemental sense, and something else again in the planetary scale.

Pale silvery blue is the colour for working on Zodiacal principles. Gold is the King or High Priest colour. Black stands for domination over the underworld. Alex has a sash of red, white, black, blue and gold cords stitched together. 'When you see me wearing that inside the Circle,' he says, 'you'll know there's something big coming up.'

The planetary scale of colours is as follows (for convenience, I have added the corresponding Sephiroth of the Tree of Life, which are dealt with in Chapter 9):

Saturn: Black (Binah, 'Understanding')
Jupiter: Deep sky blue (Chesed, 'Mercy')
Mars: Red (Geburah, 'Strength')
Venus: Green (Netzach, 'Victory')
Mercury: Vermillion; some say yellow or silver   (Tiphareth, 'Beauty', and Hod, 'Glory')
Sun: Gold   (Twisted together, the combination
Moon: Silvery white   of Godhead in Kether. 'Crown')
Earth: Olive, citrine, russet and black (Malkuth, 'Kingdom')

For one operation of cord magic which any psychologist would endorse independently of its occult interpretation, a green cord is traditionally employed. Forty knots are tied in it, which makes it the 'Witch's Ladder'.[6] It is used for straightforward auto-suggestion.

Suppose, for example, a colleague at work (call him Jim) has the knack of upsetting you, throwing you off your stroke, and making you feel inadequate. You want to make yourself less vulnerable to him. So you formulate your wish in a short, precise sentence, such as 'Jim cannot disturb me'. Immediately before falling asleep, you take the Ladder in your hand, and either in an undertone or mentally, you repeat 'Jim cannot disturb me' once for each knot till No. 40 is reached. With each repetition, you envisage the wish as already realized. If you wake during the night, take your Ladder and do it again. In the morning, if possible before you are fully awake, do it yet again. Quite simply, you are imprinting a new attitude to Jim on your subconscious mind, conditioning a new reflex to the Jim-stimulus. Keep it up night after night until Jim has been reduced to human proportions.

The Ladder can equally well be used for self-healing or for the breaking of bad habits. But a word of warning: do not use it for a new wish until you are absolutely satisfied with the results of the last one, or your subconscious (which is tortuous but not very bright) will only become confused.

(Another, from Alex: only use the Ladder for wishes which have to do with the personality, including, of course, its psychosomatic aspects. It will *not* work with bingo or one-armed bandits, so don't waste your time.)

The Akashic purple cord may also be made into a Witch's Ladder, but only for use within its own spiritual terms of reference, once you fully understand what they are.

Ladder work can be done within the Circle (taking advantage of the Cone of Power) as well as in bed (taking advantage of the relaxed grip of the conscious mind over the subconscious). It is up to the individual to discover by experiment which is effective for him; maybe both, especially if the problem is stubborn.

There are many spells which can be worked in the Circle, and this is perhaps the activity which the man in the street most readily imagines witches carrying on—though, with all respect, the man in the street usually has it slightly wrong. He thinks that witches believe that certain physical actions, performed with certain physical objects, will automatically bring about certain results. Witches believe nothing of the kind, unless they are exceptionally naive (for which weakness, believe me, membership of Alex and Maxine's coven is a healthy antidote).

For the witch, the object used in a spell is a symbol, a focal point for a psychic operation. The prime mover is the will, the object is a channel for concentrating that will, Circle and coven are means of amplifying it, and the ritual is a means of clarifying it, making it specific, and directing it.

To use a motoring metaphor—the physical object is the driver's map, symbolizing and epitomizing the place he is aiming at, his will is the fuel in the tank , the coven is the engine, the Cone of Power is the rotary force produced by fuel and engine, and the ritual is the transmission. Given an accurate map, pure fuel, and a sound car, the driver gets where he wants.

A very simple example is a time-honored love spell. Two needles large enough to be manageable, are taken to represent the man and the woman. The point of the 'male' needle is inserted in the eye of the 'female' needle, and the two are bound together with thread of the planetary colour appropriate to the situation. The symbolism could hardly be plainer, but the ritual can (and indeed should) be elaborated to give the occasion substance in the minds of the operators—to give the power something to work on, so to speak. For instance, each needle can be named and blessed. The female needle can be held by a woman and the male needle by a man. The pair should be in emotional sympathy, and if they are lovers so much the better. Words are needed, of course; and they may be traditional, or made up for the occasion, but in either case in verse.

'Of spells, the exact words matter little if the intent be clear, and you raise the true power and sufficient thereof,' says the Book of Shadows. 'Always in rhyme they are . . . in rhyme the words seem to say themselves; you do not have to pause and think "What comes next?'' Doing this takes away much of your intent.'

Reasonable advice, so let us make up a little rhyme for our two needles.

John be sharp
Mary be bright;
Thread of Venus bind them tight.
Sun by day,
Moon by night,
Bring them hourly new delight;
Love and laughter,
Joy and light—
Thread of Venus bind them tight.

Unremarkable, but it jingles, and it took me three and a half minutes to compose, so it would serve the purpose. Every coven must have at least one who could do as well or better, and he might be appointed Coven Rhymester.

(As to the ethics of love spells, that is up to the coven, and it depends very much on the circumstances of the case. Sympathetic encouragement of a pair who would be helped by a little prodding, or who seem attracted but inhibited, is one thing; selfish manipulation is quite another, and verges dangerously on the black.)

Another popular spell, which is actually referred to in the Book of Shadows, is the Candle Spell. A new candle is taken into the Circle and consecrated. A Pentagram is inscribed on it with the white-handled knife, while the operator recites:

Upon this candle I will write
What I receive of thee this night.
Grant what I wish you to do;
I dedicate this rite to you.
I trust that you will grant this boon,
O lovely Goddess of the Moon.

(One of the less admirable bits in the Book of Shadows; it sounds like something out of a Christmas cracker, and does not even scan. Over to the Coven Rhymester for improvement.)

The candle is mentally charged with the wish, and is then wrapped in paper of the planetary colour of the person for whom the work is being done. It is given to him, and he is told to light it during the appropriate planetary hour (*see* App. 3) and to allow it to burn itself out. As it burns, the spell will start working for him.

Another candle spell, for healing, uses a needle. Candle and needle are consecrated, and the needle named to represent the patient. The needle is stuck in the side of the candle, and the candle lit. The concept to hold here is of power building up as the candle burns down to the needle, and being released for healing work when the needle is reached.

The use of a wax image to represent a person is the best-known (if least understood) witch's spell of all. Like all other spell objects, the image is a concentration channel of the kind I have already explained, but perhaps a more thorough-going device than some of the simpler symbols. It is given ritual 'birth' (usually by the High Priestess with the assistance of the High Priest) within the Circle, and the appropriate spell is performed on it. That such images have in the past been used maliciously, often with terrible effect, no one can deny, and doubtless there are black operators who do so use them today. But in white covens they are used for healing—or, at most, for 'restraining'.

An example of the restraining use was when a friend of Alex's, a woman journalist, was encountering obstruction from the jealous and possessive secretary of a man with whom she had to work professionally. Alex performed a wax-image spell, binding the image with blue cord. From that day the secretary (who knew nothing about the spell) became friendly and co-operative, and the journalist was able to complete her work.

Alex once created a sensation—and some misunderstanding—by producing a wax image on the Simon Dee Show on television. It represented, he announced, an ex-witch who had 'exposed' him in a Sunday newspaper, and he proposed to prick it from time to time. One result was a good deal of humourless counter-challenging from certain Wiccan circles who do not view Alex or Alexandrians kindly. In fact, as Alex told me with a grin, 'It was only his conscience that I was pricking,' Typically (for Alex seems quixotically unable to carry a grudge), he was drinking beer with his 'victim' in a Notting Hill pub three or four weeks later.

For healing work, an interesting alternative to the image is the body of another witch within the Circle. I have seen Alex locate and cure back-ache for the pregnant wife of one of our witches, by concentration and the direct laying-on of hands on the patient; but he also uses, and teaches, the 'stand-in' method. The stand-in concentrates on the absent patient, 'thinking herself into her', while the healer concentrates on the stand-in. By this two-stage contact, it is possible, as Alex has demonstrated, both to diagnose and to cure. Naturally, the stand-in should be of the same sex as the patient.

One other type of work should be mentioned here: the creating and employing of spirits with their own independent consciousness, either in the form of a simple 'elemental' for a specific purpose, with a lifespan limited to the achievement of that purpose, or in the form of a 'guardian angel' which remains its creator's companion.

This is a phenomenon which is very difficult for the non-occultists to swallow, yet it has a long and well-documented history. The works of the late Dion Fortune (who was not only an occult leader but also a professional psychiatrist at a world-famous London Clinic) are full of instances of it—including malevolent ones which she had to deal with in dead earnest during her practice.

These beings (so Dion Fortune maintained, and Alex agrees) are not separate entities in the literal sense, but are sectors of the operator's mental make-up rendered independently active; deliberate and constructive split personality, so to speak. An elemental of this kind may be likened to a complex—a group of mental factors associated with a particular idea, which have become organized into a recognizable unity. Everyone knows how a complex (an aversion to cats, or our reaction to 'Jim') can behave as though it were a force independent of our conscious will. The witch goes one better, deliberately constructing it and sending it off to work, briefed by his will.

I have watched Alex build such an entity for a specific task of healing, and give it a localized home; in this case, a Martini bottle. (The true meaning of the 'genie in the bottle'.) Within his own Circle, he concentrated on the elements. Fire was the key one, because of the nature of the illness to be cured, but the elements had to be balanced on the 'tetrapolar magnet'[7] so first he mentally filled his body with 'Air of Air', the quintessence of that occult element. Next, Fire of Fire, mentally drawing on solar heat by visualizing the Sun God.[8] 'The Air,' he said, 'will keep the Fire burning.' He then transferred these balanced opposites to the astral plane, and proceeded to complement them with the other pair—Water of Water and Earth of Earth. So the balance was complete, but not yet conscious or charged with the healing command. Next he surrounded himself mentally with the deep purple of the Akashic Principle—'nothing can touch me while I'm in it'—impregnated the entity with the healing desire while he visualized the patient, and willed it into the bottle.

'I want a slow cure,' he ordered, 'not too drastic because fire burns . . . I want the healing to be completed by 25 December . . . I give you consciousness, in the names of the God and the Goddess and the rulers of the elements . . . Go, do the work, work at sunrise and at sunset, seven minutes each time . . . If you feel your power failing, come back to the bottle, rest awhile, be restored, and then return to the healing . . . And on 25 December, at seven o'clock in the evening, cease to be.'

Alex then banished the Circle, and told me: "There's the spirit in the bottle, and it will go on working independently of me.'

I asked if a spirit which had been treated in this way ever became obstinate as the deadline approached, and resisted its own end.

'Yes, occasionally,' Alex said. 'It happened to me. You get a sudden "*Uh-h*" feeling that something has gone wrong in your own elemental make-up. When you've identified the trouble, you fill a bath with hot water, purifying it exactly like the water in the Circle, and bless and add salt. Then you get into the bath with the bottle, open it, and banish the spirit; return it to the water element. You dissolve all its elements out of the bottle into yourself, off the inner plane, exhale them into the universe. You say "Now you cease to be", and let the bath water run out, back to the primal source. Then it really ceases to be.

'The same with an image; sometimes it can get a little too conscious and start living off the person it's working for. You get the bath water so hot that you can manipulate the wax and break it up, and you banish it in the same way. And it really works.'

An entity of the 'genie in the bottle' kind may be created by an individual, or on a more complex level by two or more people, or the whole coven. An example of such a co-operative creation is 'Michael', whose beginning is described in Chapter XX of *King of the Witches*. Michael is still very much around; sometimes he speaks through a tranced Alex, in a very identifiable voice, and we have all talked with him at these times. On other occasions, he is merely a presence, friendly, but often obstreperous, with a tendency to take over the ritual. (I have heard Alex mutter tetchily: 'Oh, Michael,—off out of the Circle!' which seems to restore order.) In general he is a useful and effective spirit: Alex and Maxine can both set him to work on a problem and leave him to it. So, I understand, can Paul, his other creator, but Paul is out of touch with Alex at the moment, and I have never met him.

The creation of a 'Guardian angel' (or 'Body of Light') is similar in some ways, but always individual and always permanent. In psychological terms, while a created elemental may be called the deliberate hiving-off of a complex, the guardian angel may be likened to one's own super-ego given independent consciousness. (I say this with some diffidence, as a layman meddling with psychiatric definitions, but I think it will give other laymen an idea of the concept.) 'It is your true self, in fact your God-self,' says Alex, 'your higher consciousness. You have to develop every aspect of it, and know yourself so completely that you can separate it off and give it a consciousness, make it think separately, make it travel anywhere at will. (This was the purpose of Egyptian initiation.) It is "myself made perfect, whom no man hath seen at any time".'

Obviously this is a matter of long self-analysis and self-training.

There is no set ritual. Because it is so personal, it has to be left to one's own imagination and ingenuity, as does the form in which one visualizes the entity.

'You devise what you are going to be like and look like—physically, mentally, astrally and spiritually,' Alex says, 'and you build these images and merge them all together. Then you transfer your consciousness into this, till you can see with its eyes, hear with its ears, taking the five senses from the physical plane on to the inner plane.'

The actual technique for consummating this transfer has parallels with that of astral projection; but that is a matter for Chapter 12.

Giving independent life to one's own higher consciousness, so that one can consult it, converse with it, and set it to work, is far from easy. But if it can be achieved, some might think it worth all the rest of their Wiccan training put together.

---

[1]Though some witches say this should only be done when the moon is waxing. Some indeed will not work 'on the dark side of the moon' at all.

[2]See Appendix 2. A verse form of the Charge is often used here, beginning
> All ye assembled in my sight,
> Bow before my spirit bright;
> Aphrodite, Arianrhod,
> Lover of the Horned God . . .
but for me at least it is far less moving than the prose version.

[3]The remarks on reincarnation (p. 38) may also be relevant to this.

[4]I wonder if the children's 'Ring-a-ring-a-roses' ending with 'we all fall down', as well as its suggested association with the Great Plague, echoes the pattern of older witch dances?

[5]For an interesting and practical thesis on elemental qualities and their relation to personality traits, see *The Purpose of Love* by Richard Gardner.

[6]The Witch's Ladder does not have to be a knotted cord; it can be a string of forty 'worry-beads', or a woman witch can make her traditional amber and jet necklace of forty pieces so that it can also be used as a Ladder. The Ladder, like the rosary, is simply a device for counting without diverting one's attention to the process.

[7]The balance of elements as arranged round the Circle (*see* Fig. 3, p. 45).

[8]To visualize the Sun God for healing purposes, the image that Alex himself uses is that of the Christ figure 'with his beautiful red hair and his hands up, and the rays of healing coming from them'.

6.

The Great Rite

When a witch has developed to the point where he (or she) is ready to leave the coven and form his own—and has acquired the stature and authority needed for the valid initiation of other witches—he is taken through the Second and Third Degree initiation rites.

The Third Degree ceremony culminates in the Great Rite, the sexual ritual which has aroused so much pious horror and prurient curiosity in those who do not understand it, and which is the main target of 'exposures' in newspapers whose calculated formula is to combine pandering with self-righteousness.

Before explaining what the Great Rite means to witches, I must disappoint the horrified and the curious by saying that the Great Rite can be either actual or purely symbolic, and that (in Alex's view at least) both are equally valid. Since I joined Alex and Maxine's coven, symbolic Great Rites have outnumbered actual by two to one. The choice rests entirely with the people concerned, and if they decide it should be actual, everybody but the couple leaves the room before the ritual becomes at all intimate. Nobody even knows, nor are the couple asked, if consummation has occurred. 'Whether it has or not,' Alex says, 'They are given the title, because if they're so sincere that they've taken it that far, it's taken for granted.'

There are covens in which the others do not leave the room, but go to the edge of the Circle and turn their backs; Alex regards this as both inhibiting and distasteful.

By 'actual' I mean that the rite which I shall describe culminates in sexual intercourse within the Circle. By 'symbolic' I mean that the rite follows the same course, but culminates in the Blessing of the Wine with chalice and the athame in token of male-female union. The key to both is that the union is at all levels—physical (whether through bodies, or through chalice and athame), astral, mental and spiritual. The couple are, for the moment, the God and Goddess as well as themselves; they are Microcosm and Macrocosm.

Witchcraft has always been a fertility religion. In earlier, earthier days when fertility of man, beast and field was a plain matter of survival, activities to bring it about were concerned more with necessity than with taste or morals. Today, when technology determines agricultural fertility, and human over-population is a major problem and individual childlessness a minor (though sometimes distressing) one, spiritual fertility becomes more important to religion than physical.

To some people, that may sound like a hypocritical rationalization, or in plainer words, a nice excuse for an orgy; but anyone who is looking for any orgy will be wasting his time in a genuine Wiccan coven. He would do better to find some like-minded friends, and some drink, and throw a party.

The orgy used to exist in the Craft, certainly—when the coven worked itself up with dancing under the moon and then paired off into the woods. Its fertility purpose was direct; it offered periodic release from a harsh round of existence; and it had the admirable effect of giving the plainer girls a chance. Any girl who became pregnant could be sure of a 'handfasting'—if necessary enforced by the coven, because some at least would have seen who it was she disappeared into the woods with. Such rough-and-ready methods are no longer necessary.

But even in those days the spiritual aspect was present, in that the resulting children were regarded as gifts from the Goddess. And sometimes a couple would seek the Goddess's blessing in a more planned and purposeful way—the woman placing herself on the altar, and ritual and invocation being used to lead up to consummation. Man and woman called down the God and Goddess upon themselves to ensure not merely fertility, but a divinely protected and favoured child. That was a consciously religious act, and the ancestor of the Great Rite.[1]

In modern Wicca, the Great Rite is approached in much the same spirit. The couple are identified ritually with the God and the Goddess, and they unite as a sacred and symbolic act into which they try to draw all levels of themselves. The 'child' they seek is the spiritual stature which will entitle them to lead their own coven.

Critics are entitled to accept or reject this concept, but I do not think they are entitled to be scornful or shocked about it. If a couple merely wanted to make love, there are easier ways. Nor can it be attacked as hypocritical, because witches regard man and woman as beings of many levels, all of them equally important, and in a sense equally holy. So to attempt to open up all these levels in one ritual act is an honest and complete expression of their belief.

Sex is the most personal of all relations, and involves two unique individuals, which is why it is left to them to choose between the actual and symbolic form. The Third Degree rite is ideally between two people who are going to found a new coven together as High Priest and High Priestess, but it may equally well be between the High Priest or High Priestess of the parent coven and an individual who is ready for the status. Or one of the pair may be merely a First Degree witch who will be working with the new High Priest or Priestess, but is not personally taking the Second and Third as yet. It all depends on the circumstances.

The High Priest-High Priestess partnership is necessarily close, and must be harmonious, but there is no reason why it should not be platonic. It often happens that such a pair, each happily married to someone else, goes through the Great Rite symbolically and proceeds to found a successful coven with no hurt to anyone. In fact, if they are working and developing properly, they should be a better wife and husband for it.

In a word, the 'actual' Great Rite is normally between husband and wife or between established lovers.

On the question of opening-up of levels, the degrees of initiation can be directly related to the Cabalistic Tree of Life. I explain this, all too briefly, in Chapter 9, but perhaps I may anticipate here by saying that while Wicca operates in the main on the bottom triangle of the Tree—Malkuth, Yesod, Hod and Netzach (physical, astral, intellectual, emotional)—the whole of the Tree is interlinked,[2] and in the Third Degree ceremony in particular the whole of it is brought into play. Thus the symbol of the First Degree initiation is the inverted triangle corresponding to the bottom of the Tree. The symbol of the Second Degree is the upright pentagram which embraces the Tree from Malkuth up to Tiphareth, Geburah and Chesed (transformation, strength, compassion). With the Third Degree this is crowned by the upright triangle which completes the Tree by bringing in the three Supernals Binah, Chokmah and Kether (formative mother, creative father, divine spark). This reaching-up is also expressed vividly by the Egyptian symbol associated with the Great Rite, the hieroglyph *ankh-ka* or 'soul-life'. The inverted triangle and the upright pentagram, are used respectively in the First and Second Degree anointing.

Fig. 7 (a). Triangle of the
First Degree.

Fig. 7 (b). Pentagram of the
Second Degree.

Fig. 7 (c). Pentagram and
Triangle of the Third Degree.

Fig. 7 (d). The Ankh-ka,
symbol of the Great Rite.

The Second and Third Degree initiation rituals involve two new names. In the Second Degree, the witch is formally given a new name which she has chosen beforehand, and by which she may be known in future within the coven, though usually it will only be used on ritual occasions. In the Third Degree she is given the Secret Name of the Goddess, which she may use in future instead of Aradia (or whatever name the coven uses in the First Degree). She will use this secret name in an undertone, or simply within her mind, whenever anyone is present who has not taken the Third Degree. This rule accords with the theory that the effect of 'Names of Power' is lessened when they are widely known and used, a theory with sound psychic principles to back it.

I refer to the witch as 'she' for no other reason than that I used the example of a male initiate in describing the First Degree rite, so this time I will maintain the balance by assuming a lady. If the initiate is a man, the main difference is of course that the High

Priestess conducts the initiation instead of the High Priest.

The initiate is bound and blindfolded as before, a blue cord round the knees being added to the red cord round the wrists and neck, and the white cord round one ankle, which are used in the First Degree.

She is not kept waiting at the edge of the Circle or challenged, because she is already a witch and therefore belongs within it.

The High Priest leads her to east, south, west and north in turn, proclaiming at each point: 'Hear, ye Mighty Ones; Mary, a duly consecrated Priestess and Witch, is now properly prepared to be made a High Priestess and Witch Queen.'[3]

The coven now does a ring dance to the Witches' Rune (see pp. 13), after which the initiate kneels before the altar and the white cord is bound round her other ankle.

The High Priest says: 'To attain this sublime degree it is necessary to suffer and be purified. Are you willing to suffer to learn?'

The initiate answers: 'I am.'

The High Priest says: 'I purify thee to take the Great Oath rightly,' and the bell is rung three times.

The ritual 'scourging' follows. As in the First Degree, there is a set number of strokes divided into four groups, each number having a symbolic significance.

'I now give thee a new name—Levanah,'[4] the High Priest tells her. 'Repeat thy new name after me, saying: "I Levanah, swear . . ."'

The initiate repeats the oath, phrase by phrase: 'I, Levanah, swear upon my mother's womb, and by my honour among men, and my Brothers and Sisters of the Art, that I will never reveal, to any at all, any of the secrets of the Art, except it be to a worthy person, properly prepared in the centre of a Magic Circle such as I am now in. This I swear by my hopes of salvation, my past lives, and my hope of future ones to come, and I devote myself and my measure to utter destruction if I break this my solemn oath.'

Now comes the moment of the formal handing-on of High Priestly power, in what may be called the Apostolic Succession of witchcraft. The High Priest kneels beside the initiate and places his left hand under her knees and his right hand on her head. He says: 'I will all my power unto thee'—concentrating all his will on doing just that.

The initiate's ankles and knees are untied, and she is helped to rise. The High Priest moistens the little finger of his right hand with consecrated oil, and saying 'I consecrate thee with oil' he touches her right breast, womb, left breast, right hip, left hip, right breast again, and womb again—thus completing and sealing the Pentagram of the Second Degree initiation.

He dips his little finger in the wine and repeats the Pentagram, saying 'I consecrate thee with wine.'

Finally he kisses each spot in the same sequence, to the words: 'I consecrate thee with my lips, High Priestess and Witch Queen.'

The blindfold and the remaining cord are untied from the newlymade High Priestess.

As in the First Degree, all the tools are now presented, but this time with a difference: the initiate immediately uses each in turn. First she carries the sword round the Circle, re-casting it. Next she does the same with the athame. When she accepts the white-handled knife, she picks up a new unlit candle which is ready on the altar, and with the knife she inscribes an upright pentagram on it. This candle will light her first altar when she forms her own new coven.

She waves the wand to each of the cardinal points, and then shows the pentacle to each. Then she carries the censer round the Circle

The cords are used to illustrate a traditional Wiccan principle. With them she binds the High Priest who has just initiated her, and he kneels, saying: 'Learn, in witchcraft, you must ever give as you receive, but ever triple. So where I gave thee three, return nine . . .' and so on, numbering and trebling each of the groups of 'lashes'. The initiate takes the scourge, and administers the trebled number of strokes as instructed.

'Thou hast obeyed the Law,' says the High Priest, 'but mark well, when thou receivest good, so equally art bound to return good threefold.'

The High Priest is untied, and tells her, 'Having learned thus far, you must know why the Wicca are called the Hidden Children of the Goddess.'

The rest of the Second Degree ritual is an enactment of the Legend of the Descent of the Goddess into the Underworld, the full text of which will be found in Appendix 1. If it is properly done, it can be beautiful.

Normally, the initiate will take the part of the Goddess, and the High Priest that of the Lord of the Underworld. Or if it is a male initiate, he will act the Lord of the Underworld and the High Priestess the Goddess. Another member of the coven acts as Narrator, and yet another as Guardian of the Portal.

Whoever is to play the Goddess takes off her necklace, if she is wearing one, and lays it on the altar. Then she goes outside the Circle and is dressed in a veil and jewellery. The Lord of the Underworld wears a crown, and stands with the scourge and sword by the altar in the God Position (arms crossed on his breast).

The Narrator reads: 'In ancient times, our Lord, the Horned One, was (as he still is) the Consoler, the Comforter. But men knew him as the dread Lord of Shadows, lonely, stern and just. But our Lady the Goddess would solve all mysteries. . .'

As the story unfolds, the Goddess advances to the edge of the circle, where the Guardian of the Portals challenges her with sword or athame. She takes off her veil and jewels, and leaves them outside the Circle. The Guardian binds her with a cord, and leads her inside.

'Such was her beauty that Death himself knelt, and laid his sword and crown at their feet, and kissed her feet . . .'

The Lord of the Underworld does so, and the question and answer, plea and refusal, complaint and explanation continue till the Goddess submits to Death's scourge and admits: 'I know the pangs of love,' He raises her, gives her the Fivefold Kiss, and unties her. He takes her necklace from the altar and puts it round her neck; she picks up the sword and crown and returns them to him.

Then they stand side by side before the altar, he in the God Position with arms folded, she in the Goddess Position, feet astride and arms outstretched to form the Pentagram, while the Narrator completes the reading.

Finally the High Priest takes the initiate by the hand, holds his athame in the other, and proclaims at each of the cardinal points: 'Hear, ye Mighty Ones; Levanah has been duly consecrated High Priestess and Witch Queen.'

The Third Degree ritual—the Great Rite itself—can take several forms, differing slightly according to whether an individual or a couple is taking the degree. I will assume that it is a couple, and for simplicity I will call them the Man and the Woman to distinguish them from the presiding High Priest and High Priestess—though of course the Man and the Woman now also hold that status.

(Although the Great Rite is the heart of the Third Degree ritual, the Book of Shadows also lays down that it should be observed at the end of various seasonal rites, as will be seen in Chapter 7. On such occasions, it is carried out by the coven's High Priest and High Priestess, either symbolically or actually.)

To begin the ceremony, the High Priestess stands with her arms folded across her breast in the God (or Osiris) Position, and says to the High Priest: 'Blessed be. Ere I dare to proceed with this sublime rite, I must beg purification at thy hands.'

The High Priest gives the High Priestess the Fivefold Kiss, and ties her wrists with a cord. Then he gives her a symbolic 'scourging', and unties her.

Now the High Priest and High Priestess take the Man and the Woman to each cardinal point, proclaiming: 'Hear ye, Mighty Ones; twice consecrated and holy Levanah, High Priestess and

Witch Queen, and Geminus, High Priest and Magus, are properly prepared, and will now proceed to erect the sacred altar.'

The High Priestess says: 'Now again I must beg purification.' But this time it is the Man who ties the Woman, 'scourges' her, and unties her.

'Now I must reveal a great mystery,' the High Priestess says, and again assumes the Osiris Position while the High Priest gives her the Fivefold Kiss.

The Woman lays herself down in the centre of the Circle, face upwards, head to the north, with her arms and legs outstretched in the Pentagram position. A veil is laid over her body.

If the rite is to be symbolic, High Priest, High Priestess and coven stand around the Circle facing inwards. If it is to be actual, they now begin to leave the room. The Man recites the Incantation, kissing the Woman after every few lines, and in due course unveiling her.

Assist me to erect the ancient altar, at which in days past all worshipped.
The great altar of all things.
For in the old time, Woman was the altar
Thus was the altar made and placed,
And the sacred place was the point within the centre of the Circle.
As we have of old been taught that the point within the centre is the origin of all things,
Therefore should we adore it;
Therefore whom we adore we also invoke.
O Circle of Stars[5]
Whereof our father is but the younger brother,
Marvel beyond imagination, soul of infinite space,
Before whom time is ashamed, the mind bewildered and the understanding dark,
Not unto thee may we attain unless thine image we love.
Therefore by seed and root, and stem and bud,
And leaf and flower and fruit do we invoke thee.
O Queen of Space, O Jewel of Light,
Continuous One of the Heavens;
Let it be ever thus
That men speak not of thee as One, but as None;
And let them not speak of thee at all, since thou art continuous;
For thou art the point within the Circle, which we adore.
The point of life without which we would not be;
And in this way truly are erected the holy twin pillars.
In beauty and in strength were they erected
To the wonder and glory of all men.
Altar of mysteries manifold,
The sacred Circle's secret point—

Thus do I sign thee as of old,
With kisses of my lips anoint.
Open for me the secret way,
The pathway of intelligence,
Between the gates of night and day,
Beyond the bounds of time and sense.
Behold the mystery aright—
Five are the points of fellowship;
Here where the Lance and Grail unite,
And feet, and knees, and breast, and lip.

When the Great Rite has been solemnly consummated, Man and Woman exchange their new witch names. From this moment, too, they may use the Secret Name of the Goddess.

If the Rite is to be symbolic, the Woman lays herself down in the same way, and the Incantation is the same, but she rises when it is time to consecrate the wine.

I would like to add a personal memory of the first time I was present when the Great Rite was performed in actuality. We had withdrawn from the room and shut the door, and were talking very quietly, exchanging nervous cigarettes because several of us were new to such an occasion.

After a while the door opened and the Woman walked out. She was an averagely plain girl, but at that moment the Goddess was truly upon her: she was beautiful, calm, dignified, and utterly unselfconscious. She walked through the naked coven neither avoiding nor seeking our eyes. We stood to let her pass, the smokers instinctively taking their cigarettes from their mouths. There was no hint of either embarrassment or salaciousness; for a while, that London flat was a temple.

If that was an orgy, I have never understood the meaning of the word.

[1] It may also have been the basis of propaganda stories about the Black Mass and the sacrilegious use of the body of a naked virgin as an altar. To the hostile propagandist, half-truths are always more useful than outright inventions.

[2] The division of the Tree into triangles is shown in Fig. 11, p. 113.

[3] For a male initiate, 'High Priest and Magus'.

[4] A Moon Goddess name. The witch chooses a name which she feels matches her character or aspirations. For myself, for instance, I have chosen the name of an historical Egyptian scribe, which seemed appropriate to my profession.

[5] From 'O Circle of Stars' down to 'do we invoke thee' is, except for the substitution of 'thine image we love' for 'thine image be love', a passage from the Gnostic Mass in *Magick in Theory and Practice* by Aleister Crowley.

7.

The Seasonal Festivals

Says the Goddess: 'Ye shall dance, sing, fe ist, make music and love, all in my praise. For mine is the ecstasy of the spirit, and mine also is joy on earth . . . Let my worship be within the heart that rejoiceth; for behold, all acts of love and pleasure are my rituals.'[1]

Wicca is a creed of joy: among other things, of joyful communion with the great annual cycle of the fertility of nature. So witches celebrate the key points of this cycle with festivals. The urge to do so seems a basic factor in the human religious instinct. The four main festivals, within a day or two, occur in almost every pagan religion, and with appropriate saintly labels they have survived ineradicably in the Christian calendar.

These four great festivals are February 2, Candlemas; April 30, May Eve; July 31, August Eve; and October 31, Hallowe'en.

They are linked with the agricultural and herd-raising year, rather than with the astronomical one. But witches celebrate the latter as well, at the two solstices (June 22 and December 22) and the two equinoxes (March 21 and September 21). These four are lesser festivals, and in some racial traditions and periods of history they do not appear at all. The fact that today's witches do celebrate them seems to me another pointer to the twofold nature of modern Wicca, with its roots on the one hand in the age-old fertility cults of the countryside, and on the other in the almost equally ancient, but more sophisticated, wisdom of the astronomer-priest's temple and the magician's study.

What is in the modern witches' minds as they celebrate these festivals? I doubt if many would give the naive answer of one lady when she was asked why she performed her rites: 'Because the sun wouldn't rise in the morning if I didn't.' The days when worshippers believed that only their ritual and their sacrifices (including, at one time, that of their human god-king) kept the solar cycle in motion are gone, in literate communities at least.

That does not mean the witches' eight festivals are now mere excuses for a party. A Wiccan festival certainly is a party, and a good one too; but a party with a purpose—of putting oneself in tune with the rhythm of the Macrocosm, of plugging oneself in to the mains, so to speak. As we have seen already, the essence of Wicca is that it teaches levels of consciousness; and the festivals are one of the means by which the necessary channels are strengthened.

From a more mundane point of view, witches are people, they are each other's friends, and like anyone else they enjoy get-togethers which are enhanced by a sense of occasion. Tradition says that in the old days the esbats or routine meetings were single-coven affairs, while the sabbats or main festivals brought two or more covens together, and this custom is often observed today.

The eight festival rituals which follow are, basically, as they are given in the Book of Shadows; but they are (and are meant to be) elastic and adaptable, according to mood, circumstance, the people present, and whether the meeting is indoors or outdoors (and, if the latter, the weather). This is true of all the Wiccan rituals, of course. The Book of Shadows gives the bare bones, but the flesh is that of the coven's creative imagination.

Individual feelings decide how the instructions are to be interpreted. For example, the Book of Shadows lays down, for most of the festivals, that a phallus or phallic wand should be carried. This is certainly in keeping with the festival's fertility-cult origins, but how visually explicit the implement should be is a matter of taste. One traditional symbol is a plain wand tipped with a pine-cone, and Alex considers it quite enough. It may be decorated with a black and a white ribbon; Alex suggests this is the true form of the caduceus, or Mercurian staff with its intertwined twin serpents.[2] I refer to it throughout as the 'wand'.

February 2—Candlemas

This is the classical Lupercalia or Feast of Pan. More anciently still, it is the celebration of the Goddess's recovery from giving birth to the new year's Sun God, coming as it does six weeks after the winter solstice. The same concept has survived undisguised in the Christian festival of the Purification of the Blessed Virgin Mary; on an individual level, its equivalent is the largely obsolescent

Christian rite of the Churching of Women.

The High Priestess, carrying the wand, leads the coven with a dance step to the chosen site. No chants are laid down. She may choose her own, or use the Witches' Rune (*see* p. 13). The Volta Dance follows: in other words, lively dancing in couples. (The Volta Dance came from Italy via France in the sixteenth century. It was regarded as rather shocking at the time, because social dancing up to then had been of the square or circle type, and the Volta was one of the first in which individual couples actually held each other. It was an ancestor of the waltz.)

The High Priestess casts the Circle in the usual way. The High Priest then enters the Circle, with a sword in his right hand and a wand in his left. He lays these on the altar and gives the High Priestess the Fivefold Kiss. The High Priestess says 'Blessed be', and gives him the Fivefold Kiss in return.

She then recites this invocation.

Dread Lord of Death and Resurrection,
Of Life, and the Giver of Life;
Lord within ourselves, whose name is Mystery of Mysteries;
Encourage our hearts,
Let the Light crystallize itself in our blood,
Fulfilling of us resurrection;
For there is no part of us that is not of the Gods.
Descend, we pray thee, upon thy servant and priest.

If there are any new witches to be initiated, this is done now. Cakes and wine follow.

Next, says the Book of Shadows, comes 'the Great Rite, if possible'. This is laid down for most of the festivals, as befits a fertility-cycle celebration; it may, of course, be symbolic.

The Formal rituals over, feasting, dancing and games complete the occasion.

One traditional Wiccan game is the Candle Game. For this, the men form a ring facing inwards, either sitting or standing. The women stand in a ring outside them, 'standing on something if too short,' as the Book of Shadows considerately allows. The men pass a lighted candle from hand to hand, deosil (clockwise), while the women lean forward and try to blow it out.

The man who holds it when it is blown out gets three flicks of the scourge from the successful blower, and must give her the Fivefold Kiss in return. The candle is relit and the game proceeds.

For this, the Symbol of the Wheel must be used. It may be a plain disc, or an eight-spoked wheel, or the pentacle will do. Alex and Maxine use a circular mirror which has a broad frame, also circular, decorated as a twelve-pointed star.

This Wheel is placed beforehand on the altar, flanked with burning candles, or with fire in some form—torches, or small tripods with fire in their cups.

In the centre of the Circle is either a cauldron full of inflammable material, or (out of doors) a bonfire ready to be lit.

The High Priestess casts the Circle and invokes the Lords of the Watchtowers. Then she stands in the west, and the High Priest in the east, both carrying wands. The High Priestess recites:

We kindle this fire today
In the presence of the Holy Ones,
Without malice, without jealousy, without envy,
Without fear of aught beneath the Sun
But the High Gods.
Thee we invoke, O Light of Life;
Be thou a bright flame before us,
Be thou a guiding star above us,
Be thou a smooth path beneath us;
Kindle thou within our hearts
A flame of love for our neighbours,
To our foes, to our friends, to our kindred all,
To all men on the broad earth;
O merciful Son of Cerridwen,
From the lowliest thing that liveth
To the Name which is highest of all.

The High Priestess then traces the Invoking Pentagram (*see* p. 48) in front of the High Priest with her wand, and hands the wand to him, together with the scourge.

The Maiden (*see* p. 57) strikes a light and hands it to the High Priest, who lights the cauldron or bonfire. He (carrying a wand) and the High Priestess (carrying a sistrum) lead the dance, with the rest following in couples. Each couple must leap over the fire.[3]

'The last couple over the fire before it goes out should be well purified,' says the Book of Shadows. This means, in practice, a ritual 'scourging' and a good deal of laughter. The penalized man must then give the Fivefold Kiss to each of the women, and his partner to each of the men—'or any other penalty the High Priestess shall decide'.

These penalties, like the 'forfeits' at children's parties, depend on the High Priestess's ingenuity and sense of humour. On one occasion Maxine ruled that all the men were too proud, and that they should become beasts of burden. She promoted the women to be various legendary queens, and they rode the men side-saddle round the Circle till their pride had been suitably humbled.

And so to the cakes and wine.

The Spring Equinox is obviously an occasion for decorating the room with daffodils and other spring blossoms, and also for honouring one of the younger women by appointing her the coven's Spring Queen and sending her home afterwards with an armful of the flowers. This may equally well be done on May Eve.

April 30—May Eve

This, the Gaelic fire festival of Beltane, is also known as Rood Day or Roodmas (moved by the Church to May 3), and in Germany as Walpurgis Nacht, or the Eve of St. Walburga's Day. St. Walburga was a Sussex-born woman saint who emigrated to Germany and died there about A.D. 780. Interestingly, Walburg is an old Teutonic name for the Earth Mother.

In classical times, April 30 was the festival of Pluto or Hades, god and king of the underworld, whom witches regard not as the ruler of a Hell of torment, but in a more kindly light. While his call is inexorable, he also presides over the soul's necessary rest before its next reincarnation, and it was he who taught the Goddess the secrets of witchcraft to pass on to mankind.[4]

The May Eve/May Day festival is the oldest of them all, and the one that has survived with the maximum of popular vigour and the minimum of Christian refashioning. One does not have to be a psychiatrist to see the meaning of the beribboned may-pole, and it is surely significant that the workers' movement which grew out of the Industrial Revolution chose May Day as its major celebration.

Hobby horses are a feature of several surviving local May customs, and in the Wiccan May Eve festival the Book of Shadows says 'if possible ride poles'. The High Priestess leads the coven with a quick trotting step, singing:[5]

O do not tell the Priest of our Art,
For he would call it sin;
But we will be in the woods all night
A-conjuring Summer in.
And we bring you good news by word of mouth
For woman, cattle and corn,

For the Sun is coming up from the south
With oak, and ash, and thorn.

A ring dance follows, after which the High Priestess casts the Circle. The Book of Shadows specifically mentions Drawing Down the Moon (*see* p. 57) for this occasion; Alex says it should in fact be done at each of the festivals. The Book also calls for the 'purification' of everyone in the Circle, including the High Priest at the High Priestess's own hands, but Alex does not favour an excess of this symbolic scourging.

The prescribed ritual for May Eve is one of the least detailed in the Book. Apart from the above, it calls only for cakes and wine and 'the Great Rite, if possible, in token or truly'. Perhaps its authors, whoever they were, felt that this was the time of year when most could be left to the coven's inventiveness and sense of fun.

June 22—Summer Solstice

The Midsummer festival is naturally a favourite with British witches, being the one they are most likely to be able to celebrate out of doors without discomfort, which also makes it that much easier for more than one coven to get together.

The cauldron, filled with water and decorated with flowers, is placed before the altar. The High Priestess casts the Circle, and then stands in front of the cauldron with her wand raised. The High Priest stands to the north behind the altar, and the coven form a large ring facing inwards, men and women alternately.

The High Priestess says:

Great One of Heaven, Power of the Sun, we invoke thee in thine ancient names—Michael, Balin, Arthur, Lugh, Herne; come again as of old into this thy land. Lift up thy shining spear of light to protect us. Put to flight the powers of darkness. Give us fair woodlands and green fields, blossoming orchards and ripening corn. Bring us to stand upon thy hill of vision, and show us the lovely realms of the Gods.

She then traces the Invoking Pentagram in front of the High Priest with her wand. He comes forward, deosil round the altar, picking up his own wand and the scourge. He plunges the wand into the cauldron and holds it up, saying:

The Spear to the Cauldron, the Lance to the Grail, Spirit to Flesh, Man to Woman, Sun to Earth.

Saluting the High Priestess over the cauldron, he takes his place among the coven. The High Priestess, still carrying her wand, picks up sprinkler which has been placed ready on the altar, and stands by the cauldron. She says:

Dance ye about the Cauldron of Cerridwen, the Goddess, and be ye blessed with the touch of this consecrated water; even as the Sun, the Lord of Life, ariseth in his strength in the sign of the Waters of Life.

The coven dances clockwise about the altar and cauldron, led by the High Priest. The High Priestess sprinkles them all with water from the cauldron as they pass her.

Cakes and wine are followed by 'dances, rites and games as the High Priestess shall direct'. If the meeting is out of doors, there may also be a bonfire in the Circle, and in the British climate Midsummer is usually a better occasion for bonfire-jumping than the Spring Equinox.

July 31—August Eve

This is Lammas, the Gaelic fire festival of Lugnasadh, and the Eve of Lady Day. Anciently it is the Feast of Bread, the time of year when the divine priest-king was sacrificed in the fields and his body scattered. The grain made into bread represented his body.

In the Book of Shadows, the prescribed rite is even more cryptic than that for May Eve. Poles should be ridden, and a ring dance is followed by the casting of the Circle.

The High Priestess traces the Invoking Pentagram in front of the High Priest, saying:

O Mighty Mother of us all, Mother of all fruitfulness, give us fruit and grain, flocks and herds, and children to the tribe, that we be mighty. By thy Rosey Love,[6] do thou descend upon thy servant and priestess here.

Everyone salutes the High Priestess, and the cakes and wine are taken.

Unless the High Priestess feels moved to expand the prescribed rite, such brief forms would usually be combined with the normal work of a coven meeting.

September 21—Autumn Equinox

For this festival, the altar is decorated with pine-cones, oak sprigs, acorns, ears of grain, or other symbols of autumn.

After the Circle has been cast, the coven stand in a ring facing inwards, men and woman alternately. The High Priest stands to the west of the altar and the High Priestess to the east, facing each other. The High Priestess recites:

Farewell, O sun, ever-returning Light,
The hidden God, who ever yet remains,
Who now departs to the Land of Youth
Through the Gates of Death
To dwell enthroned. The judge of Gods and men,
The horned leader of the hosts of air—
Yet, even as he stands unseen about the Circle,
So dwelleth he within the secret seed—
The seed of newly-ripened grain, the seed of flesh;
Hidden in earth, the marvellous seed of the stars.
In him is Life, and Life is the Light of man,
That which was never born, and never dies.
Therefore the wise weep not, but rejoice.

Then she hands the High Priest the wand, and picks up a sistrum; they lead the dance three times round the altar.

The Candle Game is played, followed by cakes and wine and any other dances and games the High Priestess decides on.

October 31—Hallowe'en

November Eve, All Hallow Eve, the Gaelic fire festival of Samhain or Samhuin, strikes a more eerie note than the other festivals. It is the summer's end, when the powers of the underworld are felt to be growing, with its gates opened and all its forces let loose—the evil as well as the good. Non-witches used to bar their doors and windows on Hallowe'en, and use candle-lit pumpkins to frighten the evil spirits away, a custom which has become attenuated (particularly in America) into a children's game.

Witches were less defensive; they faced the season actively by calling on friendly spirits. Modern witches do the same, deliberately trying to contact dead friends and relatives—all too successfully, according to Alex, who admits he does not like Hallowe'en. 'They are dead; leave them in peace,' is his attitude.

'Sometimes I see my grandmother in the smoke from the cauldron during the Hallowe'en ritual. I loved her very much while she was alive, but she's moved on, and we have no need of each other now.'

The ritual begins with a walk or slow dance, the coven bearing torches or candles, led by the High Priest and High Priestess carrying wands. The Witches' Runes, or any other suitable chant, is sung to a slow tempo.

When it is finished, the High Priest and High Priestess trace the Invoking Pentagram with their athames, while the High Priestess recites:

Dread Lord of the Shadows, God of Life, and the Giver of Life—
Yet it is the knowledge of thee, the knowledge of Death.
Open wide, I pray thee, the Gates through which all must pass.
Let our dear ones who have gone before
Return this night to make merry with us.
And when our time comes, as it must,
O thou the Comforter, the Consoler, the Giver of Peace and Rest,
We will enter thy realms gladly and unafraid;
For we know that when rested and refreshed among our dear ones
We will be reborn again by thy grace, and the grace of the Great Mother.
Let it be in the same place and the same time as our beloved ones,
And may we meet, and know, and remember,
And love them again.
Descend, we pray thee, in thy servant and priest.

Each woman then gives the Fivefold Kiss to the High Priest, as the personification of the God.

No precise method is laid down for inducing visualization of the dead friends. The choice depends on the individual coven, who may have found this or that system most effective in their own experience. Alex and Maxine favour the smoking cauldron.

Cakes and wine, dances and games follow, and if the right attitude has been achieved, there will be a sense of those others taking part.

Of all the eight festivals, this is the one where the Book of Shadows insists most emphatically on the Great Rite. If it is not possible at the time, the Book says the High Priest and High Priestess should celebrate it themselves as soon as convenient, 'in token, or if possible in reality'. The point presumably is that since the Hallowe'en ritual is intimately concerned with death and the dead, it should conclude with a solemn and intense reaffirmation of life.

This is the festival of the rebirth of the Sun God, the shortest day of the year, after which he steadily grows in strength and influence towards his midsummer peak. The ancient astronomer-priests were able to calculate the summer and winter solstices exactly— which suggests that they, too, were concerned with putting themselves and their flocks in tune with the yearly cycle, and not with deluding themselves that they were actually bringing it about. They were less naive, and had a truer sense of both scientific and spiritual realities, than some of the historians who have claimed to interpret them.

That does not mean their rituals were empty or hypocritical; on the contrary. 'Putting themselves in tune' meant drawing the maximum benefit for mankind from that cycle, and to this they applied both their spiritual wisdom, and the scientific knowledge of which they were also the public guardians. In some civilizations, certainly, their function degenerated, and the light was lost in bloody sacrifice, fear, obscurantism, and the cynical maintaining of their class status. But in the best, the light burned clearly. In ancient Egypt above all, it proved itself by inspiring and guiding the longest lasting and (ups and downs notwithstanding) one of the most stable civilizations in world history.

It is the same light which, in modern conditions and with the added advantage of modern knowledge, today's witches are trying to recapture.

The Winter Solstice is the true New Year, astronomically as well as spiritually. Christianity acknowledged the religious significance of the turn of the year when it settled on December 25 (January 6 in the Eastern churches) as the date of Jesus' birth, after three or four centuries of argument, during which March, April and November were all strong contenders. In fact, while most scholars would allow the Gospel accounts of Christ's ministry and death to have at least a foundation of historical fact, the legends of His birth (as given by Matthew and Luke and subsequently embellished) bear all the hallmarks of a far older tradition—that of the Goddess giving birth at the Winter Solstice to the promised new Sun God, who would in due course die (or be sacrificed) as a prelude to rebirth (or resurrection).

The celebration of this birth is explicitly in the Incantation of the Wiccan Winter Solstice rite.

The ceremony begins as usual with the casting of the Circle and the summoning of the Lords of the Watchtowers. For this occasion, the Cauldron of Cerridwen (the symbol of immortality)

90

is placed towards the south of the Circle, wreathed with holly, ivy and mistletoe, and with fire inside it (which may be merely a candle). 'There should be none other light,' says the Book of Shadows, 'except the altar candle, and those about the Circle.'

After the Drawing Down of the Moon, the High Priestess stands behind the cauldron, and the coven form a ring facing inwards, men and women alternately. The High Priest stands facing the High Priestess with a bundle of unlit torches or candles and the Book of Shadows. One of the coven stands beside him with a lighted candle so that he may see to read.

The coven starts to move slowly round the Circle, deosil. As each one passes the High Priest, the latter lights a torch or candle from the fire in the cauldron and hands it to him, until everybody has one. A real fire is now lit in the cauldron if only a candle has been used so far, and the High Priest reads the Incantation:

Queen of the Moon, Queen of the Sun
Queen of the Heavens, Queen of the Stars,
Queen of the Waters, Queen of the Earth,
Bring to us the Child of Promise!
It is the Great Mother who giveth birth to Him;
It is the Lord of Life who is born again;
Darkness and tears are set aside when the Sun shall come up early.
Golden sun of the mountains, illumine the land,
Light up the world, illumine the seas and the rivers;
Sorrows be laid—joy to the world!
Blessed be the Great Goddess, without beginning,
Without end,
Everlasting to eternity, Io Evo[7] He! Blessed be!
Io Evo! He! Blessed be!
Io Evo! He! Blessed Be!

During the Incantation, the coven circle slowly. They join in the chant of 'Io Evo! He! Blessed be!' and finally the High Priestess joins the dance, leading it with a quieter rhythm.

The burning cauldron is pushed into the centre, and the dancers jump over it in couples. The last couple over before it goes out 'should be well purified, three times each, and may pay an amusing forfeit as the High Priestess may ordain'. Sometimes the cauldron is relit several times to prolong the fun.

And so to the cakes and wine.

¹From the Charge (*see* App. 2).

²The black and white ribbons are also regarded as symbolizing the two pillars of Solomon's Temple, Boaz (black) and Jakin (white), which stand for duality, the unity of balancing opposites. These pillars are a recurring theme in occult symbolism—for example, in the High Priestess card of the Tarot.

³Indoors, a fire may not be practicable, so the High Priestess may devise an alternative. At our last Spring Equinox, Maxine had us all kneeling in the centre facing outwards, while the Wheel (mirror outwards) was rolled along the floor hand to hand, several times round the outside of the group. The mirror caught the candlelight very prettily; Maxine is a natural choreographer, no bad thing in a High Priestess.

⁴See the Legend of the Descent of the Goddess, Appendix 1.

⁵The Book of Shadows says 'singing', but no tune is given.

⁶This strange phrase is as Alex copied it from his grandmother's Book of Shadows . . . The invocation is unique, being the only occasion when the High Priestess calls down the Goddess upon herself. In all other rites the High Priest calls down the Goddess upon the High Priestess, while she stands mute.

⁷'Io Evo!' is the Greek Bacchanalian cry of joy. Perhaps its nearest translation is the Australian 'Good-oh!'

8.

Clairvoyance

Clairvoyance (literally, 'clear-seeing') is the faculty of perceiving facts, objects, situations and events, either actual or potential, by means other than the physical senses. In the narrow definition, it means apprehending such information in the form of visual images, whether 'actual' or mental. More generally (and in this book) it includes seeing in the sense of 'I see what you mean'.

Clairaudience ('clear-hearing') is a similar faculty, but in that case the information comes as though heard instead of seen. For simplicity I include this, too, under the general heading of clairvoyance.

Alex maintains that everyone is clairvoyant if only he will let himself be, and that the faculty can be awakened, developed and trained. I think most people would agree that the gift of intuition appears to be widespread, particularly among women: 'hunches' arise without prior mental working-out, or obvious sensory data, to back them. We rely on intuition far more than we realize, if only because we simply have not enough time to apply conscious thought to all the thousands of major and minor decisions that have to be made each day of our lives. So we play our hunches, and whether we like the word or not, we are using clairvoyance. The man in the street would confine the word to the more spectacular and 'supernatural' manifestations of the gift, but these are merely the same thing developed to a high pitch, where vague awareness becomes certainty. Effective and reliable clairvoyance is, in essence, intuition understood, trusted and trained.

How to explain it is another matter, and worth a book (at least) by itself. On an orthodox psychological level, it may be said that the subconscious mind has absorbed all the known data from the conscious mind, and has gone on working on them underground. It arrives at an answer, and throws it up into consciousness. This sudden emergence of the answer often appears miraculous (and therefore untrustworthy) to the conscious mind, because it believes no work has been done on the problem. In fact the work has been done, but below the level of awareness.

When we decide to 'sleep on a problem', it is precisely this process which we are setting in motion. It works, and not only with emotional problems; scientists and mathematicians use it, too.

But this explanation, while certainly part of the truth, is not enough for all the phenomena involved. It cannot account for precognition (the foretelling of future events) except in so far as this is an extrapolation from known factors. For example, it would not account for the first prediction which Alex gave me personally, as recorded on page 4. There was no possible way in which I, or Alex, or my agent (whom Alex had no yet met), or even Thames Television, could have known at that stage that I would be writing a *Special Branch* episode, or what the fee (which my agent negotiated, not I) would be. (At the very most, Thames Television may have had my name in mind among those of other writers. But as every scriptwriter knows, when it comes to storylines and contracts, many are called but few are chosen.)

Nor can it account for many cases I have known in which Alex has given sound advice and accurate predictions over the telephone to, or about, people he has never met. One brief example: X was distressed about her fiance, Y, with whom she had quarrelled. Alex told here to ring Y at a certain time on a certain day at his office. She was sure that he would not be there, and even if he was, that he would be unable to talk. Alex insisted. She rang—and not only was he there, but he was alone and answered the phone himself.

Alex had never met or spoken to Y, and had no 'natural' way of knowing his movements, but he gave her his advice with absolute certainty. (Both Alex and X told me about this independently.)

To explain such cases, one has to go beyond the limits of conventional psychology into the realms of telepathy, the collective unconscious,[1] and the theory of levels. This is no place to propound such theories in depth, so I will confine myself to the practical ways in which witches actually use clairvoyance.

Highly-developed clairvoyants such as Alex seem to be able to draw their material 'out of the air' if necessary, without artificial aids, but most people need what may be called a 'trigger' to set them working.

Such triggers can give rise to a lot of misunderstanding, because they include, perfectly justifiably, such things as tea-leaves. Used mechanically to give an automatic answer according to set formulae, tea-leaves (or Tarot cards) deserve all the scorn the sceptic pours on them. Used as triggers, as catalysts to initiate a psychic process, as stimulators of the trained intuition, they are in a different class altogether.

The function of the trigger is to help into consciousness relevant symbols which are hesitating on its threshold. (Psychologists use the ink-blots of the Rorschach test in exactly the same way, and nobody calls them witches.) From there, the clairvoyant's intuition and experience carry the process forward to the interpretive stage.

Triggers are many and various. Physical objects include, apart from tea-leaves, molten lead poured into the water, the crystal ball, patterns in the fire, and even rings of froth on a beer-glass. The first time I saw Alex pick up a comparative stranger's beer-glass in a pub and start telling her things about herself, I must admit I thought he was pulling her leg. But her bewilderment at his accuracy made me think again.

'Guinness is best,' Alex told me cheerfully. 'Its froth is deeper, richer, and lasts longer.' Then, more seriously, 'It's not so much the thing itself, but the symbols it arouses in your mind, your reaction to the symbology, and the interpretation you put on it.'

Tarot cards (see the next chapter) are a far more complex trigger, once they have been mastered, because their symbology is unendingly rich and deep. Even without knowledge, they can be helpful. Alex tells of one woman whom he was trying to convince that she, like anyone, had clairvoyant powers. He gave her a Tarot pack (which she had never seen before) and told her to lay some cards out, choosing her own pattern. She did so, protesting that she had no idea what they meant. 'Never mind,' he told her, 'choose someone in the room you feel the message is for, and tell a story from the pictures.' Gaining confidence, she went ahead.

'Her message was excellent and useful,' Alex told me. 'It fitted, because the truth has been thrust on her.'

Individuals differ in the triggers which they find effective. For example, Alex does not advise new witches to spend a lot of money on a crystal, because it may not suit them. He recommends a cheaper substitute which suits almost anybody: dissolve copper sulphate crystals in water to a satisfying blue-green solution, pour it into a spherical flask (a laboratory flask is ideal) of which the neck has been cut off short either with a glass-cutter or by lighting a ring of cotton-wool soaked in methylated spirit, and cork and seal it without any air-bubbles. Then mount the flask upside-down on a stand lined with black velvet. 'It's the best crystal of all,' he says. 'It's peaceful, relaxing, and it induces the right state of mind.'

A trigger need not be a physical object at all. The clairvoyant may ask the querent[2] to give two or three numbers, and may then use number symbology to start off his train of thought. Or he may ask for random symbols from the querent's mind, and use these to provoke his own symbols.

Or the clairvoyant may use psychometry—taking an object in his hands which belongs to the querent, or to an absent person with whom the reading is concerned, and sensing its psychic 'charge' (again, in terms of the symbols which it provokes). Physical contact with the querent himself—touching his hand, for example—can serve the same purpose. In fact I suspect that palmistry, when it is effective, is really psychometry rather than a mechanical reading of lines.

Another class of trigger has a slightly different purpose, to detach rather than to stimulate. To this belong the swinging pendulum, the stroboscope, the stared-at candle flame, and also the ancient but dangerous methods of flagellation, restrictions of blood circulation, mortification of the flesh, fasting, and the stupefying vapours of the Delphic oracle. The main object of all these is to induce a trancelike detachment from the clairvoyant's surroundings, so that the symbols which arise are more vivid and undistorted by other influences.

In fact, though, both classes overlap, because deliberate concentration on a coal fire, or a crystal, or even tea-leaves, has some detaching effect, while at the same time providing the stimulus for images to arise. For the beginner (apart from the dangers of some of the other methods) these gentler approaches are to be preferred, and have the added advantage that the conscious mind remains clear for interpretation of the symbols. It is significant that the pronouncements of the bemused priestesses of Delphi were cryptic and that the querent was left to interpret the symbols himself, often disastrously.

With practice, the ability to discern and interpret symbols improves, and artificial triggers become less and less necessary. Results strengthen the apprentice clairvoyant's confidence in the symbols he sees, the interpretation he puts on them, and the relevance of fresh symbols that come to his mind as the interpretation develops. These fresh symbols at first look like mere 'free association' (if free association ever is 'mere'), crossing over into other categories—for example, from colour symbolism to Tarot symbolism to numerology to the Zodiac and back—but (again through results) he learns to trust them.

I was present recently when Alex gave just such an 'untriggered' clairvoyant reading to a man querent.

'I see a ball of wool, untidy—whatever you do, you always have to fasten a knot in it somewhere; it's never complete, always a flaw, you're never quite satisfied. Eventually you'll get what you're looking for in life. You won't buy the ball of wool, you'll start making it yourself from the raw materials, and there won't be flaws in it as you go along . . .

'I see a bunch of flowers, chrysanthemum, snowdrops and violets, tied by a blue wide ribbon which is all out of proportion to the smaller flowers, but not to the chrysanthemums . . . You'll have problems concerning rule and authority——that's blue, the Jupiter colour—— and it's in your home . . . The snowdrop comes through at the hardest time of the year. It's a delicate thing, it is absolute pristine purity. To get your rule, to fasten everything up with blue ribbon, you've got to wait till the really hard time comes, and then the purity and tininess of this seed of truth will start to come out . . . With the violet, which comes in the spring, things are fresher for you; unsettled conditions in your home are going to improve tremendously; there's a health condition which will improve, too.

But watch out between the end of October and the beginning of February for something absolutely new opening out in a business direction. This is the chrysanthemum, very deep bronze on the outside but very pale gold in the centre, which is excellent . . . Flower symbols often give you the time of year, you know. Rule, authority—there's some condition in your home life where you must put your foot down. Let them all say what they want to say (really, I don't know what it is I'm on about) but you make the final decision . . . Watch out for the five months October to February, even the symbology in the 5; 5 is the Hierophant in the Tarot, who wears a triple crown: there are three people ruling in one roost, but each has his own individuality, you get clashes, you need the big blue ribbon to bind everything up, kindly and gently . . .

'There should be quite a lot of money coming into the place, because the three flowers are all to do with money—don't ask me how, I don't know. Within the next five or six months. The snowdrop's the younger person, the violet the older lady; the chrysanthemum, you. Only one flower smells to me, the violet. Something very good there, something very real and worthwhile . . . But it's you who must bind the three up with the blue ribbon, there's got to be a balancing somewhere, an understanding. I don't know what this relates to, it's not my affair to know it . . . I can see the older lady's face, with lines around the eyes, not of age, but of eye-strain. Perhaps she should change her glasses? And she should go to bed early oftener, and you take her up a drink. . .'

After the man had gone, Alex said, 'Once you start on clairvoyance, you can go on opening it out for a long time. It must start with the imagination, hence all these mind-control exercises I give to my classes. Then the imagination must be guided, so that it becomes image, controlled imagery. Then the imagery can be called upon to produce images in harmony with another person who wants help, and they start throwing up the symbols for you. It's not telepathy, because that's unconscious, and this is very deliberate . . . Then you act on the symbolism and predict the outcome of the thing.

'If people don't understand, give it to them all the same. Your own relations with the person you're helping can affect what you see and say, because you want to please him. You have to detach yourself from this, and develop the attitude of getting something and giving it to him whether he believes it or not. The witch must do his work and then forget about it . . . Sometimes, if it's someone you love, the message has to be really drastic for it to force itself through.

'You succeed by constant practice, and by having the courage to do it. You may miss the mark sometimes at first, but that'll happen less and less as you go on . . . There's far more clairvoyance around than people realize, if only they'd dare to use it.'

A good way to start, Alex says, is to take the Tarot and learn the approximate symbolism of each card. Then to start working with them, by laying them out and trying to relate them to a particular problem and to each other. 'After a while you'll suddenly find that behind all this you're awakening something else. Other images are coming though, and you can interpret them.'

Incense can be helpful, and with this, as with all the other idioms of symbology—colours, plants, animals, the gods and goddesses of various pantheons, numbers, Hebrew letters, astrology, the Tree of Life, the Tarot—it is well worth while to study the traditional tables of correspondence given, for example, in Aleister Crowley's *Magick in Theory and Practice,* or more fully in his *777.* These correspondences may seem largely fortuitous at first glance, but the more you study them the more you realize they are not. And even if you are unconvinced of their universal validity, on a purely personal level they will equip you with a spreading web of associations which will make it that much easier for you to practise clairvoyance by following trails of symbology which branch out naturally and rewardingly.

Highly-developed clairvoyants can often see (I mean literally, with their eyes) phenomena which are invisible to the rest of us. Alex, for instance, says that he often knows that a stranger has undergone initiation into Wicca or some occult fraternity before he even speaks to him, because he can see a little silver disc 'about as big as a half-crown' glowing just above the stranger's head. I asked if this was a faculty of astral vision, like the ability to see a person's aura and its significant colours, but Alex thought it was on a higher level, spiritual rather than astral.

In fact, clairvoyance in general would seem to operate on the mental and spiritual levels rather than on the astral, which is just as well, because the astral plane (*see* Ch. 12) is notoriously one of illusion, where considerable experience is needed before one can be certain of the significance of what one sees. If, therefore, clairvoyance were mainly an astral function, reliable clairvoyance would be a monopoly of the advanced worker. But fortunately, since it is mainly mental and spiritual, the beginner's efforts can be useful, even if rudimentary, right from the start.

I have suggested that much of the information received symbolically in clairvoyance comes from the collective (and intercommunicating) unconscious, and the very fact that it is received symbolically supports this, because symbology is the only language the unconscious can speak. But the question arises—does some of it come from non-human, or human but discorporate, entities? I think that some of it must do. In Alex's case, for example, a lot of precise information comes from 'Michael' *(see* p. 70, who strikes me as operating (if he will forgive the description) as a kind of psychic leg-man for Alex, gathering and passing on not merely feelings but facts. Since Michael (however you explain him) is unquestionably conscious, he has no need of symbology but speaks to Alex directly. It was Michael who told Alex that X should ring her fiance Y at a particular time, in the example I gave earlier. And how would one communicate '11.15 a.m. on Thursday' by symbology?

For beginners, however, the source is veiled; they are merely aware of the symbols; all they need is the confidence to let them come, and the intelligent insight to interpret them.

To demonstrate that everybody has this ability if he will only use it, Alex suggested an experiment. At our next class, I was to look around the people present, write the names of three of them ('the more unlikely the better') on a piece of paper, and hand it to Alex, who would use my chosen three as guinea-pigs.

When the time came, I chose B, a shy lady who cam regularly with her husband to classes but seldom opened her mouth; C, a girl and G, a man, who were the newest attenders of each sex.

Alex took the paper, read it, grinned, muttered, 'Isn't he a bastard?' to Maxine, and called on B.

'Shut your eyes for about a minute,' he told her, 'and see what symbols come up. Then decide who you think they're for.'

I did feel a little guilty about my choice of B, because she was paralysed with self-consciousness and could produce nothing. But her shyness, paradoxically, broke the ice a little. Alex told her not to worry, she would find it easier next time, and turned to C.

C concentrated for her minute, and then said, 'I've got a picture of N with a silver chain round his neck, and a silver disc on the chain . . .I've tried to think of everybody else in the room, but I can only see N with that round his neck.'

'Good,' said Alex. 'Interpret what you think it is.'

'Oh, dear . . . To me it's a chain of office of some sort. That's all I can think of.'

'Well, I can tell you what it is,' Alex told her. 'The chain represents eternity, and the magic circle, and it's made of silver, the metal of the Moon Goddess. The disc is the full moon. And like the witch's necklace, it's a female symbol round the man's neck—and that's what N is looking for, in fact a woman witch he can work with as his High Priestess . . . Now, open it out further than that. Try to put a time to it, when he will be able to wear the chain of office.'

'I don't know, I just get the feeling it's not very long,' C said. 'He looked very much as I see him now, not any older.'[3]

'Fair enough,' Alex told her. 'Now, G . . .'

G produced something for me: 'I see Stewart and a briefcase—so much in it that he can't cope with it . . .' No need for interpretation—and how right he was!

After the three I had named, Alex asked for volunteers. M came up with a symbol for J: 'A bird, something like an eagle, but not a bird with feathers, it's metal or something like that . . . The wings are beautiful, but from the neck upwards it's ugly, really ugly . . .' The symbol meant nothing to M, but for J it had an exact meaning connected with her work.

Next, L produced for P 'a whirlwind, going up and up to a point, and getting higher at the top—no, I don't know what it means.'

Alex, however, did. 'P wants realization, and we've been working for her. The cone of power which the coven's been raising, it's coming to a point, and in the very near future you, P, will hear what you've been waiting to hear. You know what it is—I don't want to let it out to the whole crowd . . .'

I listened, absorbed, as others spoke, some understanding their symbols, some merely passing them on. Suddenly, to my surprise because I had been giving all my attention to the others, two symbols came very clearly to me.

The first was a picture of the Tower of Babel, like a tall wedding-cake, with tiny figures confusedly occupied on its various tiers. The second was a tangled pattern of the underground roots of a tree, weaving and looping through each other.

Before I had attached any meaning to these pictures, I knew they were for H, a studious and knowledgeable, if sometimes tongue-tied, third-degree witch, so I described them to him.

'Right,' said Alex. 'Try to interpret them.'

I thought for a moment. 'I suppose it means he's trying to base what he's doing on too much of a tangle of influences and ideas, so confusion's growing out of the top of it.'

'Just what I've been telling you privately,' Alex said to H. 'That you must finish one thing at a time. You've got too many things going on and never completed, your roots are all over the place, and instead of a trunk growing out of them, there's a Tower of Babel.'

After the class, H agreed with the assessment.

I had been impressed by the class experiment, not so much because the instances 'proved' anything, but because they confirmed the fruitfulness of the technique of catching and developing symbols. And when it happened to me quite spontaneously (the symbols and the knowledge that they concerned H all taking me unawares) the technique became a reality for me personally instead of a mere hypothesis, however intellectually convincing. It was a small thing, certainly, but it was my first conscious act of clairvoyance. I say 'conscious' advisedly, because it also made me realize that such symbols had been populating my mind all my life. I had simply never asked myself what could be done with them, or to whom they might be addressed. So Alex was right. Everybody can be clairvoyant if he realizes how to go about it.

Next day I repeated the experiment (silently) in relation to a woman I knew professionally quite well but domestically not at all. Thinking of her, I saw first a thick-set shrub, round, tight-leaved, and a few feet tall. Then, vividly, a metal ring round a wooden shaft of some kind, like a part of a walking-stick or umbrella.

Interpretation? The outline of her personality is clear, but her private life is impenetrable to her professional friends. We can see the leaves but not the stem. Something holds that personal life in an unbreakable ring; the ring is iron or steel, not gold, so it is not a wedding ring. Being a ring, it is endless and with no way out, but it is strong, smooth, and fits the shaft perfectly, so as well as constraining it, the ring holds it together and prevents it splitting. Although it represents an impasse in one sense, in another it represents stability, continuity, reliability. Perhaps she is as happy with the steel as she would be with the gold. The remarkable sweetness of her occasional smile suggests it . . .

Obviously, clairvoyance could become a habit. And why not?

[1]Although Jung was the great propounder of the concept of the collective unconscious, I realize that this use of his phrase exceeds what he meant. He applied it to the common racial memory, inconceivably ancient, in which the archetypes persist. I use it in the extended sense of such writers as Rosalind Heywood (*The Sixth Sense* and *The Infinite Hive*) who suggest that the collective unconscious can and does intercommunicate, and is the actual channel of telepathy.

[2]A general term for the person seeking a divinatory reading.

[3]C had only met N once before, and had no knowledge of this wish of his.

9.

The Tarot and the Tree

Two things are inseparable from the Western occult tradition, the Tarot pack, and the Cabalistic Tree of Life; and if witches of the old days knew little or nothing of the Cabala and only some of them had the Tarot, modern Wicca is deeply influenced by both.

At first sight, the Tarot is merely a pack of cards, some of which have a family resemblance to the modern playing pack; and the Tree of Life is a simple diagram of ten circles with Hebrew names and twenty-two connecting lines. Yet each is the blueprint of a philosophy of the universe, the quintessence of a wisdom so ancient that nobody can pinpoint its origin; Chaldea, Egypt, Atlantis, according to your school of thought. And Tarot and Tree are intimately interrelated.

The Tarot consists of seventy-eight cards, and is clearly the ancestor of the bridge-player's pack. Fifty-six of them are divided into four suits—Cups (corresponding to Hearts), Swords (Spades), Wands (Clubs), and Pentacles (Diamonds). Each suit has the Ace to Ten and the Knave—in between the Page and the Queen. (The Knight is sometimes called the Prince, and the Page the Princess.) The four suits represent the four occult elements—their usual allocation being Cups for Water, Swords for Air, Wands for Fire, and Pentacles for Earth, though some (including Alex) transpose Air and Fire (*see* p. 139). These fifty-six cards are known as the Minor Arcana (or 'lesser mysteries').

The remaining cards, numbered 0 and 1-21, are the Major Arcana ('greater mysteries') or Trumps Major; and apart from 0, the Fool, whose debased descendant is the Joker, they bear no relation to the modern pack. And yet they are the heart of the Tarot. The modern pack may be called the Tarot with the guts taken out, and I suspect it was the Church which was responsible for the evisceration. Until recently at least, the Church has frowned on cards as 'the Devil's picture book', but only, as far as the four suits were concerned, in relation to the minor sin of gambling. With the Major Arcana, however, it must have smelt brimstone, the heretical world of divination, lurking pagan gods, and a philosophy not worked out in the cloister. Unfair, in fact, because Christian interpretations of the Major Arcana are possible and have been made. But I cannot help feeling that priestly suspicion whittled the pack down to the the tolerated fifty-two (the Knight having somehow fallen by the wayside in the process).

It would be impossible, in half a chapter, to analyse the Major Arcana in any depth, and in any case there are almost as many interpretations of them as there are interpreters. Which is not to say that all but one (or even a majority) of them are wrong. The Tarot is so rich in symbolism that anyone who starts to study it will find meanings behind meanings. Like any set of symbols, it is a mirror which interacts with the observer as though it were itself a living organism.[1] But to give some idea of the Major Arcana to those who have never seen a Tarot Pack, here is a brief description of each card. From the many Tarots currently on sale, I have taken as standard the Waite pack,[2] not because it is the most attractive (unfortunately it is not) but because it is generally accepted as being the most accurate in its symbolism.

1. The Magician (also called the Magus or the Juggler). A young man holding up a wand in his right hand, and pointing to the earth with his left. On a table before him are the four elemental symbols, and above his head is the sign of eternity or infinity ∞ (also known as the sign of the Holy Spirit). He is the Magus, the Adept, the human being integrated on all planes, the will liberated through understanding. His gesture refers to the basic occult principle 'That which is above is as that which is below, but after another manner'.

2. The High Priestess (also called the Female Pope, Pope Joan, the Temple Virgin, Occult Science). A young woman seated between the pillars Boaz and Jakin[3] and in front of the veil of the Temple. On her lap, half-hidden, is the scroll of the Tora, the Secret Law. She is crowned with the disc and horns of Isis, and the crescent moon is at her feet. She both offers occult wisdom, and guards it. She is at the same time virgin and mother. Waite says she is 'the spiritual Bride of the just man, and when he reads the Law she gives the divine meaning,' and adds 'there are some respects in which this card is the highest and holiest of the Greater Arcana'.

3. The Empress (also called the Celestial Mother). A seated woman, crowned and bearing a sceptre. While the High Priestess is virginal and secret, the Empress is fecund and of this world. She is action, fertility, the Earth Mother; in some packs she is shown as pregnant. In a sense she is the equilibrium of Cards 1 and 2.

4. *The Emperor*[4] A throned ruler, also with crown and scepter. In many ways, the virile counterpart of the Empress. He, too, is of this world; executive power and intellectual wisdom. In one sense, says Waite, it is he who 'seeks to remove the Veil of Isis; yet she remains *virgo intacta*'; intellect alone will never enter the secret Temple.

5. *The Hierophant* (also called the Pope). A seated priestly figure with a triple crown. He is 'the ruling power of external religion', in contrast to the High Priestess who symbolizes the inner secrets. This does not mean he merely represents an empty outward show (though he can degenerate into it), but that he stands, at his best, for the public expression of those truths which have their root in the hidden occult wisdom common to all such forms.

6. *The Lovers*. A young man and woman turning toward each other, with the sun shining down on them. In the Waite pack they are a naked Adam and Eve, innocence before contamination, with an angelic figure blessing them from above. In other packs, this is a Cupid figure with bow and arrow. A card of human love, with many implications: discriminating choice, equilibrium of male and female principles. Also, as Eden Gray puts it in *The Tarot Revealed*, 'the self-conscious intellect represented by the man does not establish direct contact with super-consciousness (the Angel), except through Eve (the subconscious)'—which is, in psychological terms, the secret of Wicca.

7. *The Chariot*. A figure in armour riding a chariot drawn by two sphinxes, one black and one white, which he controls by a wand or sword. (In some packs the sphinxes are horses.) This, too, is a card of equilibrium, and of triumph: the charioteer progresses confidently by controlling, with his will and knowledge, the twin forces of power and love, of Boaz and Jakin. He has learned the secret of polarity, of the positive resultant of contrasting forces.

8. *Strength* (also called Force, Fortitude, of the Enchantress).[5] A woman closing (or in some packs opening) the jaws of a lion. Above her head is the same eternity symbol ∞ which is above the Magician (in some packs this symbol is formed by the curves of their hats). Her strength is not brute force, nor courage in the ordinary sense, but the power of spiritual development, of holy innocence. She is sometimes described as the feminine counterpart of St. George with his Dragon.

9. *The Hermit*. A cloaked and bearded man, carrying a lantern and a staff. He is often interpreted as a seeker after wisdom, but is perhaps better seen as one who has already attained it, whose

lamp is not to guide his own feet, but to show the way to those who follow him.

10. The Wheel of Fortune. A wheel bearing on its rim the letters T—A—R—O (which can also be read as R—O—T—A, wheel) and the Tetragrammaton.[6] Circling with it are the jackal-headed Egyptian god Hermes-Anubis (representing the upward evolution of consciousness) and the serpent Typhon (representing cosmic energy manifesting as form). Above the wheel is a sphinx—equilibrium again, stability within movement. In the corners of the card are the four creatures of Ezekiel[7]—man or angel, eagle, lion and bull, all of them winged. They are unchanging reality in the midst of which the universe, and human life, are in constant flux. It is this flux within constancy, rather than any crude idea of 'luck', which the card stands for, in spite of widely differing symbols from pack to pack.

11. Justice[8] The traditional figure of Justice, with sword and scales (but in this case not blindfolded) sits throned and crowned between two pillars. The symbolism is straightforward, and once more involves the recurring theme of equilibrium.

12. The Hanged Man. A youth hanging upside down, by one ankle tied to a T-cross of living wood. His other leg is bent to form a cross with the first, and his hands are behind his back. Round his head is a golden nimbus. 'It is a card of profound significance,' says Waite, 'but all the significance is veiled.' Sacrifice is an oversimplified interpretation. The concept of the Dying and Resurrected God is here--and in human sense, transformation and awakening: 'a reversal of the mind rather than of the body', as Eden Gray suggests.

13. Death (also called the Skeleton Reaper). In the Waite pack, a skeleton in armour rides a white horse and carries a banner with a white rose signifying life. On the horizon beyond him is the gateway of immortality. Most other packs show a skeleton with a scythe, but the Death card does not necessarily stand for physical death—rather, for the death of the old self followed by rebirth, renewal. Most occult fraternities' initiation rituals include a symbolic death and rebirth (as does the Wiccan second degree with its story of the Descent of the Goddess and her conquest of Death) so card 13 may also be said to symbolize Initiation.

14. Temperance (also called the Angel of Time, and—by Crowley—Art). A winged angel, neither male or female, bestrides earth and water, and pours liquid from one chalice to another. In one sense, the essence of life is moving from past into future; in another, male and female principles are uniting. 'Temperance' here has nothing to do with teetotalism, but means tempering, combining, harmonizing; yet another aspect of Equilibrium.

15. The Devil. A horned devil with bat's wings squats on an altar, to which are chained a male and a female figure. In the Waite pack these two recall the Lovers of Card 6, 'as if Adam and Eve after the Fall'. The man and woman are not degenerate, however. Their faces are intelligent and their chains are loose. The card does not imply damnation, but rather the inevitable stage after knowledge has banished innocence, and before it has been liberated by understanding. Matter is the master at present, but is destined to become the servant.

16. The Tower (also called the Lightning-Struck Tower and the House of God). A tower being struck by lightning and bursting into flames; two human figures are falling from its summit. In a way this parallels the last card. While that concerned the trap of materialism, this concerns the trap of intellectual pride and dogmatism. The flash of spiritual insight is demolishing the structure of false reasoning. In the Waite card, the sky is raining drops of light in the form of Hebrew 'Yods', symbolizing the cosmic life-force fertilizing material existence. The lightning destroys so that the Yod may rebuild.

17. The Star.[9] A naked girl, youth and beauty personified, kneels on the land with her right foot in the water. She has a ewer in each hand, and is pouring the Waters of Life impartially onto land and sea. A huge eight-pointed star, surrounded by seven smaller stars, shines down upon her. She is the Great Mother, eternally young, eternally renewing creation, giving life to both mind and to matter. In turn, she herself is a manifestaion of the ultimate, limitless source of cosmic energy represented by the Star.

18. The Moon. A dog and a wolf are baying at the waxing Moon, which has a woman's profile. Beyond them, a path winds between two towers to a hilly horizon. In the foreground is a pool from which a creature like a lobster is crawling onto dry land. A card of levels of consciousness: man's half-evolved nature is drawn towards (though it fears) the reflected light of the imagination— which can lead it forward into the astral plane. Behind is the depth of the unconscious, from which nameless things emerge.[10] The light, although of the imagination, is not illusory, for the Moon, too, is sending down the Yods of the life-force.

19. The Sun. A naked child, riding a white horse and carrying a red banner, emerges from a walled garden. The Sun, many-rayed and with a man's face, shines benevolently down on him. (Other packs show two children, on foot.) This time the light is not reflected, but direct: the full light of understanding which completes the evolutionary cycle by restoring innocence, but now fulfilled and balanced by wisdom. The garden—the whole of Nature—turns toward man for its final development, and fully self-conscious man leads it forward into the new phase.

20. Judgement (also called the Last Judgement, the Angel, and—by Crowley—the Aeon). The archangel Gabriel blows his trumpet from the heavens, and men, women, and children emerge from their open coffins, arms upraised. Not the Last Judgement in the traditional sense, but the call of the Supernal, heard and answered within, and bringing transformation.

21. The World (also called the Universe). A dancer, naked except for a drape across her loins, holds a wand in each hand. She is framed by an oval wreath of leaves. In the corners of the card are the same four creatures of Ezekiel which appear in Card 10. The World is a card of completion, of attainment, 'the restored world when the law of manifestation shall have been carried to the highest degree of natural perfection,' says Waite, adding that it can also refer to the beginning of the cycle when 'all was declared to be good, when the morning stars sang together and all the Sons of God shouted for joy'. Eden Gray again puts it in psychological terms: 'The dancer represents the final attainment of man, the merging of the self-consciousness with the subconscious and blending of these two with the superconsciousness.' This tallies with the tradition that the dancer's drape (which appears in all packs) hides the fact that she is really hermaphroditic—the final equilibrium of male and female principles; not sexless like a milk-and-water Victorian angel, but containing both forces.

0. The Fool. A young man, richly dressed, steps unafraid to the edge of a precipice; a dog romps at his heels. In one hand he carries a wand (the will) to which is attached a wallet (stored memories, the riches of the Universal Subconscious), and in the other a white rose (freedom from mere animality). His gaze is towards the sky, not the abyss below. He is not a Fool in the modern sense, but a holy innocent; the Spirit of Aether, as Crowley calls him. In fact he has more in common with the mediaeval court Fool, often the only man whose wisdom and wit the King could trust, because it was completely untrammelled by convention or respect for rank. He enters this world in search of experience, but is not of it, a Yod about to plunge into the abyss of manifestation. That is why he is numbered 0: he is everywhere but nowhere, universal, but bound to no hierarchy. A Fool, but no fool, he is the free-ranging spirit of humanity.

The Tarot is an alphabet of symbolism with which whole volumes of ideas can be spelled out. It is almost an anticlimax to say that it can be used for divination, too. But it has a very real function in that sphere, as I indicated in the last chapter. At one extreme, certainly, it can degenerate into mere party-trick fortune-telling, with a whole set of traditional meanings for each card, mechanically applied, which seem to bear little relation to the occult symbolism, at least of the Major Arcana.

But on a higher level, the Tarot can be a catalyst for one's own psychic insight. There are several systems and layouts for Tarot divination, given in many books[11] and, properly used, they all have their advantages. The thing that matters is to use their readings as guide lines and hints on which the power of one's intuition can work. Then they can be astonishingly (sometimes disturbingly) provocative of ideas which seem beyond the reach of unaided insight. Used mechanically and without concentration, on the principle of 'press the button and out comes the answer', they are a waste of time.

A friend of mine, highly intelligent but without any occult training, bought a Tarot pack and tried several divinatory readings out of curiosity. They proved so accurate that she was frightened into putting the pack away for good. I am certain that the reason lay not in the cards themselves, so much as in the fact that she was naturally intuitive and used the Tarot correctly by instinct, so that it triggered off her unsuspected powers.

The Tarot Major Arcana, and less richly the Minor Arcana, have their correspondences and cross-references with every sphere of occult study, from Astrology to the Elements and the 360° of the Magic Circle—but most intimately of all, with the Cabalistic Tree of Life.

The Tree of Life, like the Tarot, is too vast a subject for a few hundred words. On this, too, many books have been written[12] and many more will be, but no work on modern Wicca would be complete without at least a basic description of it and a few pointers to its significance.

I have touched on the Cabala in Chapter 2; the Tree of Life is its map, 'the ground-plan of the Western Esoteric Tradition', as Dion Fortune describes it. To put it in the simplest terms, it portrays the steps by which the unknowable Ultimate, which manifests itself 'downwards' to produce the Universe and Man as we know them; and correspondingly, the steps by which Man evolves 'upwards' through various levels of consciousness and being to re-identify himself with his source.

Fig. 8 below shows the plan of the Tree. It consists of ten spheres or Sephiroth (singular, Sephira) connected by twenty-two paths. The Sephiroth are generally referred to by their Hebrew names because this identifies them at once as Sephiroth, whereas such words as 'Kingdom' or 'Strength' do not.

Each of the twenty-two connecting Paths is traditionally associated with one of the Tarot trumps, and I have so marked them. It would be too much of a diversion to discuss these associations here, but any reader who likes to think them over should find the study interesting.[13]

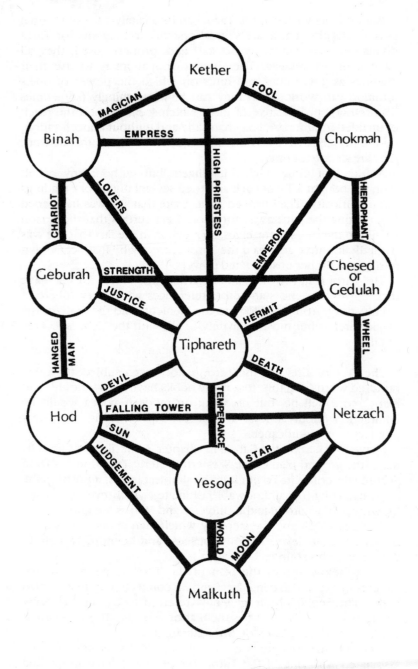

Fig. 8. The Tree of Life.

Fig. 9 shows the natural sequence of the Sephiroth, which is the same both upwards and downwards; Fig. 10 shows the three Pillars into which the Tree may be divided vertically; and Fig. 11 gives the three Triangles into which it may be divided horizontally.

The top Sephira, Kether, is the highest conceivable by human consciousness. Beyond this is the Unmanifest, or 'Negative Existence', which the Cabalists divided into three planes of Veils. First, 'Ain', Negativity; second, 'Ain Soph', the Limitless; and finally, 'Ain Soph Aur', the Limitless Light. It is out of Ain Soph Aur that Kether becomes manifest. The three Veils are by definition unknowable, so their names are merely useful symbols for what cannot be grasped, and are employed much as the mathematician uses the term 'root minus one'.

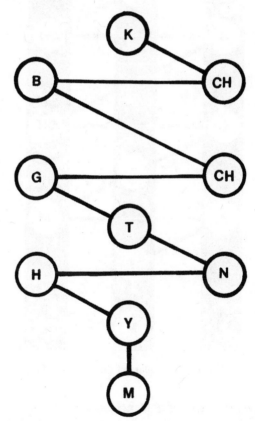

Fig. 9. Sequence of Sephiroth of the Tree of Life (upwards and downwards).

The Cabala sees evolution as a progressive series of manifestations. (In this concept, the Hidden Wisdom of Israel was far ahead of its public legends; the Tree of Life can be equated with modern scientific cosmology; Genesis 1 to 3 cannot, except symbolically.) Each Sephira therefore preceded the next in time, but subsequently coexisted with it in space, overflowing into it, so to speak. Each can be thought of as feminine, negative, receptive in relation to the one before it, and masculine, positive, active in relation to the one that follows it. Each includes within itself both polarities.

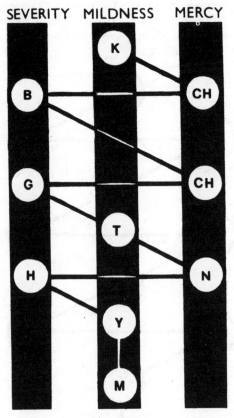

Fig. 10. The Pillars of the Tree of Life.

The Universe, including Man, includes within itself all the Sephiroth, which is why the process of individual development 'upwards' is not so much a climbing, as an opening-up and realization of what is already within us in potential. When a witch says 'Wicca teaches levels of consciousness' he could equally well put it that 'Wicca opens up progressively higher Sephiroth'.

The ten Sephiroth, in descending order, are:

1. Kether (Crown). The first manifestation, the Prime Mover, 'I Am That I Am', pure being without form, and, until it gave rise to Chokmah, without activity. In theological terms, to attain consciousness of Kether is to achieve union with God. Its magical image is an ancient bearded king, seen in profile.

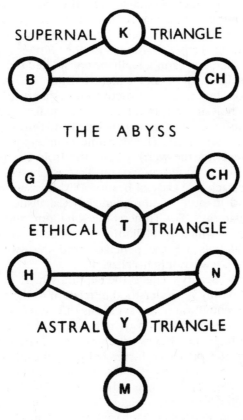

Fig. 11. The Triangles of the Tree of Life.

2. Chokmah (Wisdom). Activity begins; Kether becomes dynamic in Chokmah, but it is as yet a dynamism without organization, a pure rush of cosmic energy. Chokmah is the Supernal Father, the Yod of the Tetragrammaton, the impregnating force of the universe. Its God-name is Jehova, its symbol the phallus, and its magical image a bearded male figure.

3. Binah (Understanding), Force becomes organized in form; Binah, the Supernal Mother, the Sanctifying Intelligence, is the feminine principle balancing Chokmah. Inert in itself, it receives Chokmah's boundless but undirected energy and sets it to work.

This paradox of inertia and creativity is reflected in two of its names—Ama, the dark sterile Mother, and Aima, the bright fertile Mother; also in its allocation both to Juno and to Saturn. Binah's God-name is Jehova Elohim (*see* note 16, p. 117), its symbols are the yoni and the chalice, and its magical image is a mature woman.

4. Chesed (Mercy). (Also called Gedulah.) This is the first Sephira below the Abyss which separates the Three Supernals from the rest of the Tree (*see* Fig. 11). Actual manifestation, as the finite mind can conceive it, only begins below the Abyss. Chokmah is the all-begetting Father; Chesed is the Jupiter sphere, the protecting Father, and cannot really be considered separately from the next Sephira, Geburah, which balances it. As Binah is formative, so Chesed is constructive, the sphere of archetypal ideas. Its symbols are the solid figure, the equal-armed cross, the sceptre; and its magical image is a crowned and throned king.

5. Geburah (Strength). The dynamic counterpart of Chesed, Geburah is severity, the warrior king, the Holy Destroyer, Mars, 'as necessary to the equilibrium of the Tree as Chesed, the Lord of Love, and Netzach, the Lady of Beauty'.[14] This essential balance is acknowledged in pure (if unrecognized) Cabalistic terms every time a Christian says 'For Thine is the Kingdom, and the power, and the glory'—which is 'Malkuth, ve Geburah, ve Gedulah'.[15] Geburah's symbols are the pentagon and the sword, and its magical image is a warrior in his chariot.

6. Tiphareth (Beauty). This is the Sephira which, more than all the others, can only be understood in relation to the whole of the Tree. It is the equilibrium and synthesis of Chesed and Geburah, and also of Hod and Netzach. It is the central point of the six Sephiroth which lie below the Abyss. Cosmically, above Tiphareth are the planes of force, below it the planes of form. Humanly, above it is the point of transmutation. In terms of levels of consciousness, Tiphareth is where the mind 'changes gear'. Exoteric religion can see no higher. In Christian terms, it is the Christ-figure, the Redeemer, Tiphareth the Son showing us Kether the Father; in Greek terms; Dionysos or Adonis; in Roman, Apollo; in Egyptian, Osiris; it is the Illuminator as well as the Sacrificial God. Symbols of Tiphareth are the Rosy Cross, the Calvary Cross, and the truncated pyramid; its magical images are a majestic king, a child, and a sacrificed god.

7. Netzach (Victory). This is the Venus Sephira, the realm of the emotions, and instincts, of the group mind, of the life-force of Nature. Like Chesed and Binah, but on a lower plane, it balances with its opposite Hod as force to form. Netzach is peopled by elusive beings hovering around the frontiers of manifestation. Above Netzach, concepts can only be perceived by abstract intuition; here, the developing mind begins to see them as astral forms, subjective in the sense that the individual 'invents' them in his own associative terms, archetypal in the sense that he draws on the collective symbolism of the group mind, actual in the sense that they mirror aspects of a higher reality. It is easy to be deceived on these lower Sephiroth, the Plane of Illusion, but there is much wheat among the chaff, and one of the main functions of Wiccan training is to teach the witch to tell them apart. In fact, since the ten Sephiroth correspond to the traditional ten degrees of occult initiation, the lower Sephiroth are the specific province of the three degrees of Wicca. Practically, it is impossible to put the Sephiroth in water-tight compartments, because they all affect each other, and in one sense each degree refers not merely to one Sephira but to the 'leap' from it to the next, but in general the bottom four Sephiroth may be called the home ground of Wiccan Activity. The God-name of Netzach is Jehovan Tzabaoth, the Lord of Hosts;[16] its symbols are the lamp and girdle, and the rose; its magical image is a beautiful naked woman.

8. Hod (Glory). The sphere of Mercury, of Hermes, of the intellect, where universality is finally differentiated into individual human minds. Hod represents form on the astral plane, as its counterpart Netzach represents force. All the god-forms which man has personified belong to Hod. It is the sphere of magic, because it is the magician's intelligent will that creates the necessary forms, but they can only be 'ensouled' by drawing on Netzach, the sphere of emotion and empathy. (As I said in reference to the Emperor card, intellect alone cannot enter the secret Temple.) Hod's God-name is Elohim Tzabaoth, the God (or male-female dual principle) of Hosts. Its symbols are the occultist's Names and Versicles and Apron (known also to the Masons), and its magical image is a hermaphrodite.

9. Yesod (Foundation). Sometimes called the Sphere of the Machinery of the Universe; its associated spiritual experience is the vision of that machinery. In old rabbinical phraseology, Yesod 'purifies the emanations' of the other Sephiroth, 'proves and corrects' them, and is responsible for unity of design. It is the sole channel by which these emanations are transmitted to the physical plane, and is therefore essential to any magical operation which is meant to take effect in that plane. It is the sphere of the Akashic Principle of Astral Light, the universal psychic ether which is the raw material of the astral plane, denser than mind but more tenuous than matter, and forming the organic link between the two. It is the first sphere the witch (or any other occultist) contacts as he begins to learn to 'rise on the planes', or open up levels of consciousness. Yesod is also the Moon-sphere, in an eternal condition of cyclic flux, which again has an important bearing on magical operations. Within this rhythm is included both the chaste

Diana and the Fertile Isis. In Christian terms, it is the sphere of the Holy Spirit. Yesod's God-name is Shaddai el Chai, the Almighty Living God, its symbols, perfumes and sandals[17]; its magical image, a strong and beautiful naked man.

10. Malkuth (Kingdom). The manifest universe, the sphere of the elements both occult and physical, the end product of involution through which all life must pass before it can complete its development by 'climbing' back to its source. All the emanations of the Tree come, through the organizing filter of Yesod, to Malkuth, where they crystallize into concrete form. Yet Malkuth is not only matter, it is also the Earth-soul, 'the subtle, psychic aspect of matter; the underlying noumenon of the physical plane which gives rise to all physical phenomena'.[18] Magically, Malkuth is the sphere of divination, of the use of material objects (including the Tarot) to provide answers to non-material questions. As I have already hinted, this can only be done by establishing an effective link with at least the bottom triangle of the Tree. The God-names of Malkuth are Adonai Malekh (the Lord who is King) of Adonai ha Aretz (the Lord of Earth). Its symbols are the altar of the double cube, the equal-armed cross, the magic circle, and the triangle of art. Its magical image is a young woman, crowned and throned.

These are bare bones; so much more could be said. For example, the Sephiroth can be allocated to parts of the human body (*see* Note 2, p. 137). And one could discuss the Qlipoth (Hebrew, 'harlots'), the 'awful forms, dangerous even to think upon' which are the evil counterparts of each Sephira, thrown off during the phase of disequilibrium before it fulfilled itself by giving birth to the Sephira below. The fully-developed occultist must understand the Qliphoth so that he can control and limit them.

But on this question of evil, one final point should be made clear. There is no question of equating the upper planes of the Tree with good and the lower, grosser planes with evil. To the Cabalist, all Sephiroth are equally holy—necessary phases in the cosmic process. And if the Right-Hand Path means anything, the witch—who operates primarily on the lower Sephiroth—must accept this equality of holiness.

1. Some outstanding minds have drawn inspiration from the Tarot; T. S. Eliot, for example, in *The Waste Land.*

2. Designed by Pamela Colman Smith under the instruction of Arthur Edward Waite, published and exported by University Books, Inc. New York, and on sale in most occult bookshops.

3. *See* note 2 p. 92, also Card 7 below.

4. On the paths of the Tree (Fig. 8) Aleister Crowley interchanges Emperor and Star, for reasons too complex to be gone into here.

5. Numbered 11 (thus changing places with Justice) in packs earlier than Waite, and still by some.

6. The four Hebrew letters Yod, He, Vau, He—simply, the Name of God, but in a more fundamental sense, the formula of the cosmic creative process.

7. Ezekiel 1:10.

8. Otherwise numbered 8—*see* note 5 above.

9. *See* note on the Emperor.

10. An archetypal concept, like so much in the Tarot. Jung, analysing the symbols in a patient's dream, writes: 'The water signifies the unconscious, or rather, the state of unconsciousness, of concealment; for the crab too is something unconscious, in fact it is the dynamic content that lies concealed in its depths.' *(Collected Works* 2nd. edn., Vol. 7, p. 89)

11. For example, *The Pictorial Key to the Tarot* by A. E. Waite; *The Book of Thoth* by Aleister Crowley; *THe Tarot of the Bohemians* by Papus; and for a simple modern approach, with the added advantage of plenty of white space to write notes, *The Tarot Revealed* by Eden Gray. Though published in America, all these are on sale in Britain.

12. For example, *The Kabbalah* by C. D. Ginsburg; *The Mystical Qabalah* by Dion Fortune; and *A Practical Guide to Qabalistic Symbolism* by Gareth Knight.

13. Including the fact, already mentioned, that Crowley (and others following him) interchange the Emperor and the Star.

14. Dion Fortune, loc. cit.

15. Some witches, including Alex, use the Cabalistic Cross during Circle-casting. In full it is 'Kether' (facing east, right hand to forehead with palm open to left), 'Malkuth' (facing south, right hand to waist), 've Geburah' (facing west, hands palm-to-palm to right shoulder), 've Gedulah' (facing north, hands to left shoulder), 'le olham' ('forever'—hands central). 'Glory' is the literal translation of Hod, but in another sense it is a legitimate meaning of Gedulah or Chesed.

16. I have only given some of these God-names, because most of them are incomprehensible except to a Hebrew scholar. But they are very revealing, because the Bible uses them with great precision and with full awareness of their Cabalistic meaning. By identifying the original Hebrew God-name in any Bible passage, one can place it on the Tree, and the passage is illuminated in terms of the Hidden Doctrine. See, for example, note on p. 29.

17. 'Put off thy shoes from thy feet, for the place whereon thou standest is holy ground.' The magician makes his own holy ground by wearing consecrated sandals.

18. Dion Fortune, loc. cit.

10.

Magic

A witch works with elemental forces. A magician works with the essences behind these forces. A witch works naturally, largely instinctively, as a rule in a coven but occasionally alone. A magician works methodically, with exact knowledge of what he is doing, as a rule alone but sometimes with helpers.

Their basic aim is, or should be, the same: the spiritual development of the individual witch or magician, and the expanding of his consciousness.

Some witches, and some magicians, would draw a sharp dividing line between the two. There are witches who believe that anyone practising one of the various systems of magic disqualifies himself from Wicca. There are magicians who (as one of them, though himself more tolerant, has put it) 'wouldn't be seen dead with a witch'.

Everyone is entitled to, and indeed should, choose his own path. It may be Wicca, or one of the systems of magic, or (if he feels he can handle them) both, and it is difficult to understand why anyone who finds the two compatible, in terms of his own personality, needs, and state of development, should rouse such fury in certain sectarian minds. In particular I see no reason why someone like Alex, who began as a witch and developed himself into a magician, should not stay within Wicca if he wants to, and devote part of his energies to it, if only to help and train newer witches and to make his experience, understanding, and wider horizons available to them; any more than a professional orchestral conductor should be criticized for singing pop songs with his children and teaching them how to sing in tune.

After all, Wicca *is* magic, mostly sympathetic and nature magic in a simple tradition. A witch's coven raises power in an elementary way (in both senses of the word 'elementary') and applies it by methods which have been evolved through trial and error over the centuries rather than by academic understanding. It has its own unique beauty, it strikes a deep chord in human nature, and it works.

In this sense, a magician proper is a more advanced, more sophisticated, more scholarly and more highly-developed witch. Similarly, any witch who takes his work seriously, and really tries to understand what he is doing, is already beginning to be a magician even if he was only initiated last week.

That is why the three degrees of Wicca provide one (though only one) of the valid ways of setting foot on the occult and magical ladder.

Wicca is not for everybody (though it would be good for a lot of people who do not realize the fact). Magic is for even fewer, because it can be a rigorous and lonely path.

A magician, to the man in the street, is someone who can wave a magic wand and perform miracles.[1] It is true that the magician, like the witch, can and does produce results in divination, healing, manifestation, evocation, exorcism, the psychic 'charging' of talismans and so on which seem to break the rules of mundane cause and effect. In fact, these phenomena merely show that the magician has a better understanding of the rules (and of the rules behind the rules) than has the man in the street. He does not flaunt his powers, nor use them unnecessarily, nor try to 'prove' them publicly, nor even care if they are believed or not; because to him, they are by-products of his real purpose—his own spiritual development. He will use them to help someone, if he is asked, but not to show off.

If spiritual development is his aim, why does he not join a church or synagogue or mosque? The same question cannot be asked of a witch, because in his own way he has done just that—joined a religious group with a congregation, common beliefs, and regular services. But the lone magician?

Israel Regardie in *The Art and Meaning of Magic* uses the simile of a man who wants to reach the roof of a ten-storey building. Conventional religion tends to attempt to jump from ground to roof, while magic recognizes the existence of the floors in between and uses either the stairs or the lift.

In either case, it is a graduated process—an evolution, if you wish. Man, holds the magical theory, is a more or less complicated creature whose several faculties of feeling, sensation, and thinking have slowly been evolved in the course of aeons of evolution. It is

119

fatal to ignore these faculties . . . the whole man must evolve, and not simply little bits or aspects of him, whilst other parts of his nature are left undeveloped at a primitive or infantile level of being. Moreover, these faculties must be so trained as to be able to 'take' the enormous tension sure to be imposed upon them by so exalted but nevertheless so powerful an attainment. Each faculty must be deliberately trained and carried stage by stage through various levels of human and cosmic consciousness so that gradually they become accustomed to the high potential of energy, ideation, and inspiration that must inevitably accompany illumination and an extension of consciousness.

This stage-by-stage development of the entire human being is the whole aim of magic. It can be most easily understood (in the Western tradition at least[2]) by relating it to the Tree of Life. The ten 'grades' of magical progress correspond, in ascending order, to the Tree's ten Sephiroth which I outlined in the last chapter. There are many different attitudes to this scale of grades, but the generally accepted one is that of the Golden Dawn: Zelator, Theoricus, Practicus, Philosophus, Adeptus Minor, Adeptus Major, Adeptus Exemptus, Magister Templi, Magus and Ipsissimus. (The name for this highest grade, which means literally 'one's very self' or 'most truly oneself', expresses the goal of all Western magical systems.) The grades may also be indicated by a number code: $1° = 10^{\Box}$ for Zelator, $2° = 9^{\Box}$ for Theoricus, up to $10° = 1^{\Box}$ for Ipsissimus. (Also found is $0° = 0^{\Box}$ for Neophyte, who is not yet related to a Sephira.)

Alex emphasizes that these grades are only a sliding scale, and tend all too easily to become 'a snob thing'. A true magician regards them merely as convenient labels for certain spiritual experiences achieved by the appropriate techniques, preparations, and rituals; and only he knows when he has undergone those experiences and the grades are genuinely his.

'Some occult fraternities,' Alex says, 'have made the higher grades so unattainable that people are afraid to do the rituals that go with them. They don't realize that in ordinary life you can attain Godhead, but you only get a glimpse of it, a feeling of it; it wouldn't do for you to be in it all the time. In fact you may attain the grade without doing the rites. You can devise your own rituals; you don't have to follow any particular way. For example, you may decide that your Geburah aspect—the forceful, energetic Sephira—needs strengthening, so you find, or adapt, or devise, the appropriate rites of Mars, and when you know in yourself that you have achieved the result you need, the balancing of that aspect of yourself and the spiritual experience that goes with it, then you have that grade.

'An order can put itself out of reach with all the expensive robes and trappings and intellectual snobbery it attaches to the various grades. The Golden Dawn did, and today it's not so powerful as the Wicca. Aleister Crowley said he was writing to help the grocer, the factory girl, the mathematician and everybody—and then put whole paragraphs of his rituals into classical Greek!

'Fine feathers make fine birds, but some things are carrion when you eat them...The basic Circle is four candles and the furniture pushed back; it's the symbology you put into it that matters.'

There are many systems of magic, suited to individual temperaments, and because their basic principle is the same, they overlap; so any names that are attached to them indicate their particular emphasis rather than watertight categories.

'Ritual magic' can be applied to them all in varying degrees, because the technique of magic is a ritual one—on the principle which I have already explained of using ritual to bring the Microcosm in tune with the Macrocosm, thereby achieving results which transcend the individual's unaided power.

'Ceremonial magic' lays emphasis on the robes, colours, tools, weapons, incenses and so on which are used, and on planetary correspondences and hours (*see* App. 3). In ecclesiastical terms, it could be called 'high'.

'Hermetic magic' goes to the other extremes; it aims at dispensing altogether with material accessories, and achieving its results by mental, psychic, and spiritual development alone. Hermetic philosophy stems from Hermes Trismegistos, the Thrice-Greatest Hermes, a figure who may have been actual, mythological, or (as so often happens) actual with mythological accretions. Tradition says that Abraham's wife Sarah found his body in a cave tomb clutching a tablet of emerald on which the philosophy was inscribed. The earliest known versions of the Emerald Table are in Arabic, and it had been translated into Latin at least by the twelfth century A.D. Its first sentence is: 'That which is above is like that which is below, and that which is below is like that which is above, to achieve the wonders of the one thing'[3]—the fundamental axiom of all magic, occultism and witchcraft. Hermetic philosophy is based on seven Principles—of Mind, of Correspondence, of Vibration, of Polarity, of Rhythm, of Cause and Effect, and of Gender.

'Cabalistic magic' lays emphasis on the Tree of Life, with rites appropriate to its various Sephiroth. Just as 'the Tree of Life is the ground-plan of Western occultism', so also Cabalistic concepts pervade the whole of Western magic.

Emphasis apart, it is not really possible to separate these approaches in any definitive way. The same magician may refer to himself interchangeably as 'ritual' and 'ceremonial', and express himself in both Cabalistic and Hermetic phraseology. He chooses a particular system to suit himself, but all the systems express the same principles in their own terms, just as English, German or French can express the same ideas, while each gives them a slightly different viewpoint.

Whatever his system, the magician normally works in his own 'temple'. If it is all possible, he sets a room aside to be used for nothing else. He keeps it locked and only he goes into it, apart from a few (if any) whom he may ask to work with him from time to time. He decorates it to his own taste, which may be simple or complex. For example, he might paint walls and ceiling the colour of the night sky and dot it with stars, if that helps him; he might colour his four walls the red of fire, the blue of air, the green of water, and the yellow of earth, in whichever compass directions his particular system places these elements; or he might have everything a restfully neutral shade to avoid distraction.

He will certainly have an altar, and on it the pentacle for earth, the wand for air[4], the sword for fire[4], and the cup or chalice for water, plus candlesticks and a censer for incense. He may have a Circle marked on the floor, or indicate it with four candles as the witch does—or more likely do without it altogether, since the whole temple is his 'Akashic Egg' and a Circle is really superfluous. There is little point in preparing, decoration and consecrating a room for magical working and then leaving bits of it outside.

Paintings, sculptures, embellishments, these again are up to the magician; and if he uses them, they can be changed for particular rites. For example, one magician invoking Isis might be helped by pictures of her behind the altar, while a another might find they limit his imagination.

Many magicians find background music helpful—suited to the rite, from disc or tape.

A magician, unlike most witches, works robed. His robe may be ornate and of silk, or plain and of cotton, but in either case (like all his tools, and those of witches) it will be consecrated and used for no other purpose.[5]

Most magicians, according to their system and their purse, will build up a stock of robes and candles of different colours for different rituals, also 'accessories' of different metals, and incenses of different perfumes.

The sources from which modern magicians derive their rituals are many, though they are in a common tradition and often derive from each other. The most modern major source is the Golden Dawn (see Israel Regardie's or R.G. Torrens' book, both of which I referred to in note 9, p. 30). An important nineteenth-century source is Elihas-Levi, in particular his *Transcendental Magic*.

Of the mediaeval grimoires, the most important are *The Greater Key of Solomon* and *The Book of Sacred Magic of Abra-Melin the Mage*. The traditional author of the *Key of Solomon* was King

Solomon himself, but the oldest actual manuscript among those from which the de Laurence edition was compiled (all in the British Museum) dates from about the end of the sixteenth century. Abra-Melin, a Jewish magus of Wurzburg, was born probably in 1362 and wrote his book for his son Lamech about 1458, in his ninety-sixth year. The de Laurence edition was translated from a French manuscript version of the original Hebrew, in the Bibliotheque de l'Arsenal in Paris. Both these translations, the *Key* and *Abra-Melin,* were made by S. L. MacGregor Mathers, a leading light of the Golden Dawn. A useful anthology of the 'meat' of all the classical mediaeval grimoires is the somewhat alarmingly named *Book of Black Magic and of Pacts* (also de Laurence) by Arthur Edward Waite, another Golden Dawn leader, of undoubted learning but annoyingly patronizing style.

The oldest existing source is the Egyptian *Book of the Dead* (English translation by Sir E. A. Wallis Budge), and for many magicians this beautiful collection shines more clearly than anything which has followed it.

The whole tradition of the Cabala (which in any case underlies much of the rest) is a framework particularly suited for devising one's own rituals, which some find preferable to a rigid adherence to mediaeval forms.

The traditional rules for making robes and tools are often quite impracticable today; for example, linen woven from thread spun by a virgin during the waning moon is not generally so labelled in department stores. Nor could many modern urban magicians obtain wood to make a wand by finding a hazel or nut tree which had not yet borne fruit, and cutting a branch from the tree with a single stroke of a magic sickle at sunrise on the day of Mercury, the sickle itself having been made by a formula which involved magpies' blood. Such formulae were written during the Middle Ages, partly for their symbolic significance, and partly to make them deliberately difficult and discouraging for any but the most dedicated. (Also, some of the more bizarre ingredients were in fact code names for others, not necessarily sinister, but secret and handed on by oral tradition only.) Being a magician in the twentieth century has quite enough difficulties to deter the casually curious, and as for symbology, it is now considered better for the magician or witch to blend tradition with individuality and work out his own.

I am sure my athame is none the worse for not having been tempered in the blood of a black cat and juice of hemlock, as the *Key of Solomon* lays down. It was consecrated in a Circle, it has cast Circles and traced Pentagrams, it works for me, and that is enough.

Witches, as I have said, work with elemental forces. Their year is based on the nature festivals, their God and Goddess are nature deities, and they invoke and banish power with the Pentagram of Earth. Their work certainly involves the other three elements, and the astral plane—but all in their earth-related aspects. Of course a highly developed witch's efforts have much higher overtones, and he is conscious of them, and studies and strengthens them (another reason for saying that every good witch is a magician); but in general a coven's work is firmly earth-based.

A magician, however, uses the invoking and banishing Pentagrams of Fire, Air, Water and Spirit as well (see Fig. 5, p. 49), and is constantly expanding his knowledge and understanding of these realms. He invokes them not merely to tap the raw force of each, but to contact the entities behind them. His Gods are not earthbound; they are heaven-Gods. He has no God, and many Gods. None, in the sense that he recognizes a universal, eternal divine principle as the source of all, but accepts that it is unknowable directly by man while he is still man. Many, in that he personifies this unknowable ultimate into a hierarchy of entities which are knowable and contactable. These entities are not convenient mental fictions, but realities. At the lower end of the scale he can command them or make friends with them, and on the higher planes he can learn to raise himself to identification with them. For, to the occultist, it is a fundamental characteristic of the unknowable divine life-force that it manifests in self-conscious entities on each of the planes, a hierarchy which includes man on the physical plane of manifestation and elemental nature-spirits on the astral, as well as what the Christian calls angels and archangels on the spiritual. (See Chapter 12).

And yet, although real, the Gods are in one sense man-made. The aspects of Godhead which man personified as Osiris, or Isis, or Mercury, or Aphrodite, have acquired over the centuries what may be called 'public images' which have in turn achieved reality as channels of communication from the human level. The image of Osiris has become the spiritual call-sign of that aspect of divinity, a pathway to the God marked with the psychic footprints of millions of men and women, just as usage keeps open a right of way across a field. So the Gods live; from the human standpoint indeed they are more truly alive than the Unknowable Ultimate which they manifest. Isis exists, because as one of the self-conscious aspects of manifested Ultimate she has always existed. She exists for us in the robe and symbols of Egypt because that is how man clothed her as he became aware of her, and a man could doubtless pioneer his own, but trodden paths are easiest. She overlaps with others—Demeter, Diana, the Virgin Mary, Astarte— because all aspects of the One must inevitably overlap to a greater or lesser degree, but that does not prevent each being real, approachable and responsive as a unique entity.

A magician's highest Gods are those with him whom he can still identify himself in his highest moments of spiritual consciousness. 'And ultimately,' says Alex, 'there comes a point where you must accept that there is something beyond you that you will never comprehend, and while I can sense it, I can never actually put my hands on it or describe it. From my own point of view I have to say: "Nothing on my altar, only Truth." If I had to symbolize it I would put a blood-red rose there, because it stands for the fulness of life and the purity and spirituality of all things, and even when the rose has gone the perfume remains.

'But if you came to me, in the initial stages, I would have to introduce my past experience and comprehension of what I thought the Gods were. I haven't discarded them; what they've done is to enrich my experience to a higher comprehension of what is behind them but if you ask me what is behind them, I can only say I don't know. And yet I've all the faith and belief in the world in my Gods and Goddesses.

'You've watched me Drawing down the Moon. I go into the Circle, kiss Maxine on the lips, and from that point I'm invoking the Goddess. To me, it means that the Goddess is veiled in mystery, hidden inside a representative in the Circle. When I go down down on my knees, I'm looking up at the night sky, midnight blue with twinkling stars in it, and Maxine isn't there. And gradually, through my own illumination and understanding of the Goddess, I want her to reveal herself as she really is, inside the Circle, in her beauty and purity as a Goddess—as absolutely pure womanhood that can open the circle to infinity and bring all the children in. So the veil is gradually drawn away and Maxine stands there naked.'

No man can spend all his time at the level of consciousness where he faces the Gods—or even higher, where he briefly feels on his cheek the wind of the great Silence. No man could stand it. Much of a magician's time is spent working with entities of a much less exalted level, and these he does not invoke or identify with—he evokes and commands. He may order them for information, for divination, for mental or physical healing. Alex has his own views on this relationship.

'A good magician makes a friend of any spirit he's working with,' he insists. 'They should be as master and devoted servant, with a complete understanding between them both, and mutual respect. It says in the book that you should never let a spirit take command at any point, or he will master you. But I don't believe this, because I put trust in spirits, give them the experience of doing earth work for mortals in their own right, using their own discretion. I give my spirits—not all of them, but some of them—scope to move around, in their own sphere and out of it. Because I always feel there may come a time when they can be born, and I might be denying them the chance.'

Even this lower magic is not used wastefully. A good magician does not reject or ignore 'normal' science. His attitude is to embrace it and push beyond its present frontiers. He will therefore only use magic on a problem which 'normal' science cannot solve, either from inadequacy or because circumstances frustrate it.

'If a person comes to me with a fertility problem,' Alex says, 'I ask if all the medical and psychological measures have been taken first. Only then do I use magic, by getting in touch with the appropriate spirit and sending it to do the work.'

Although Alex sometimes uses ritual, he no longer has to; in that sense his magic is often Hermetic. I have seen him cast a Circle round himself mentally, sitting in his characteristic posture of relaxation with his left leg over one chair-arm, and then proceed with magical work, explaining each stage to me as he went along. From that same armchair he talks to people who come to him with problems, and he deals with them without leaving it for anything more magical than fetching an ash-tray.

One example both of his magical methods and of his absolute confidence in them—is the way he deals, when necessary, with pregnancies. Women often come to him asking him to end a pregnancy by magic. Before agreeing, he always satisfies himself first that it is morally and legally justifiable, and that the woman cannot afford a normal abortion in a clinic. More than that—he may pull strings with doctor friends to get her into a clinic at a reduced fee. Only as a last resort will he use magic.

'There was a girl only recently who had tried everything, and had no money,' he told me. 'She said she really believed I could stop it. I pointed at her womb, without touching her or giving her anything to take, and said, "Yes, it's stopped. It won't grow anymore. You will have a very heavy period, and by the end of September you'll be clear of it." No ritual, no nothing. It ceased to be, by command—the spirit working. I've done it many times, and there's no pain involved.

'Another girl, almost three months pregnant—I got the clinic fee reduced by more that half for her, but she still couldn't afford it, and she was desperate. So I told her, "I don't care if you believe me or not—it's stopped!" Michael was shouting in my mind "Three, three, three". I told her, "Within three days you'll be perfectly all right. Don't let it happen again, because I can't help you any more." She's happily married now.

'When I point at the womb and say the words, I picture the pentagram (which represents that particular foetal microcosm) crumbling. It goes down with a roar and a crash of thunder, drops into powder and disappears...At the same time I realize that I'm taking life—I have to absorb that spirit into my being and become responsible for it. That's where the magic and the wisdom come in.'

I asked if the pointing ever failed. 'Never,' Alex replied. 'Not ever.'

Which provokes a final thought for this chapter—the terrible responsibility that his powers place on the magician. Because he works alone, he is even more face to face with his conscience than the witch. Black Magicians do exist, and although they run the daily risk of coming up against a stronger defence and destroying themselves by the boomerang effect of their own power, they can do a lot of damage while they last. By the nature of things, they are self-destructive, because in attempting to scale a path which should be used for spiritual progression, they are attacking heights where the price for black working grows more astronomical with every step. Some do turn back, but the agony of such a reversal and of the subsequent purification—as Alex remembers all too well—is more than most men have to courage to face.

Fortunately, although the black magician can (literally) get away with murder undetected by his ordinary fellow citizens, white magicians have their own ways of smelling his rat. Part of the regular work of white magicians, and of effective occult fraternities in general, is to act as a kind of radar, sweeping the psychic horizon for the echoes of black working. The more serious and powerful the offender, the harder it is for him to cover his traces, and the moment he is detected, a silent battle opens of which only those involved are aware. If he persists, the battle can only end one way, because in a showdown, those of the Right-Hand Path can always call on the biggest reinforcements.

And if anyone does not believe me, he should read Dion Fortune's works, especially her *Psychic Self-Defence* and her novel *The Secrets of Dr. Taverner* (which, although fiction in form, deals with real cases).

In Britain at least, there would seem to be more white magic than black around—and it is more powerful.

1. The conventional story-book illustration of a magic wand has a glowing five-pointed star at its tip. I wonder how many illustrators realize how accurately they are portraying the drawing down of power by the Invoking Pentagram, which the witch or magician traces and visualizes in the air? An example of the remarkably tenacious survival of symbolism, even when unconscious.

2. Briefly, the Eastern tradition aims at the elimination of the ego, while the Western aims at its perfection. Not so opposed as they may appear, because they are simply two ways of looking at the union of the ego with the ultimate Godhead.

3. In the Latin version: *'Quod superius est sicut quod inferius et quod inferius est sicut quod superius ad perpetranda miracula rei unius.'*

4. Some systems attribute the wand to fire and the sword to air. Neither attribution is 'wrong', as long as the operator feels in tune with it. The same is true of the attribution of elements to the compass points. *See also* p. 139.

5. Alex occasionally wears long robes for public occasions, but like other magicians or witches who do this, he keeps separate robes for the purpose and would never wear those particular ones for magical working or in the witches' Circle.

11.

Healing

Healing is a major part of the work of a witch, both within the coven Circle and alone. Many different methods and principles are involved, some of which are 'pure' witchcraft, and some magical in the sense I explained in the last chapter. Within these categories, too, there are subdivisions.

'Pure' witchcraft healing can be roughly divided into herbalism, the sympathetic magic of charms and spells, and what may be called the 'unaided' direction of will; only roughly, because the three overlap and shade into each other. For example, directed will enters into herbalism and charms; and 'unaided' will usually involves at least some simple aid to concentration, such as the cords.

Herbalism is a subject on its own, too complex to be gone into in this book, but I have already given a couple of examples of it on page 63. The point to be borne in mind is that Wiccan herbalism concerns more than the purely medicinal properties of certain plants, which are acknowledged by the most dogmatic materialist. It also involves (a) the occult significance of the herbs themselves[1] and of their methods of preparation and use, and (b) the concept of the impregnation of the material means with the healing wish. I have already described on pages 69-70 the technique of the 'genie in the bottle' by which, in effect, a part of the healer's own mental being is given temporarily independent existence and consciousness and sent to carry out a specific task. A witch who gives a patient a herbal remedy does the same thing on a more limited scale, loading the remedy with a strongly impressed healing wish that is also, in a sense, a detached and independently acting part of himself.

The same is true of charms and talismans. They are appropriately chosen and made according to the system of correspondences—or, if you prefer, of psychic resonance—and charged with the healing wish.

Methods of group working for healing purposes vary from coven to coven. In Alex's, cord magic as described on p. 61 is the basic system, and is carried out at most of the coven meetings. The wax image or the human stand-in (*see* p. 68) are also used within the Circle for diagnosis and healing. Such spells as the candle-and-needle spell (p. 66) can of course be executed alone, but there is a lot to be said for consecrating and preparing the objects as a coven, with the added solemnity of group ritual, even if those objects are to be used later and elsewhere. It depends on the human material. A healer confident of his powers may feel happier working alone if the coven lacks experience, but on the other hand a coven which is used to working together, and is aware of past successes, can 'charge' objects with more power than most individual witches are capable of raising. After all, that is what a coven is for.

Diagnosis is essentially a clairvoyant art, and the wax image or the stand-in is a focus and stimulant for that clairvoyance in the same way as a crystal or a Tarot layout, though in a sense more direct because it is a similarly-shaped substitute for the patient's body. The advantage of the wax image is that it has no ailments or biological characteristics of its own to confuse an inexperienced clairvoyant. The advantage of a human stand-in is, first, that he or she is roughly the same size as the patient and no mental magnification is necessary; and second, that he or she is a more effective 'demonstration model' for teaching others.

Alex can diagnose by either of these methods, or with the patient present (though without having to touch him), or with the patient absent and without the aid of image or stand-in. I say 'can' instead of a more cautious 'claims to be able to' because I have seen him do it, accurately and often to the surprise of the people concerned. I asked him to describe his method.

'By imagination I create the body of the person,' he said. 'If he is there, I look at him; if he is not, I visualize him in his own room. I close my eyes and hold the image for a moment. Then I start to see a blue light, the aura, round his head and crossing in two main bands over his chest and round his back, like the snakes of a caduceus. Now the image itself begins to disappear, leaving these lights, but the shape remains vaguely inside, and the lights guide the play of the bone and muscle structure.

'Then at certain points I see blotches. Some of these cross the light in very positive places, and some are only vague with spaces in between. Some things I see directly—bad teeth for example look cloudy in the head, fillings more solid, and a denture a big blot in the mouth. Tuberculosis looks cloudy, smoky. Others give symbols—I see cancer like a lobster or a scorpion, wherever it is in the body, very dense and black. Rheumatism is like a hairy anemone in the joint, branching upwards and downwards. Boils, carbuncles, cysts, seem to come towards me...

'While I'm doing all this, I have the feeling that there's someone much bigger behind me, telling me how I should go about things—laying on of hands, or whatever it is—and roughly how long it's going to take, how many times the person should come to see me, whether he's going to take the advice I give him or neglect it, whether he's going to be cured in this life or is going to have to be taken out of the body to be cured in another life...and roughly how long he's going to live in this life'

'Do you ever tell him how long he's going to live?' I asked.

'I have done, on occasion, but very rarely. I don't like doing it.'

Alex's method of diagnosis is the same whether the patient is present or miles away. 'Sometimes I've had watches and things sent to me, and I've diagnosed by psychometry; you name it, I've probably had it.

'Sometimes the sickness is just a mind sickness, and the only way I can treat the person is by talking to him, being a spiritual father, ridding him of his guilt feelings and complexes...Just recently I've talked a man out of suicide by knocking his props away—convincing him of eternal life, so that he realized suicide was no way out.

'As for laying on of hands, that's been known since time immemorial. In Ancient Egypt, people went to the Healer Priests for it. I can use it without the sympathy of the patient; he may stand there disbelieving that it's going to work, and I can make it work. I understand the electrical and magnetic passes; I neutralize every single thing that's in him, and then start to fill him with healing vibrations. I visualize the body and the aura being cleansed and filled with the purification of fire. Then comes the laying on of hands, literally giving pure energy which clears away the condition. It may have to be done several times, or sometimes you can get immediate reaction so that the trouble doesn't return.

'When I'm ready to work, I find my hands starting to feel warm (even now, talking about it) and the tendons start to pull, the palms to radiate. In certain shades of light you can see it coming from your hands like cigarette smoke or phosphorescence.

'For myself I don't think of any particular "name of power"; I just realize that I've got a potential within my own body, and I understand what the elements are and how to direct them.'

To the magician, all things are magical. Alex is just as likely to prescribe asprin as to make a spell, because to him the technical skills of doctor or pharmacist are just as much 'Rites of Tiphareth' (the healing Sephira) as the candle and needle or the laying on of hands. 'Spiritual healing should be practised in the churches with the surgeons and doctors.' he maintains. 'Once the priests *were* the surgeons and doctors; now you have two separate divisions, passing the buck to each other.'

He often prescribes warm olive oil applied to the afflicted area. 'This is the healing unction, the holy anointing oil. Though the true holy anointing oil—the oil you were initiated with, for example—is olive oil plus another quite simple ingredient which mustn't be revealed. You must be in a state of grace to prepare it, with purification rites. And you may never sell it, though in special circumstances you may give it away.'

Alex's healing (indeed, his whole outlook) is closely bound up with the Tree of Life. When he is 'cleansing and refilling a patient,' he visualizes the Tree as aligned with the body.[2] He sees first himself, and then the patient, as the middle pillar of the Tree, and works for equilibrium of the patient's outer pillars, his Boaz and Jakin. 'I draw all the power down from Kether, all through the person, right down into manifestaion.'

I have watched him do this, passing his hands down the patient's sides and finishing by flicking his hands outwards at about knee level as though he were shaking away the imperfections.

This Tree visualization is related not merely to the patient's anatomy, but also to his personality, his psyche, his spiritual content. Some of the placings of the Sephiroth on the body may seem arbitrary at first sight (Netzach, the emotional and occult Sephira, on the left leg?) while others are clearly appropriate (Geburah, the active and combative Sephira, on the right arm)—but without going too deeply into the rationale of these placings, they do have one immediate practical advantage. They symbolize the basic occult principle of 'as above, so below'—the correspondence of Macrocosm and Microcosm which the healer needs to keep firmly in mind. They provide at the same time a useful conceptual framework whereby he can see the patient as a complex of spiritual, mental, astral and physical levels, and can treat all these levels simultaneously without 'losing track'.

When he is doing healing work of this kind, Alex likes to start by washing his hands, with a purification ritual. Then he gets a fresh bowl of water (or, better still, has somebody else bring it to him) and starts. 'I go through each Sephira, right down the Tree, with water on my fingers. It's not necessary to touch the patient—only his aura. When I've finished, I dry my hands on a spotlessly clean towel, and the water's thrown away.'

The same Tree of Life concept can be applied to cord-magic healing. 'You direct your desire to the point of all being—your Godhead, your Kether—and from there it must emanate out again for the patient to receive it. It's a conscious desire for the patient to be healed. You bind your will on the cord, at the same time directing the desire to the centre, where it's given out again.'

Obviously, the better integrated the healer is in himself, the more effective his healing. 'One of the most famous is an excellent man, he's healed thousands of people, but the healing very rarely lasts longer than a year, which shows that there's something wrong in his spirit.'

This points again to one of the reasons why witches work in covens. In some ways it is easier (or at least more likely) for a group to be well integrated than for an individual. A voluntary mixture of ages, sexes, callings and personality, regularly working together because they enjoy it and need it, presided over by a High Priest and High Priestess sympathetically on the watch for potentialities to be encouraged or frictions to be resolved, can develop into a balance and useful unit. That may sound more like a counsel of perfection than a description of any real-life coven, but even partial success in achieving such a standard pays off handsomely. (Sociologists are always pointing to the harm done to modern urban society by the disappearance of the 'extended family'. A well-mixed coven, even of normally imperfect human beings, can do a lot to refill that vacuum working as it does in a stronger atmosphere of family-type intimacy than the average church or club.)

The impulse to carry out a particular piece of healing work may come without warning, particularly within the Circle. It may or may not be combined with trance. I have seen Alex go suddenly into a trance state and start speaking in Michael's unmistakable voice. Then he gives a message to various people in the group, some of them diagnostic combined with recommendations for treatment, some of them advice or prediction unconnected with healing. When these messages have been addressed to me, or to someone else in connection with circumstances of which I have been aware or have learned about afterwards, I have found them to be to the point. Some of them might conceivably be attributed to Alex's subconscious mind drawing shrewd conclusions from known facts, but some of them could not possibly be.

Alex develops, like anyone else, and more and more often recently these messages have been coming through without any trance state, and in his normal voice. 'There are times,' he says, 'when I just suddenly feel pushed up on to my feet. I don't know what I'm getting up for, except that it's either clairvoyance or healing for someone in the room. And while I'm standing up, without any magic Circle or invocation or anything, I feel one of my spirits (more often than not, these days, it's Michael) filling my body till I'm much bigger, hiding inside me and controlling me. Magicians say you shouldn't allow this to happen, but I do.

'Then I feel as though I'm being pulled up through a big hole in the back of my head, and something else is walking in. Not "them", whoever they are; they're doing it from a distance, and this is an emanation, a power that they're using, and they can use it better through me than by an indirect healing.

'And yet I remain fully conscious...I would like to work like this all the time, instead of going into a trance state, but it still seems to be a very imperfect thing. When I do go into a trance state, I'm not consciously aware afterwards of what's taken place or what's been said, but over the next two or three days bits and pieces are given back to me, so that I can check whether other people have received what they were meant to get.'

Often Alex himself does not know what the messages mean. He passes them on with the interpolation 'I don't know I'm on about'—but usually the recipient knows. They may be very relevant to facts in his private life of which Alex must be unaware. I have received several such messages from him myself, including a spontaneous but correct diagnosis of two physical ailments for a friend of mine whom Alex had not met for months.

Alex's healing powers have been with him for a long time. His daughter Janice (now grown up with a daughter of her own) benefited from his ministrations when she was a few hours old. Born in dry labour, she had been taken straight off to hospital by ambulance because her left foot was twisted round so that the toes were pointing backwards. Two or three hours later the doctor brought her back and told Alex regretfully that nothing could be done until Janice was about fourteen.

'I kept the baby with me downstairs,' Alex says. 'And then suddenly I had this impression, from my own spirit teacher, that I had to get olive oil and warm it. I anointed the foot, and then simply put it straight. Just twisted it forward. I was very apprehensive while I was doing it, but I knew I had to. She's been almost perfect ever since. It's only in very cold weather that she walks with a very slight limp...It got into the papers—not through me—and the doctor, poor man, was nearly struck off, because they tried to imply he was involved in spiritual healing at a time when it was very controversial. But he knew nothing about it till I'd done it.'

Alex suits the treatment to the patient, not merely physically but spiritually. After he had appeared on the Simon Dee television programme, a day nursery matron phoned him. A devout Roman

Catholic, she had no desire to be a witch but was convinced that a spirit of goodness emanated from Alex, and believed he could help her. For many years she had had a form of rash on her cheeks and chin, due to a hormone imbalance more appropriate to adolescence than to her thirty-five years. Hospitals and Harley Street had been unable to cure it.

'When she came to see me, she kept insisting on her devotion to the Catholic Church. I have a cross which was given to me by Maxine's mother, and which is reputed to have belonged to Padre Pio, the Italian saint who died in 1968. I told her to hold it for a few minutes and absorb what it implied. She said a few Hail Marys with it in her hand, then pressed the amethysts of the cross against her cheeks, and left...All I did was supply the symbol and the Mother Goddess in another aspect.

'About a week later she rang to say her own doctor was wondering how her face had suddenly cleared up. A newspaper had been attacking me, and she offered to appear on any TV programme to prove that I had all the gifts I claimed...Her trouble hasn't returned.'

Straight psychology, perhaps—which Alex uses as shrewdly as any professional psychiatrist. But his gifts of intuition and of clairvoyant diagnosis often enable him to pinpoint a trouble, and deal with it, in one session where it would take a conventional practitioner weeks of probing. A few months ago a young man was carried into the Sanders' flat by a mutual friend, in the middle of a severe asthmatic attack. Alex laid his hands on the back of his neck, and within ten minutes the attack had cleared.

'Then I told him: "You're a homosexual, and your guilt about it is causing these attacks. Go away, be yourself, and accept what you are as a natural part of your life." He's only had two very mild attacks since, and he had been having them almost every day.

Alex admits, though, that some cases are more stubborn. At the time of writing he is treating a young professional man who is obsessed by two forms of perversion, one fairly common and one unpleasantly bizarre. For the first time in many years, Alex is using a series of hypnotic tests to get right down to the trouble, which he suspects had its roots in the man's last incarnation—the type of case in which Dion Fortune was so expert.

'I've tried to reach it by my usual methods, and I can't, so I've got to go back right to the moment of conception, in case he becomes too much involved with that former life...He's one of the most difficult patients I've ever had.'

Difficult he may be; but to me, admittedly a very slight acquaintance, he has looked a changed man in a few weeks.

To return to more strictly Wiccan methods, and to another admission of Alex's. 'Dealing with warts—some witches would call my method black. I find the only way I can get rid of them is by wishing them on someone else, someone who's already ugly, with boil marks I can fill up with the warts...There was a girl who had fifteen of them on her body, and wanted me to cure them. So I wished them on to a man's neck, in the pub. He'd been aggressively rude to me, in that same pub—a man who should of known better. He had nothing to do with me, and there was no reason for him to attack me publicly. So he got fifteen warts, and the girl lost them.'

Clairvoyant diagnosis needs to be kept in trim by practise. 'Sometimes, if you're too involved with a person, you may not see the wood for the trees,' Alex points out. 'Several years ago I was staying in the same house as a hospital dietician. One day she and I and another girl were walking along, and for a joke I'd lifted her on to a wall—she was a very tiny person. She said, "Oh, don't, I feel ill"—so I put her down, thought "period", and dismissed it.

'About two in the morning, a horrible scream came through to me in my sleep. Another man and I dashed into her bedroom, and found her hanging out of bed and coughing up a large patch of her stomach-lining. She had cancer of the stomach and I hadn't known...We took her to hospital, and for three days and nights I was in a private ward with her; she wouldn't be separated from me. I had my hands literally glued to her feet, giving her healing through them. She refused all transfusions, saying that life was pouring out of me into her. That woman is hale and hearty today, and the wall of her stomach is completely healed.'

Another hospital worker, a nurse, is known to me personally. She is one of Alex's witches, and she had suffered from cystitis all her life. Alex laid his hands on her head, willed the trouble away, and she has never had it since.

Yet another of our friends who would do anything for Alex and Maxine is a young man who, two years ago, was an advanced heroin addict, kept lingeringly alive by his prescribed dose and written off as incurable. Alex cured him in a fortnight. Today he is a normal, clear-eyed man in a regular job.

Sometimes merely becoming a witch seems to have a curative effect in itself. One Scottish engineer came to London for initiation by our coven, a ceremony in which I took part. He did not mention that he had suffered from hiatus hernia all his life, was obliged to be very careful about his food, and could not drink beer or spirits.

Staying with the Sanders for a few days, he felt prompted for some reason to eat and drink everything they ate and drank. He came to the pub with the coven and drank as we did. He has continued taking exactly what he likes ever since, and has had no more trouble. I have just heard from him that an X-ray has shown the hernia to have been healed, and that his doctor is very puzzled.

'Initiation put him in touch with the cosmic forces,' Alex explains, 'and the first thing the Goddess did for him was to clear this obstruction that had haunted him all his life. I didn't even know about it till he told me.'

Folk-singers Dave and Toni Arthur are also witches, and have a six-year-old son Jonathan. 'When they first came to see me, last year,' Alex says, 'they were testing me, like everyone does. They showed me Jonathan's forefinger: it was missing at the first joint—nail and root had gone. He'd had an accident with a lawn-mower, slicing off tip, and the doctor had had to take more off to give a flap of skin to cover it.

'They asked me, "Can you do anything with this?" I said it was most unlikely, and they were expecting a lot; but I told Michael to get working on it.

'They were initiated, and went on tour. Five or six months later they came to see us. "Have you seen Jonathan's finger? Nobody can understand it—look at this." The finger was still short, but a complete nail was growing, although the doctor had said the root was gone. And the finger itself was about an eighth of an inch longer than it had been...Michael did the work there, not me; but I was the instigator.'

Finally, another child case, this time a patient whom Alex did not even see. The father of one of our women witches (himself a devout Christian) works in a hospital—in a non-medical job, but he has contact with patients. He was very affected by the case of one little boy who was suffering from mercury poisoning.

This boy had been in and out of the hospital for weeks, having tests and treatment, and was making no progress. Our witch's father worried about him, as the case seemed 'pretty hopeless', so he appealed to Alex for help, though with considerable misgivings. Alex gave absent treatment, and within a week or two the boy was discharged. A later test showed he was clear of the poisoning.

Father's bewildered comment: 'Witchcraft works!'

1. A useful little book is *The Occult Properties of Herbs* by W. B. Crow.

2. The traditional correspondences are: Kether, the cranium; Chokmah, left side of the face; Binah, right side of the face; Chesed, left arm; Geburah, right arm; Tiphareth, breast; Netzach, left leg and thigh; Hod, right leg and thigh; Yesod, genitals; Malkuth, feet and anus.

12.

Worlds of the Elements

It is one of the fundamental beliefs of witchcraft (and of occultism in general) that the universe is populated by a whole hierarchy of intelligent entities in addition to those which are materially visible in the human and animal kingdom.

These entities range 'downwards' from the Unknowable Ultimate. First come the highest expressions of that Ultimate which the human mind can grasp and communicate with. To the witch, these are the supreme male and female principles of Godhead, the Horned God and the Mother Goddess. Next, the beings which govern the fundamental categories of existence symbolized by the elements of air, fire, water and earth, and their respective hierarchies. The Christian calls these archangels and angels. Some witches do the same, while others prefer to use the names which have no dogmatic associations; this is a matter of personal choice.

Man is not at the bottom of the scale, even if one excludes the animals. More primitive than man in their stage of development are the elementary, or nature, spirits. In the occult view, everything we see around us, including man, has evolved from these. Man is in fact a synthesis of the four elementary essences, and the more balanced the synthesis, the more highly developed the individual. Striving for such a balance is the central aim of occultism—of the magician in his temple, the alchemist in his laboratory, and the witch in his coven.

This concept of a hierarchy of beings operating on the spiritual, mental and astral levels, which is shared in one form or another by all religions, is of course rejected by the materialist; but even to him one must point out that, as a working hypothesis, it gets results.

Strictly speaking, there are not four elements but five, the fifth being the Akashic Principle, the spirit element which pervades them all and from which they all stem. The magic Circle expresses this perfectly. Its four quarters represent the four elements—air in the east, fire in the south, water in the west, earth in the north—but the Akashic Principle is the medium in which the Circle itself is formed. The Circle, as we have seen, is really a sphere, sometimes known as the Akashic Egg.

The Akashic Principle can also be thought of as a multi-dimensional recording medium, in which everything that has ever happened has left its mark. Advanced adepts acquire the gift of 'consulting the Akashic Records' for information on their own and other people's past lives, a method referred to several times in Dion Fortune's works, particularly in *The Secrets of Dr. Taverner*.

A recent book giving clinical examples of the technique is *Many Lifetimes* by Joan Grant and Denys Kelsey.

The placing of the four elements in the witches' Circle (*see* Fig. 3. p. 45) and the Tetrapolar Magnet is not merely a ritual convention. The witch strives all the time he is in the Circle to be conscious or them and to put himself in tune with them, till they become permanent parts of his concept of the Circle on all levels of consciousness. The actual placings may differ in various parts of the world (for example, in the Southern Hemisphere, where the sun passes from east through north to west) or in various traditions, but the ones I have given are those generally used in the Wiccan Circle. Obviously it is better to decide on your placings and keep to them, if you want them to become instinctive.

The same is true of the attribution of the tools. The Pentacle stands for earth, and the Cup for water, in everybody's book, but there are two traditions concerning the Sword (or athame, with which it is interchangable for all purposes) and the Wand. Alex attributes the Sword to fire and the Wand to air, and I too find this the more natural correspondence, but other workers reverse them. Either way is right if the operator is happy with it. Again, the main thing is to choose one set of concepts for yourself and stick to it.[1]

Air is the element of intellect, of the life-principle. Its governing entity is Raphael (Thoth, Hermes), the instructor, the traveller, the healer of wounds. The virtues of air are diligence, dexterity, optimism, joy of living; its vices are frivolity, boasting, squandering

Fire is the element of action, of the light-principle. It is ruled by Michael (Beltane), the Solar diety, the victor over injustice and ignorance. The virtues of fire are courage, daring, enthusiasm, valour against evil; its vices are anger, jealousy, vindictiveness, hatred.

Water is the element of fertility, of the love-principle. It is ruled by Gabriel, who turns force into form, and whose traditional horn is a double fertility symbol—male phallus and female cup. The virtues of water are compassion, tenderness, receptivity, forgiveness, fluidity in the creative sense; it vices are instability, indifference, spinelessness, uncommittedness, fluidity in the treacherous sense—everything that is meant when we call someone a 'wet' or a 'drip'.

Earth is the element of solidity, of the law-principle. It is rules by Auriel, the 'Lord of Awe', the complement of Michael. The virtues of earth are endurance, responsibility, thoroughness, practicality, patience; its vices are dullness, laziness, melancholy, lack of conscience, boredom, stagnation.

These elemental concepts enter into everything a witch does. He works with them to balance his own nature; for example, with the 'Control Book' method I described on pp. 51-52. When he casts a spell, he ritually involves the appropriate element or elements. When he consecrates any object, he places it on the pentacle, touches it with water, and passes over the censer (for air) and the candle (for fire), before blessing it man-to-woman to embrace it within the polarities of a living Tetrapolar Magnet.

But he can also develop techniques for entering directly into the 'worlds' of these elements, to experience each in its undiluted form and to become aware of the entities that inhabit it—indeed, to communicate with them. In a sense this is a form of astral projection, which will be dealt with in the next chapter; one remains fully conscious all the time, but out of the physical body. Alex recommends the mastering of the elemental spheres as a first step on the path to 'normal' astral projection.

The inhabiting entities have traditional names; the sylphs of air, the salamanders of fire, the undines (mermaids, mermen) of water, and the gnomes of earth. These names have been to some extent degraded by popular fairy-tale, but to the occultist they are specific names for real beings, and their reality is underlined by the general agreement as to their natures between people who have contacted them.

Alex told me of his surprise when he first saw Arthur Rackham's illustrations of these elementary spirits in an edition of *The Ring of the Niebelungen*. 'I'm quite certain that he was in direct communication with them, otherwise nobody could draw them so well,' he said. 'Rackham's undines *are* undines, and his spirits of fire are real salamanders.'

The technique for projecting yourself into (for example) the sphere of water, of the undines, requires steady practice but is basically quite simple.

Sit in a comfortable and relaxed position where you will not be interrupted, and close your eyes. Breathe calmly and regularly; you must resist every tendency to breathe rapidly, or to hold your breath, or to tense your muscles. Calm concentration is the state to aim at.

Imagine your body to be hollow, and surrounded by all the water in the universe. When this image is clearly achieved, start bringing the surrounding water into your hollow body by breathing it into your lungs and absorbing it through every pore in your skin. As the water fills you, imagine yourself sinking gradually to the bottom of the ocean.

What you are really doing is neither sinking in a material ocean, not inventing an illusory one. You are seeking out, isolating, and submerging yourself in the water aspect of your own nature—which is real. And on the astral level of consciousness, this water-element part of yourself can become aware of, and communicate with, the entities which populate that element.

You may have to do the exercise many times, developing the experience into a vivid reality, before you make conscious contact with the undines. 'They are very elusive, in the early stages,' Alex says, 'but gradually they become clearer. They are difficult to understand, because they are flowing creatures, but you can have communication with them. You must be very courteous; meander through their life, and watch what their doing. You're not there to master them, but to learn from them about the element they live in, and the uses to which you as a witch or magician can put it. By magical ritual you can bring them to visible appearance through a human being; in fact they can sometimes enter the body of a human being and inhabit it...I've lived with a mermaid; they're very jealous, very clinging, and they can *kill* . . .

'A young merchant seaman I'd been helping with some problems turned up in this flat just after Christmas, with a girl friend. They were dancing together, and it was beautiful to watch her. She was a receptionist at an ordinary hotel, but at that moment she was like a fully trained ballet dancer. Suddenly I realized she wasn't what she appeared to be; she was watery and rubbery, and I saw a mermaid's tail . . . I told her to put on her shoes and get out; I didn't want any siren in here. She'd been possessed by an undine spirit. She's back in Australia now, a perfectly normal girl again.'

Alex relates this capacity for possession to the legend of the seal-people, undines who can come and live on land but must return to their element after seven years—'which covers the whole cycle of the Tree of Life and back again'.

The projection technique for the fire element is similar to that for water. The rules for relaxing, breathing and concentrating are the same, but this time you imagine yourself as a hollow body in the middle of an infinite universe of fire. Steadily breathe in this fire, and absorb it through every pore, concentrating it within yourself. In some ways this is the most encouraging element for the beginner because most people experience a physical sensation of rising body-heat the very first time they try the process.

Again, the fire you experience is neither actual combustion, nor an illusion. It is the genuine fire-element factor in your own nature, which you are isolating and concentrating upon. (Incidentally, quite apart from its projection purpose, this technique is a very practical device for overcoming the discomfort of chilly surroundings, as I have proved for myself.)

Salamanders, the fire-element entities, are as elusive as the undines but (as one might expect) rather more hostile to man. 'They will teach you,' says Alex, 'but they won't give in. They don't like to do the work for you at all . . . They can burn, and you should never take them for granted.

'I do tend to take them for granted, because I feel sometimes that I've really achieved the conquest of the salamanders, that I'm the boss--so I boast and do fire rituals. And instead of using them as they should be used, within the formation of a magic Circle, I do things like putting a cigarette-end on my palm to show off.

'Last time I did that, it took me three weeks to get rid of the burns. So I shouldn't boast.'

To which should be added that I have seen Alex deliberately risk burns and come to no harm, so I can only assume it depends on the purpose of the action and the frame of mind in which it was done.

Perhaps 'hostile to man' is the wrong phrase. Fire, both as a psychic element and as a physical phenomenon (or class of phenomena, for it includes both the molecular reaction of flame and the nuclear fission or fusion reactions of such things as the Sun or the Bomb), is essential to man as well as dangerous to him. To come to terms with it, either psychically or physically, he has to understand its rules and respect them. The same is true of air, earth and water; but with fire the rules are stricter and the stakes higher.

'After all,' Alex says, 'the salamanders in their truest aspect are the angels of the Sun—of Michael, Beltane, the Fire God. Life couldn't exist without them.'

Children, with their powers of temporary single-mindedness and ignorance of materialist philosophy, are natural self-projectors and do not need deliberate techniques. Maxine remembers gazing into coal fires as a little girl and talking with the salamanders (though she had not heard the name). 'I had long conversations with them, going on for hours, and nobody else could see them. I'd put the poker in the fire and they'd crawl up the handle . . . miss coal fires for that.'

Most of us can remember such experiences—maybe in other elements, according to our natures. (The fire element is a strong factor in Maxine's make-up, and there are people of her acquaintance with well-deserved psychic burns to prove it.) Most of us, in the light of our subsequent education, dismiss them as childhood fancies; but they were genuine enough, and it would do us a lot of good to reassess them. Like most things Jesus said, 'Of such is the kingdom of God' has many levels of meaning.

To project your consciousness into the world of air, of the sylphs, you use the same basic technique, but visualize a universe of air. You absorb it, with the same steady but relaxed concentration, feeling yourself to be lighter and lighter until you have a sense of floating in the element which you have isolated.

Air, the realm of intellect, is the least emotional of the four. In the make-up of human character, it is practically indefinable except in relation to at least one of the other three. Pure mind, without the mirror of love, action or solidity to view itself in, can scarcely be grasped. So to isolate that world within yourself, in order to project yourself into it and communicate with its entities, is perhaps the hardest of all. It might be impossible but for the fact that it is part of the function of these entities themselves to help you to achieve it.

'The sylphs are very hard to see—you have to be a pretty pure sort of person to see them at all,' Alex says. 'But you can make friends with them, though you have to work hard. They will teach you how to control your mind and level your thoughts out—how to be creative in the mind; this is their purpose. I have had experiences with them, but I admit I don't know a lot about them.'

As for the element of earth, this is literally our own stamping-ground, so it should be, and is, a much easier realm to explore. (It is also, as I have pointed out earlier, the witch's base of operations, though not his boundary.)

By now you should be able to work our for yourself how to set about the projection. In your relaxed position, breathing regularly, you make yourself aware of solidity, or permanence, of the earth itself. You absorb it into yourself and sink into it, knowing that you belong to it, are part of it, and can survive naturally in it.

'Gnomes,' says Alex, 'tend to be friendly. They're the easiest ones, very busy all the time. In fact, in a way we're too close to them. The earth element has provided us with so much recently—new mineral treatments in medicine, for instance—that we're "getting down to earth" and tending to ignore the other elements.

'The gnomes give you the opportunity to open up subterranean caves within yourself, within your own earth element. How much you're able to exploit the vein of gold they offer you depends entirely on yourself.'

Being so close to man, they are occasionally discernable without a deliberate act of projection. 'If you're very quick and very smart, sometimes in the country you can see them, like a shadow in the corner of your eye.'

We have been taught, most of us, to be wary of the imagination. Society pays lip-service to it, but in practice like it to be a sort of National Park with well-defined fences, within which professional artists, story-tellers and musicians are licensed to hunt and bring out trussed game (preferably of recognized species) for the orderly nourishment of the majority, the people who do the 'real' work.

The witch is a rebel against this attitude, a heretic, and therefore (society argues) an anarchist. The witch admits to rebellion, but denies anarchism, maintaining that he has a truer sense of cosmic order than most of his critics. To him, the imagination is not an enclave, but working territory—arable land producing crops.

Deliberately and methodically, he explores this territory. He regards imagination not as an escape (however therapeutic) into illusion, but as a channel of communication with other levels of reality and the beings which inhabit them. He exercises and develops his imagination in exactly the same way that a professional traveller studies foreign languages, and for the same reason: so that he can understand, recognize, and communicate, beyond his 'normal' territory.

That is why he works at exercises like the ones I have outlined in this chapter. If he is wise, he will build up to them by easy stages, starting with such mind-training homework as I described on pages 51-52. How easy or hard he finds it depends partly on his natural abilities, and partly on how encrusted his mind has become with the attitudes of contemporary materialism. But even if he seems handicapped on both counts, determination and patience will bring the breakthrough.

Different people find different approaches helpful. Many find it easier to achieve projection into an elemental world by choosing a spot in open country, preferably suited to the element. Ideally, for example, they could seek out a high hill for air, an isolated lakeside for water, a cave for earth, or brilliant sunshine (though with sensible precautions against sunstroke) for fire. Or more simply, a rooftop, a bath (not deep enough for accidents), a garden, or a fireside chair. The main requirements are freedom from interruption, and surroundings which help you to feel in tune with what you are trying to achieve.

To a practicing witch, the Circle soon becomes a very real sanctuary and focus of power, so it is reasonable to use it for these projection exercises—casting it, and then sitting within it facing the candle of the appropriate element. Any symbolism which strengthens your purpose may be added. For example, if you wish to project yourself into the world of the water element, you could cast the Circle with the Invoking Pentagram of Water (*see* Fig. 5, p. 49) instead of the usual one of Earth, and have the western candle green instead of white, placing the chalice filled with consecrated water, and the green cord, on the floor before it.

The methods—and the results—are all very personal. But if anyone who achieves the results still doubts whether they are real and valid, let him compare notes with someone else who has also achieved them. He will soon realize that two minds have, from their own individual viewpoints, looked on the same things.

1. In the case of a coven, of course, all should agree. One of the first things a new High Priest and High Priestess have to do is to make sure that the symbols they are working with mean the same to both of them, and to their coven as they build it up.

13.

Astral Projection

Occultism postulates that every living body, and every material object, has an astral counterpart, a 'double' consisting of astral substance, which is more tenuous than physical matter but grosser than mind or spirit, and visible to clairvoyant sight. Man's astral body, when thus seen, looks very like his physical body. It is equally essential to him throughout his incarnate life, because for one thing it is the bridge of communication between his mind (which operates on a still higher plane) and his physical brain and nervous system.[1]

Death is seen as a process of withdrawal: first (at physical death) of the astral body from the physical; then, over a period which may take many years, of the mental personality which was associated with it in that particular incarnation. In due course, the individual essence re-enters the lower planes for its next incarnation.

During waking life, the astral body normally coincides in space with the material body. In dreams, it is the astral body which is aware and experiences the dream-content. For most people, these two states comprise the whole of their lives, except perhaps (and particularly in childhood) for one or two isolated incidents which they may not recognize or understand.

Some, however, acquire that faculty of deliberately transferring their consciousness to the astral body, and moving about in it independently of the physical body, which is known as astral projection.[2]

Astral projection has always been an aspect of witchcraft. One significant thing which stands out among the mass of nonsense and distortion in the historical witchcraft trial reports is the repeated reference to witches 'flying' to sabbats while they were supposed to be in their beds, and where such testimony was genuine, and not merely agreement with a questioner's set formula to escape torture, it seems very likely to have been a description of astral projection.

The astral plane, in which a deliberately projected astral body moves and observes in full consciousness (much sharper than the confused astral consciousness of spontaneous dreams), is a complicated medium. It has, so to speak, one foot on the ground and one in fairyland.

At one extreme, what is observed in the astral plane corresponds closely to the physical world. It is possible for the experienced projector to transfer his consciousness at will to the astral plane (leaving his physical body inert), to wander on that plane observing places and events of which he has no normal sensory knowledge, to return to his physical body, and to report on what he has seen in such detail that it can be checked and confirmed in the material world. (Alex maintains that this faculty can be trained to a pitch where it can be used, for example, for industrial espionage.)

At the other extreme, the projected observer can leave this replica of the physical world behind, and move in worlds which have no material counterpart. And yet these worlds cannot be called illusory, because they can be shared. Astral environments 'created' by other people, or created and shared by other groups of people, can be entered and observed. Maxine tells how she once involuntarily accompanied Alex to an astral spiritualist 'heaven', occupied by spiritualists she had known. It was, literally, their Jordan. She was on this side, and they were on the far bank, dancing and singing and calling to her to join them. When she returned to her physical body she was so shaken that she was ill for a fortnight, and Alex, who had taken her there, was full of remorse.

That could of course be put down to hypnotism or induced hallucination (though both Alex and Maxine, who have a great deal of astral experience, are quite sure that it was not). But some of Maxine's other accounts of shared astral activity would be harder to explain away, especially as she herself introduced checkable factors into those activities.

She maintains, for example, that one can get into another person's dreams by astral projection.[3] 'Supposing I thought,' she told me, 'that J needed some advice she couldn't ask for. I could intrude on her dreams and give her that advice, or even healing.

'When I do that, and want the person to remember it, I give him something, some symbol, that he's not likely to forget. And more often than not he'll come to me and say: "I had a dream, and you were in it and gave me such-and-such".

'Now I find I can do it without even knowing about it; as far as I'm concerned I've just gone to sleep. The other day, C told me: "Maxine, you came to me in a dream and gave me . . . " (the symbol I do give to people, and which she couldn't have known about otherwise) " . . . and some wonderful advice".'

C is a highly intelligent girl known to both of us, and she has confirmed this to me.

R is a very normal and likeable young man who has been receiving some intensive training from Alex and Maxine in certain occult subjects. He told me how Maxine was giving much of her share of the instruction during his dreams, and he was writing it down in the morning and checking it with her. He obviously took this in his stride as a practical way of organizing his study-time.

Astral projection of this kind is, of course, the work of a highly trained adept. But even adepts have to start somewhere, and nobody finds the first breakthrough easy.

Techniques for achieving it are basically of two kinds. In the first, you will your astral body to move away from your physical body, and then will your consciousness into that displaced astral body. In the second, by imagination and will you move the 'centre of gravity' of your consciousness to a new location outside your physical body (usually by stages), and then will your astral body to join it.

With the first method, one way is to start with a part of your astral body—a hand or even a finger—instead of the whole of it, and only later to build up to the entire body.

For this you should find a chair with arm-rests, of the right size for you to sit in the 'Egyptian position'—square and upright with your legs together, so that spine, upper arms, and shins are vertical, and forearms, hands and thighs horizontal. You may find you can achieve this position in a chair without arms, by laying your forearms and hands flat on your thighs. Acquire the knack of retaining this position without either becoming tense or slumping; you should be both alert and relaxed.

Now concentrate your attention on, say, your right index finger. Visualize its astral double, coinciding with it. When this astral finger is clear and real in your mind, raise it by will alone, and will your physical finger to follow it. You may need many attempts, but persevere. In due course you will be able to raise the finger by willpower alone, without the use of muscle power.

This may sound like hair-splitting, but it a genuine mental and astral exercise, and provided you are honest with yourself, you will know in your own mind when you have succeeded.

Next (and it may be weeks later, even with daily attempts) try to do the same with two fingers, three, four, the whole hand, the wrist, the arm. Gradually you will become conscious of the reality of your astral body, and of your increasing ability to control it.

When you feel you have control over both hands, sit in the same Egyptian position, but close to the edge of a table, so that your thighs and forearms are underneath it. Now will your astral hands through the table and on to its top. Achieving this is really a breakthrough of confidence. Physical matter is no barrier to astral substance, except mentally and in the early stages.

Next, without the table, continue to build up your control of more and more of your astral body, till you can make it stand up while your physical body is still sitting.

Now try building up the concept of your astral body sitting facing your physical body and completely separate from it. Visualize every detail. You can do this with your eyes closed—or alternatively, you can sit facing a full-length mirror with your eyes open, and transfer your astral body to the mirror-image. When you feel you have achieved this, will your consciousness into your astral body.

'When I was learning,' says Alex, 'I used to sit for hours on end, building the image, forcing myself into it for day after day—but I still couldn't get there. And then suddenly, bong! I was on my feet in my astral body and walking. Sheer persistence—and that's the only way to achieve it.'

The alternative method (which requires just as much persistence) is to start by making your seat of consciousness mobile instead of your astral body. For example, you could place four or five symbols (Tarot cards would do) around the room; one on the mantlepiece, one propped on a bookshelf, and so on. Study each, and its surroundings, carefully till you know every detail by heart—the design and colouring of the symbol, the cigarette-burn on the mantlepiece, the titles and bindings of the books, and so on.

Sit in your chair in the Egyptian position, close your eyes, and take your imagination on a tour of the symbols. Mentally walk up to the first one and visualize it and its surroundings exactly, so that you can see it in full detail in your mind's eye. Contemplate it for a while, and then continue your mental walk, visualizing the turn, each step, and the halt. Then, when you have reached the second symbol and mentally turned to face it, bring its image to your mind's eye in the same way.

An interesting variation, at a later stage, is to try a tour with your 'mind's nose'. This time, instead of symbols, place around the room objects with a characteristic smell; an open scent bottle, a saucer of bleach, a burning joss-stick, a handful of cloves, and so on. Learn the route purely in terms of smell, including the background smell of the room and any localized smells belonging to items of furniture, curtains, etc. Then sit down, close your eyes, and step by step make your mental tour, using the scent-equivalent of visualization (for which unfortunately there seems to be no word, unless we coin 'olfactorization').

The same experiment can be done with sounds (a ticking watch, the hiss of a gas fire, the characteristic echo of each part of the room) and touch (various shapes and textures, feeling your way along the bookshelf).

Finally you can combine them all, so that your mental tour includes sight, smell, sound, touch, and even taste and temperature.

By this stage, you should have a real sense of your active and aware mind moving about independently of your body. There is a difference here from the first method, because whereas your astral body is real and can be manipulated separately from your physical body, your consciousness cannot actually (in any normal human state of development, anyway) locate itself outside both your physical *and* astral bodies. What you are in fact doing is getting your everyday consciousness used to the concept of astral projection, and preparing it for the breakthrough.

When that breakthrough comes (and it tends to come as Alex says, 'bong!', without warning), it will be because your mental tour has with practice become so vivid and detailed that your astral body is coaxed into taking it over. Instead of standing in front of (say) the Chariot card on the mantlepiece in your imagination, suddenly you are really standing in front of it, in full consciousness; seeing, in fact, the real thing instead of your mental picture of it, so that if for example a draught blew the card over, you would see it fall—which you would not have done on your purely mental tour, because that depended on mental images stored up beforehand.

Strong emotion can sometimes trigger off the breakthrough, as it did for Maxine.

'It was before we were married,' she told me. 'I had a small flat then, round the corner from Alex's. I wanted to be in on this big astral projection scene, and I'd been trying for months and months, sitting at the dining table struggling to bring my astral hands through it—and nothing was happening.

'There came a time when I was very broke; I literally hadn't eaten for about ten days. I walked through the little passage into Alex's road, knocking on the door, and told him: "I'm past hunger now, but I know I've got to eat." He said, "I haven't got anything—go away."

'I knew damn well he had. I went back to my own flat, and sat

150

down, took up my position in sheer temper, furious that anyone could be mean with food. I was there for about five minutes, seething.

'Then suddenly there was this clattering and banging—a great noise—oh, it was terrible . . . And I was looking at myself from the other side of the room. I saw my body in the upright position, not slumped, and I thought: "Well, I've done it now—I'll go and see."

'So I got out of the house. People had told me you could go through walls, and I hadn't believed them—but I did. I had to shut my eyes to do it, mind. I hadn't the nerve yet to cut through the houses, so I went along the passage. Alex's door was shut, of course, so I closed my eyes again, literally willing myself through it. It was a shock when I opened them again and found myself inside . . .

'Up the stairs, through the kitchen door, and there was Alex, bread and butter all laid out, and sandwich spread—oh, lashings of it.

'I was in such a blazing temper that I shot straight back into my body—too quickly, because I was terribly sick afterwards. Projection could be dangerous if you had a weak heart, because it can happen just like that.'

Alex was in the room when Maxine told me this. He confirmed the bread and butter and the sandwich spread—a little shame-facedly, as well he might.

Both Alex and Maxine can now project whenever they want to. Maxine's only break from it was when she was pregnant. 'I stopped around the second month, and it took me about a year before I was in the full swim of it again.'

Except for particular purposes,[4] though, Alex no longer practices astral projection on the physical plane—that is, to explore and observe the astral double of the physical world, and thus the events which are happening in the physical world.

'On the inner planes I will,' he says, 'but not on the physical level, for this reason: I broke the best friendship I ever had in my life because of astral nosiness . . . And I once ruined an engagement between two people because of bitterness. They had been asking for initiation and then playing about, and I set out to prove I could break it. By astral projection, I got the girl's most secret point and worked on it, bringing back information to the man and poisoning him. It was sheer astral nosiness, and I said then that I would never do it again. Incidentally, that's where industrial spying could come in—very easily.'

Once astral projection has been achieved, it takes a little getting used to. For one thing, at first you try to walk, as though you were in your physical body—until you discover that only a kind of gliding is necessary. You also discover after a while that distance is no object, and that it is possible to project yourself miles away (or thousands of miles) without any time-lag for the journey.

'And when you first try to touch an object astrally,' Alex says, 'your hand goes right through it, because your attention is directed to the physical object, which is no barrier to the astral hand. Once you realize that the object's got an astral counterpart too, and learn to observe the astral object instead of the physical one, then it will feel solid to your astral hand, because like will be touching like. But that takes a *lot* of practice.'

Some books on astral projection mention a silver cord, infinitely extendable, which can be seen during projection, connecting the physical body to the astral body. According to Muldoon and Carrington, 'The astral and the physical bodies are invariably connected by means of a sort of cord, or cable, along which vital currents pass. Should this cord be severed, death instantaneously results . . . This cord—the "Silver Cord" spoken of in Ecclesiastes—is elastic, and capable of great extension. It constitutes the essential link between the two bodies.'[5]

Alex does not agree with this concept, in fact he calls it 'a lot of rubbish, based on this text from Ecclesiastes—psychological, a safety thing to get you back in your body'.

(The text is Ecclesiastes 12:6-7—'Or ever the silver cord be loosed, or the golden bowl be broken . . . Then shall the dust return to the earth as it was; and the spirit shall return unto God who gave it.' According to *Peake's Commentary on the Bible*, the metaphor is simply of a lamp-bowl and the cord which suspends it.)

Whether other experts would agree with Alex or not on this particular point, they would certainly agree that the astral plane is very easily filled with phenomena of one's own creation, and that to one's astral vision these look as real as other astral objects which have actual physical counterparts. So the Silver Cord may well be one of these creations, a collective illusion conjured up by the desire for a reassuring life-line, and sanctified by tradition. If so, it is harmless enough, but it does point to the fact that if you wish to observe the physical world and its events during astral projection, you do have to have your wits about you, and learn to distinguish the objective from the subjective.

'Astral projection,' Alex says, 'is like a controlled dream state. In an actual dream you have no control, you're in it till it's finished. In astral projection you're conscious. Things start to appear as they do in dreams, but it's all alive. It's very difficult to convey to anyone who hasn't experienced it. Crowley, in *Magick in Theory and Practice*, is the only one who's been honest about it; he says the astral planes are what you think they are. And yet that's very much oversimplifying it.

'Once you've got the knack of slipping out of your body, you can explore the inner planes. For me, the astral plane in the initial stages of that kind of projection is exactly what it says—the star plane. It's a dark sky, like midnight. You stand there, and you suddenly realize there are tiny pinpoints of light—red, yellow, blue and green—everywhere. And as you concentrate on them, you realize it's gradually getting lighter and lighter, just like daylight, but there's nothing around you at all. Only silence.

'Then you start charging yourself with the various elements, and projecting yourself into the chosen planes . . . And that's really all you can say about it, because everyone's experience is different.'

Everyone's experience of the actual moment of projection seems to be different, too. Maxine, for example, is still aware of the 'clattering' which accompanied her first projection.

'There is another way of learning astral projection,' she says, 'and that's with the crystal. But I don't like it. The crystal pulls you in, sucks you in like a magnet . . . A horrible sensation. I prefer the clattering.'

'Yet another way,' Alex adds, 'is to visualiz⌐ a tunnel with a light at the end of it, and to walk towards it.'

One thing they both agree on. Returning from astral projection into the physical body is like a rebirth; the body feels dead, heavy, and dirty.

In reading books on astral projection you will come across the terms 'etheric plane', 'lower and upper astral planes', and 'etheric body' as well as 'astral body', so perhaps I should end this chapter by indicating how these relate to what I have said in it. I have used the word 'astral' throughout for simplicity, but, as already noted in Chapter 3, the subdivisions are finer than that.

The etheric plane, as the term is usually employed, is that which corresponds most closely to the physical. It merges with the lower astral, and it was in this zone of the planes, for instance, that Maxine caught Alex out with his sandwich spread. In the upper astral, the etheric and the physical have been left behind, and it is here that Alex experiences his sky of pinpoint colours.

Again, strictly speaking, the etheric body should be distinguished from the astral. The etheric body is closely wedded to the physical body. With it is associated the 'aura' which psychically sensitive people can see surrounding the physical body, and from which they can read much about the owner's emotional state. The astral body proper is less earthbound. Projection of consciousness is possible into either of these bodies, and for many people the first breakthrough will be into the etheric, after which the next step to the astral should be easier and may happen involuntarily.

But while you are carrying out the exercises aimed at this breakthrough, these distinctions are not really important. Once it is achieved, and you start moving on various planes, you will very soon learn—as 'Ophiel' puts it—to know where you are from the scenery.

1. A detailed description of occult views on the nature and structure of the astral body is *The Astral Body and Other Astral Phenomena* by Arthur E. Powell.

2. Among the books on astral projection which give practical advice on achieving it are *The Projection of the Astral Body* by Sylvan Muldoon and Hereward Carrington and *The Art and Practice of Astral Projection* by 'Ophiel'. Alex particularly recommends the latter as simple and sound.

3. A few days after I wrote this paragraph, a very interesting article entitled *Is Your Mind a Thief?* was published in the *Sunday Times Magazine* for 22 November 1970, by Dr. Ann Faraday, a research psychologist at University College, London. Dr. Faraday cites several consulting-room examples, from her own experience and that of other professionals (including Freud), which seem to her to point to telepathic 'invasion' of other people's dreams, and suggests that this would be a fruitful line of research 'with the present deadlock in experimental studies of ESP.'

4. For example, after the pop group performance I mentioned on p. 38, when Alex felt it necessary to return astrally to the scene for a final tidying-up of the 'psychic chaos'.

5. Muldoon and Carrington, op. cit.

14.

The Rite of Queen Hagiel

In Chapter 12 I dealt with the technique for becoming aware of, and communicating with, the primitive entities of the four elemental worlds. When a witch or magician wishes to contact a being of a higher order than these (whether he calls it angel, a spirit, or simply an entity) one time-honored method is by ritually invoking it to the Circle, and I do not think this book would be complete without a description of a typical invocation of this kind.

There is no need here to discuss yet again the nature of the reality of these entities. The principle involved is the one I discussed on pages 124-25, and practice confirms its validity, even if those who have experienced communication with such beings may interpret their experience in different ways.

We can also bypass the endless debate about whether such invocations are, properly, witchcraft or magic. They *are* ritual magic, but many witches practice them and I am sure will go on doing so; and why shouldn't they? Sensible witches regard Wicca's home ground—the bottom of the Tree—as the base, but not the boundary, of their operations. If they want to operate on other levels for particular purposes, they use the appropriate techniques. Anyone who disapproves is invited to skip this chapter.

The grimoires, and word-of-mouth tradition, are full of instructions for invoking an endless variety of spirits, both good and evil. Some grimoires give such a profusion of their names, regimentally categorized, that it is hard to take them seriously. One suspects that their authors inflated their nominal rolls in the same way that mail publicity firms do, by acquiring each other's mailing lists.

Such extravagances apart, there are entities of whom enough people have had genuine (and mutually corroborative) experience to keep any sincere practitioner occupied for a lifetime.

Of these, I have chosen one of the most charming and harmless invocatory rites—that of Queen Hagiel (a Venus concept). I say 'harmless' not because it is ineffectual, but because no one who carries it out, however successfully, can come to any harm by it—or cause any harm.

There are three varieties of the rite. Their basic method is the same, but they differ in the type of manifestation intended. The most ambitious aims at visual manifestation of Hagiel herself, in a triangle just outside the Circle. The second form involves the use of a crystal in which Hagiel is to be seen. For the third form of the rite, a suitable medium is placed kneeling in the triangle, bound and blindfolded, and Hagiel speaks through him. In all three forms, of course, the intention is to speak with Hagiel and to put your request to her.

First prepare your Circle, but do not cast it yet, because the method of casting will differ from the usual Wiccan procedures given on pages 47-50. The four candles at the cardinal points must be green, the colour of Venus. From the ceiling over the centre of the Circle, hang a lamp of green glass containing a green candle. If you are making the lamp yourself, the use of copper—Venus's metal—is sound symbology.

Just outside the Circle to the east, mark an equilateral triangle with one point to the east. If you are using a medium, it must be large enough for him to sit within it.

In the centre of the Circle, place an altar, which should be approximately square. A card table will do, but whatever you use, the floor underneath it must be clear and reachable. Cover the alter with a green cloth, and mark an equilateral triangle on it, also with one point to the east, in lighter green chalk. Stand a green candle at each point of this triangle.

If the crystal is to be used, it should be placed in this altar triangle, on the stand or black cloth with which you normally back

The altar should be decorated with roses and lilies. Wand, pentacle, censer, and consecrated water should be on the floor close at hand. You will also need either two or three pieces of paper (three for the direct manifestation method) and a pencil or pen. One piece of paper should be about eight inches square, the other one (or two) ready cut to regular seven-sided shape, three or four inches across.

Wand, pentacle and censer will of course have already been consecrated. The water is consecrated with the usual formula given on page 48, except that no athame is used. Everything else used in the rite, including paper and pen, should be consecrated at the appropriate moment by placing it on the pentacle ('I consecrate thee with the element of earth'), touching it with water ('I consecrate thee with the element of water'), and passing it over the censer ('I consecrate thee with the element of air')—but *not* passing it over the candle, because Hagiel is not invoked with fire.

Neither is it necessary to complete the consecration by blessing man-to-woman in the usual way, because this is essentially a solo rite—though there is nothing to prevent you having an assistant, to hand you what you need as the ritual proceeds.

The incense used should be powdered cinnamon.

You yourself should be robed, in azure blue silk with a green or rose-coloured girdle of material or cord. The robe need not be elaborate or expensive. A simple shift with arm and neck holes is enough, and it is a well-established occult principle that any garment, weapon or accessory made by your own hands has a certain built-in magical advantage.

You should wear the magic sword in the left side of your girdle, but it will be neither drawn nor used; this is not an occasion for the force aspect.

If a medium is being used, he should be blindfolded and bound at ankles and wrists as for first-degree initiation[1] and placed kneeling, as comfortably as possible, in the outer triangle. (By 'medium' I do not necessarily mean a professional or trained outsider. Among the varied talents which a working coven discovers within itself, there is probably at least one member who has potential as a medium, and it is part of the coven's function to diagnose and develop all such individual gifts.)

When everything is ready, take the large square of paper and mark it off with the consecrated pen into forty-nine squares (seven by seven) to make the Square of Venus, which is as follows.

22	47	16	41	10	35	4
5	23	48	17	42	11	29
30	6	24	49	18	36	12
13	31	7	25	43	19	37
38	14	32	1	26	44	20
21	39	8	33	2	27	45
46	15	40	9	34	3	28

You will notice that as with the Planetary Squares[2] each line of figures, horizontal or vertical, adds up to the same total. In this case it is 175, which in turn adds up to 13 and finally to 4—the magical number of the Goddess.

You must copy out the numbers in the correct order from 1 to 49, in their correct squares, saying 'Karnayna and Aradia bless this rite' as you write each number. When the Square is complete, consecrate it, and place it on the floor under the altar.

Take the wand, and with it cast the outer triangle. Start at the left corner, and trace out to the far corner, back to the right corner, across to the left corner, and finally out again to the far corner to seal it. Cast the altar triangle in the same way, standing to the west of it and facing east.

Now is the moment to cast the Circle. It is also done with the wand, starting at the north and moving deosil *three* times round the Circle, pointing the wand at its boundary as you would with the athame. Next you sprinkle consecrated water *once* round the boundary of the Circle, again deosil from north to north. Finally you carry the censer round once. You do not carry fire, neither do you draw down power with invoking pentagrams.

Next you take a seven-sided piece of paper, and with the consecrated pen draw the seal of Hagiel on the one side and the sign of Venus on the other. Consecrate it (again with earth, water and air only) and then trace over every line of your drawings with the tip of the wand. If you are not using a medium, prepare two such papers, consecrating them and tracing them with the wand in the same way.

One of these papers you place in the altar triangle (if you are not using a crystal) or on the floor under the altar (if you are). If you are not using a medium, place the second paper in the outer triangle. Both should lie with the Hagiel seal uppermost.

In between all these actions, do not forget to keep the censer charcoal glowing and fed with cinnamon. If you are using a medium, it will probably help him if you make sure that he inhales plenty of the incense smoke. If you have an assistant, he can attend to the censer.

You are now ready for the actual invocation. Standing to the west of the altar and facing east, you declaim: 'By Karnayna and Aradia I call thee, O thou great and holy Hagiel. Hagiel, Hagiel, vouchsafe to descend from thine abode, bringing thine influence and presence into the triangle, that I may behold thy glory, and enjoy thy society and thine aid.'

(If you are using a crystal, you should say 'into the triangle and the crystal.')

Next move deosil round the altar to the east cardinal point, and facing east, repeat the invocation. Repeat it again to the south, west and north, making five times in all.

Still moving deosil, return to the west of the altar and face east across it, looking into the crystal if you are using one, or at the outer triangle if you are not.

Fig. 12. Sigil of Hagiel.

Fig. 13. Sigil of Venus.

Wait patiently for a while, maintaining concentration on your purpose, and then say: 'Hagiel, Hagiel, Hagiel—come to my Circle.'

If your ritual has been properly prepared and carried out, physically, mentally and spiritually, you should now see Hagiel in the outer triangle or the crystal, or hear her through the medium.

There is wide agreement about Hagiel's appearance, because her image is one of the 'trodden paths' I referred to on page 125.

Alex describes her thus: 'She appears in the shape of a queen, about twenty-six or twenty-seven, with a beautiful face and figure, blue eyes, and auburn hair. She wears a mediaeval type of dress of a verdigris or green colour, embroidered with gold flowers, and gold slippers. On her head is a crown which looks like copper, with four towers. She has a very musical voice.'

Hagiel must of course not be invoked without a specific purpose, so when she manifests, you must very courteously name your request and ask her to grant it.

'If what you ask is reasonable,' says Alex, 'Hagiel will grant it, and if you reach agreement with her and she makes a promise, you can rest assured it will be fulfilled. At times, when it's necessary for you to have magical servants, she will send her own servants to you. They too will be in female form, but you'll see them for yourself. When she is leaving—and you don't tell her to go, she will simply start to go when she is ready—you will thank her for her appearance, and ask her if she will come again. It's an experience that you'll never forget.'

Once she has gone, simply blow out the candles. Tip the incense into the consecrated water and pour both away (the ordinary household plumbing will do).

If you have been using a medium, release him first and see that he is comfortable, because he well may be exhausted; but, like you, he will come to no harm. It is a good idea to have weak, sweet tea ready for him (another job for your assistant).

There is no need to banish the Circle, for the Rite of Queen Hagiel is purely an act of love.

---

1. *See* p. 15. Both ankles are bound, as for the 'ordeal'. The wrists behind the back must be secure, but the cord passing from them round the neck must be loose so that the medium does not hurt himself during a trance condition.

2. All seven Planetary Squares are given in Chapter XXII of Eliphas Levi's *Transcendental Magic*.

15.

A Witch Wedding

Witches have a wedding ceremony of their own, which they call handfasting. The dictionary defines handfasting as 'betrothal, provisional marriage, private marriage'. A witches' handfasting is all of those things. In the first place it is not, of course, a 'legal' marriage recognized by the state. Witches who want legal status for their union have a civil wedding as well, or even, if their own consciences and attitudes allow it, a church one. Under the wide umbrella of the Anglican confession, for instance, there are quite a few ministers who would in all sincerity marry couples they know to be witches. After all, a small but genuine handful of those ministers are themselves initiated witches (though I do not propose to name any of them) and a much larger number have a sympathetic interest in occultism in general.

Like so much in Wicca, a handfasting means what the witches concerned choose to make it mean. At one extreme, they may intend it as a ceremonial announcement to their friends of the Craft that they are living together and wish to be treated as a couple unless and until they change their minds. At the other, the intention is even more permanent than 'till death do us part', because it involves the concept of 'soul-mates'—a continuing relationship through all subsequent reincarnations.

The soul-mate concept is a very ancient one in occult thinking. It is reflected in the Legend of the Goddess (*see* App. I): 'To fulfil love, you must return again at the same time and at the same place as the loved ones; and you must meet, and know, and remember, and love them again.' Again, it means many things to many people. Some come to the conclusion, either through intuition or by the advance process known as 'consulting the Akashic Records' (*see* p. 139), that they have already been involved with each other in an earlier life, even perhaps that their present relationship has to deal with undischarged Karma, the burden of spiritual debit and credit carried over from incarnation to incarnation till it is finally resolved. Others, again relying on their own occult insight, may decide and accept that they are destined to a many-life relationship from now on. Yet others, without any sense of bowing to destiny, may simply decide that they wish it to be so. To these, the declaration (particularly when ritually confirmed and consummated by the Great Rite in its 'actual' form) is a committal which imposes a pattern on their future lives, and therefore probably the most serious act of magic they will ever perform.

Wiccan handfasting accepts all these attitudes, from that of the temporary union, through that of intended lifelong partnership, to that of soul-mate committal. All that Wiccan law says is that handfasting is valid in the first instance for a year and a day. At the end of that time, the couple may seek out the same High Priest and High Priestess who united them, and announce that they wish to part. If they do not, the union is regarded as continuing. Handfasting does not bind a couple for ever (or even for one life) regardless of their future feelings. However, a couple's decision that they are soul-mates, declared and ritually confirmed, does so bind them; but that is their own act, deliberately setting in motion psychic forces which they know they will not be able to reverse—not something laid upon them by any High Priest or High Priestess, even at their own request, or by any rules of the Craft.

Handfasting, then, is a celebration, and what the couple get out of is what they choose to put into it, reinforced by the presence and goodwill of their friends.

It is as joyous as any wedding, and it uses up more flowers than most. The entire Circle on the floor is composed of flowers; the couple usually bring armfuls of their own choice, to which bunches contributed by individual coven members are added. More flowers decorate the altar. Traditionally, fruit may be used as well. A crown of flowers is also ready on the altar.

The Circle is cast, High Priest and High Priestess take up their positions, then the couple are led in, usually robed as splendidly as the coven can manage—though only with outer robes over their naked bodies, as they will be removed later. Often the leading-in is done by another couple who are their special friends. These bring them to the altar and join the rest of the coven round the Circle.

Man and woman kneel—the woman on the left—and the High Priest invokes the Goddess. The beginning of the invocation is similar to the Charge (App. 2), and it goes on to ask the Goddess to give her protection 'to this son and daughter of man. Deflect evil from them and confound those who would blaspheme against the true light of thy wisdom.'

They stand, and their robes are removed for the annointing. The High Priestess anoints the man, and the High Priest the woman, according to their grade—inverted triangle for first degree witches, inverted pentagram for second, inverted pentagram and upright triangle for third—with oil, wine, and lips. (*See* Fig. 7a-c, p. 75.)

The couple kneel again, and the High Priest addresses them: 'Know that it is in the decrees of the fates that ye are to be united, nevermore to be divided. In vain against the stars preach the monk and the priest; what shall be, shall be. Wherefore take hope and joy, O children of time. And now, as I join your hands, I betroth your souls.'

(These words are traditional, obviously echoing ancient conflicts. It is up to the couple to take them as they wish to take them.)

The High Priestess takes the crown of flowers from the altar, consecrates it with the earth (pentacle), water, air (censer) and fire (candle), and passes it first over the head of the man and then over the head of the woman.

The High Priest holds his left hand over the couple, and raises his right. 'Ye Lords of the Watchtowers, O powerful God, O gentle Goddess; attest the betrothal of these young hearts . . . ' He calls on the Circle and the altar to attest it, the sun and the air. 'While the forms are divided, may the souls cling together, sorrow with sorrow, and joy with joy; and when at length bride and bridegroom are one, O Stars, may the trouble with which ye are charged have exhausted its burden; may no danger molest, and no malice disturb; but over the marriage bed, shine in peace, O Stars.'

Now the couple swear the oath, taking each other 'to my hand at the setting of the sun, the rising of the stars'—and the words of the handfasting are over.

One traditional ceremony remains. A broomstick is laid on the ground beside them, and both jump over it. Then the High Priestess picks it up, and ritually sweeps all evil influences away behind them and out of the Circle.

The High Priest traces the Pentagram in front of the newly-joined pair.

Wine and cakes are blessed in the usual way, and passed round.

The Great Rite may follow, or not, as the couple wish. If it does, again it is up to them whether they regard it as a solemn ritual consummation of their handfasting or, even more solemnly, as committing themselves to each other as soul-mates for lives to come. No one will ask them, if they do not choose to say.

When all is over—and, if the Great Rite has been celebrated, the coven have re-entered the room—the wedding becomes, like any other, a party.

16.

Endpiece

I began this book as a newly initiated first-degree witch. I finish writing it, almost a year later, as a third-degree witch, planning, with my working partner, the foundation of our own coven. Reading back over the manuscript, I find it encouraging that there is no more than the occasional phrase I want to revise, but there are one or two thoughts I would like to add, in the light of the year's experience.

One thing I learned quickly: how much of the old image of witchcraft lingers in the public mind, and how ready people are to distort and sensationalize such evidence as comes to their attention. Often these reactions would be hilariously funny if they were not disturbing.

Last midsummer, Alex and Maxine and most of their coven went up to the Midlands to join forces with another coven (as often happens at seasonal festivals) for the celebration of the Summer Solstice. The host coven had found an ideal little valley, an old quarry in wooded open country a long way from the nearest house. There we lit our bonfire and cast a huge Circle which took in a convenient rock to serve as an altar. The night was mild, the air so still that the candles burned steadily without having to be screened. We performed the seasonal ritual in very good spirits, jumped over the sinking bonfire as tradition demanded, and in general enjoyed ourselves. Nobody crept off into the woods, and apart from our nakedness there was nothing to which even a scoutmaster could reasonably object (except possibly on theo-logical grounds). The ceremony over, we got dressed and walked back to the High Priest and High Priestess's house for snacks and coffee, and then packed into our cars and drove back to London as dawn broke.

That was that, we thought. But five days later, the local paper splashed on its front page—

Mystery at Quarry

POLICE IN NAKED WITCHES PROBE

Police were called last night to a disused limestone quarry at — after rumours of nude dancing and witchcraft ceremonies had swept the village. They found the remains of a wood fire at one end of the 50-foot quarry, and a pile of sticks and a large lock of limestone nearby . . .

Two cats have disappeared from a nearby street and the villagers' theory is that they have been used as sacrifices in some strange ceremony.

Within a week, so our friends told us, the rumour had grown to ten cats with their throats cut. (And all this directed blindly at a coven whose main activity is healing, of which they have a fine if unpublished record.)

Another example occured a few days ago. One of our women witches had her purse snatched through a broken pane in a telephone kiosk. She was phoning me at the time, and I heard her scream. She told me quickly what had happened and rang off to call the police.

The thief got away, but the purse only contained some change and her front door key. More police than were strictly necessary (presumably because they were bored or because she was attractive) spent ten minutes helping her pick her front door lock, after which they all departed except one, who came in to take a leisurely statement and then left. Next day her father changed the lock and, again, they thought that was that.

A couple of days later a local paper reporter knocked on the door. Word had got around that the lady was a witch, neighbours were saying that police had descended on the house, battered on the door for ten minutes and finally broken in, searched the place and (so some declared) come away with confiscated drugs. Would she care to make any statements?

When she had stopped laughing she gave the reporter the facts. Fortunately he was an intelligent young man with professional standards, and he scrapped the news story in favour of a feature article on witchcraft with which she would help him, but in which her name would not appear.

The only thing which really stung her was the drugs rumour, because, like Alex and Maxine, she has strong anti-drug views.

Bizarre instances of neighbourly misunderstanding such as these may be jokes today (and a mere nuisance to the police) but for many centuries they would have been quite enough to send innocent people to the gallows.

One other example was merely funny. A writer on witchcraft wanted to include a chapter on Alex in a paperback he was compiling, and was interviewing him for the purpose. Alex knew the man well, and also his reputation for conviviality, so he started an evening's get together by joking: 'Now you — well stay sober, or the things I'll do to you will make Aleister Crowley look like a — boy scout!'

When the paperback appeared, the chapter (which to be fair, was otherwise perfectly reasonable) introduced Alex as 'the most flamboyant witch of them all, an Englishman who claims he is King of the Witches, and swears that one day he will make "Aleister Crowley look like a boy scout"'.

Alex laughed out loud when he read it.

Incidentally, I sometimes wish that title had never been given to him, because of the stumbling-block it has proved to so many non-Alexandrian witches who might otherwise see beyond it to the man himself. Alex admits he sometimes feels the same—but usually, I think, his ironic sense of humour relishes the commotion it causes.

He is a strange man, this Alex Sanders. A year of working with him and has given me a deep respect and affection for him, coupled with occasional exasperation at the perverse way he lays himself open to irrelevant criticism. Flamboyant he certainly is, but it is the flamboyance of a gifted court jester—and the licensed Fool was often the most intelligent man in the palace. His flair for publicity is like the strident dust-cover which sells the book, and to my own knowledge, many worthwhile people have been sufficiently intrigued by it to find out what lies behind. When all is done, he will have achieved more to clear the air on the subject of modern Wicca, and to put it in perspective, than anyone in this century (including—and I say it with no disrespect—Gerald Gardner). The exasperation will fade, the television tricks will be forgotten, but the educative effect will remain. I have no doubt that in future learned works on occultism he will rank with Levi, Crowley, Gardner and the other memorable names, and in one respect at least, sheer magical achievement, may well top them all.

Alex has often been described as an enigma, but usually, I think, by people who are content to remain baffled. His views and beliefs are clear, and he explains them clearly, describing his successes and failures with equal frankness, to those who really want to listen. Certainly he can lead the pompous up the garden (I have watched him do it, while I struggled to keep my face straight) but usually they have asked for it. His philosophy is puzzling only to those who find the whole subject of occultism incomprehensible. The enigma, to them, is that he makes it work.

With his flamboyance goes an odd streak of modesty. He may boast cheerfully about irrelevancies, while saying nothing about things that are truly worthy of admiration. I have seen him holding court in a pub, joking, teasing outrageously, carrying on half a dozen conversations at once at widely different levels—and only two or three of us would know that he and Maxine had been up several nights on end, straightening out a would-be suicide.

Maxine has two qualities in common with her husband and High Priest: genuine occult gifts, and a powerful sense of humour. Otherwise they are different—and complementary. He is learned, she is instinctive. Both are knowledgable, but whereas Alex will give you chapter and verse for pronouncements, Maxine is more likely to cite Wiccan tradition and personal experience. Purists accuse Alex (though heaven knows why it should be an accusation) of being more magician than witch; Maxine is the archetypal witch, charged with wisdom from the dark earth. She defends (and when necessary attacks) Alex like a mother-cat. I would rather cross swords with Alex than Maxine any day, because Alex would forgive me within a week, so long as I was able to laugh about it, while Maxine would give no quarter till the point was cleared up to her satisfaction.

I would not like to give the wrong impression about that, because it is often a case of 'whom the High Priestess loveth, she chasteneth'. She is likely to combine merciless criticism with encouraging predictions about one's future effectiveness. Nine-tenths of the time she is all kindliness, good humour, and very good company; but when she does decide that a reprimand is called for, everyone takes cover, and even Alex stays quiet.

Every coven has its own style and individuality, which is as it should be. Ours, for example, we intend to be small, closed, and composed as far as possible of equal numbers of men and women in compatible working pairs. We will aim at a stable membership, meeting regularly and getting used to working together, with a particular emphasis on healing. This intended pattern is no criticism of Alex, because in fact it represents his considered advice to us. Alex's coven is of necessity large and shifting, because it is a training-ground of new witches, a breeding-ground of new covens, and a winnowing-floor of wheat from chaff. (During the past year I have been constantly reminded of the Parable of the Sower.) That, too, in view of Alex's talents and his standing, is as it should be, but it is not necessarily the pattern for the typical working coven.

What have I personally gained from a year of Wicca? First of all, precisely what I had hoped to gain: confirmation that there are dormant areas of the human psyche which anyone, if he is sincere and determined, can gradually awaken and put to practical and exciting use. I know that I am only at the beginning of a long process of development, but right at the start I learned curious facts about my own mind which gave food for thought.

One small example: in trying the mental exercise of retaining a static image for a set of number of minutes (*see* p. 51), I found great difficulty at first with two-dimensional symbols such as the ankh-ka (*see* Fig. 7d, p. 75) or the Chinese yang and yin. My mind seemed to skate over the symbol, and as I concentrated on one corner of it the rest seemed misty. And yet the first time I tried a three-dimensional image—a cut rose with two leaves and a drop of water on one outer petal—it was complete and vivid. I retained that rose steadily, conscious not only of the visual picture but also of the feel of its thorns and the inverted-pendulum sensation of its weight, for the full five minutes and was surprised when my pre-set timer pinged. So next time, I 'made' the ankh-ka of quarter-inch-thick heavy metal, and found it much easier to hold in my mind.

That may sound like a minor phenomenon, but every such discovery helps you in your approach to the next step.

I have gained a sense of reawakened imagination, of cobwebs being blown out of disused corners of my mind; a new pantheistic delight in the world around and within. Added to that, a determination to follow the path and see where it leads me.

The year has satisfied me that Wicca is a workable philosophy, or religion, or Craft—however one chooses to name it. It is not for everybody. I say that, not with any arrogant implication of a Chosen Few, but because it is one approach among many, and suits certain temperaments. Mine for one; I find its symbolism beautiful, its ritual satisfying, its tolerance (and indeed encouragement) of individual attitudes civilized, its deep roots nourishing, its small-group organization comradely and effective, the work it sets out to do admirable, and its successes impressive. For me it offers (as I am sure it could for many others) a practicable synthesis of the needs of the individual, the interests of his fellow-men, and the meaning of the universe.

So I end as the Book of Shadows begins:

> Eight words the Wiccan rede fulfil:
> An it harm none, do what you will.

Appendix 1

The Legend of the Descent of the Goddess into the Underworld

In ancient times, our Lord, the Horned One, was (as he still is) the Consoler, the Comforter. But men know him as the dread Lord of Shadows, lonely, stern, and just.

But our Lady the Goddess would solve all mysteries, even the mystery of death; and so she journeyed to the underworld.

The Guardian of the Portals challenged her: 'Strip off thy garments, lay aside thy jewels; for naught mayest thou bring with thee into this our land.'

So she laid down her garments and her jewels, and was bound, as all living must be who seek to enter the realms of Death, the Mighty One.

Such was her beauty that Death himself knelt, and laid his sword and crown at her feet, and kissed her feet, saying: 'Blessed be thy feet that have brought thee in these ways. Abide with me; but let me place my cold hands on thy heart.'

And she replied: 'I love thee not. Why dost thou cause all things that I love, and take delight in, to fade and die?'

'Lady,' replied Death, 'it is age and fate, against which I am helpless. Age causes all things to wither; but when men die at the end of time, I give them rest and peace and strength, so that they may return. But you, you are lovely. Return not, abide with me.'

But she answered: 'I love thee not.'

Then said Death: 'An you receive not my hand on your heart, you must kneel to Death's scourge.'

'It is fate; better so,' she said, and she knelt.

And Death scourged her tenderly. And she cried: 'I know the pangs of love.'

And Death raised her, and said: 'Blessed be.' And he gave her the fivefold salute, saying: 'Thus only may you attain to joy, and knowledge.'

And he taught her all his mysteries, and gave her the necklace which is the circle of rebirth. And she taught him her mystery of the sacred cup which is the cauldron of rebirth.

They loved, and were one; for there be three great mysteries in the life of man, and magic controls them all. To fulfil love, you must return again at the same time and at the same place as the loved ones; and you must meet, and know, and remember, and love them again.

But to be reborn, you must die, and be made ready for a new body. And to die, you must be born; and without love, you may not be born.

And our Goddess ever inclineth to love, and mirth, and happiness; and guardeth and cherisheth her hidden children in life, and in death she teacheth the way to her communion; and even in this world she teacheth them the mystery of the Magic Circle, which is placed between the world of men and of the Gods.

Appendix 2

The Charge

The High Priest: Now listen to the words of the Great Mother, who was of old also called among men Artemis, Astarte, Athene, Dione, Melusine, Aphrodite, Cerridwen, Dana, Arianrhod, Isis, Bride, and by many other names. At her altars, the youth of Lacedaemon in Sparta made due sacrifice.

The High Priestess: Whenever ye have need of any thing, once in the month, and better it be when the moon is full, then shall ye assemble in some secret place, and adore the spirit of me, who am Queen of all witches.

There shall ye assemble, ye who are fain to learn all sorcery, yet have not won its deepest secrets; to these will I teach things that are as yet unknown.

And ye shall be free from slavery; and as a sign that ye be really free, ye shall be naked in your rites; and ye shall dance, sing, feast, make music and love, all in my praise. For mine is the ecstasy of the spirit, and mine also is joy on earth; for my law is love unto all beings.

Keep pure your highest ideal; strive ever towards it, let naught stop you or turn you aside; for mine is the secret door which opens upon the land of youth, and mine is the cup of wine of life, and the cauldron of Cerridwen, which is the Holy Grail of immortality.

I am the gracious Goddess, who gives the gift of joy unto the heart of man. Upon earth, I give the knowledge of the spirit eternal; and beyond death, I give peace, and freedom, and reunion with those who have gone before.

Nor do I demand sacrifice; for behold, I am the Mother of all living, and my love is poured out upon the earth.

The High Priest: Hear ye the words of the Star Goddess; she in the dust of whose feet are the hosts of heaven, whose body encircles the universe.

The High Priestess: I am the beauty of the green earth, and the white moon among the stars, and the mystery of the waters, and the desire of the heart of man.

Call unto thy soul; arise, and come unto me; for I am the soul of nature, who gives life to the universe. From me all things proceed, and unto me all things must return; and before my face, beloved of Gods and of men, let thine innermost divine self be enfolded in the rapture of the infinite.

Let my worship be within the heart that rejoiceth; for behold, all acts of love and pleasure are my rituals. And therefore let there be beauty and strength, power and compassion, honour and humility, mirth and reverence within you.

And thou who thinkest to seek for me, know thy seeking and yearning shall avail thee not unless thou knowest the mystery: that if that which thou seekest thou findest not within thee, thou wilt never find it without thee. For behold, I have been with thee from the beginning; and I am that which is attained at the end of desire.

Appendix 3

Planetary Hours

These are the traditionally accepted hours for operating spells which have planetary correspondences. Each day has a ruling planet; our days of the week in English are mostly named after the Teutonic forms of the planet-gods concerned.

They are: Sunday, the Sun; Monday, the Moon; Tuesday, Mars (Tiw); Wednesday, Mercury (Woden); Thursday, Jupiter (Thor); Friday, Venus (Freya); Saturday, Saturn.

The first hour after sunrise is ruled by the day's own planet, after which each hour is ruled by one of the other planets in the order Sun, Venus, Mercury, Moon, Saturn, Jupiter, Mars, and so on in rotation. Thus Monday's second daylight hour is ruled by Saturn, Tuesday's second by the Sun, etc. At sunset a new sequence starts with the fifth down the list from the day's planet: thus Monday's first hour from sunset is ruled by Venus, etc. The full list is as follows:

Hours from sunrise	Sunday	Monday	Tuesday	Wednesday	Thursday	Friday	Saturday
1st	Sun	Moon	Mars	Mercury	Jupiter	Venus	Saturn
2nd	Venus	Saturn	Sun	Moon	Mars	Mercury	Jupiter
3rd	Mercury	Jupiter	Venus	Saturn	Sun	Moon	Mars
4th	Moon	Mars	Mercury	Jupiter	Venus	Saturn	Sun
5th	Saturn	Sun	Moon	Mars	Mercury	Jupiter	Venus
6th	Jupiter	Venus	Saturn	Sun	Moon	Mars	Mercury
7th	Mars	Mercury	Jupiter	Venus	Saturn	Sun	Moon
8th	Sun	Moon	Mars	Mercury	Jupiter	Venus	Saturn

Hours from sunrise	Sunday	Monday	Tuesday	Wednesday	Thursday	Friday	Saturday
9th	Venus	Saturn	Sun	Moon	Mars	Mercury	Jupiter
10th	Mercury	Jupiter	Venus	Saturn	Sun	Moon	Mars
11th	Moon	Mars	Mercury	Jupiter	Venus	Saturn	Sun
12th	Saturn	Sun	Moon	Mars	Mercury	Jupiter	Venus

Hours from sunset	Sunday	Monday	Tuesday	Wednesday	Thursday	Friday	Saturday
1st	Jupiter	Venus	Saturn	Sun	Moon	Mars	Mercury
2nd	Mars	Mercury	Jupiter	Venus	Saturn	Sun	Moon
3rd	Sun	Moon	Mars	Mercury	Jupiter	Venus	Saturn
4th	Venus	Saturn	Sun	Moon	Mars	Mercury	Jupiter
5th	Mercury	Jupiter	Venus	Saturn	Sun	Moon	Mars
6th	Moon	Mars	Mercury	Jupiter	Venus	Saturn	Sun
7th	Saturn	Sun	Moon	Mars	Mercury	Jupiter	Venus
8th	Jupiter	Venus	Saturn	Sun	Moon	Mars	Mercury
9th	Mars	Mercury	Jupiter	Venus	Saturn	Sun	Moon
10th	Sun	Moon	Mars	Mercury	Jupiter	Venus	Saturn
11th	Venus	Saturn	Sun	Moon	Mars	Mercury	Jupiter
12th	Mercury	Jupiter	Venus	Saturn	Sun	Moon	Mars

The number of actual hours from sunrise to sunset, and from sunset to sunrise, varies of course throughout the year, and is only exactly twelve at the equinoxes. There are two ways one can deal with this. Either one can stick to the sixty-minute hour, and go on following the sequence for however many hours there are, or one can divide the sunrise-to-sunset (or sunset-to-sunrise) period by twelve, giving 'hours' of anything from about thirty-nine minutes to about eighty-three minutes in southern England. In either case, one should start a new sequence at sunrise or sunset with the appropriate first-hour planet.

The classic sources, such as the grimoires, either disagree or are unclear on the question. The first method is obviously simpler, but the second keeps the sequence unbroken throughout the week. One can only choose one's method and then keep to it.

Bibliography

ADLER, MARGOT *Drawing Down the Moon*, Boston (Beacon Press) 1981

ANON. *Book of Pagan Rituals*, New York (Samuel Weiser Inc.) 1978

BLAVATSKY, H. P. *Isis Unveiled*, New York (Lane) 1891

— *The Secret Doctrine*, 2 vols., Pasadena, Calif. (Theosophical University Press) 1963

BUDGE, SIR E. A. WALLIS *The Book of the Dead*, London (Rutledge & Kegan Paul) 1969

BURLAND, C. A. *The Magical Arts, a Short History*, London (Arthur Barker) 1966

— *The Arts of the Alchemists*, London (Weidenfeld & Nicholson) 1967

BUTLER, W. E. *How to Develop Clairvoyance*, London (Aquarian Press) 1968

CASE, PAUL FOSTER *The Book of Tokens, Tarot Meditations*, Los Angeles (Builders of the Adytum) 1968

CAVENDISH, RICHARD *The Black Arts*, London (Routledge & Kegan Paul) 1967

CROW, W. B. *A History of Magic, Witchcraft and Occultism*, London (Aquarian Press) 1968

— *Precious Stones, their Occult Power and Hidden Significance*, London (Aquarian Press) 1968

— *The Occult Properties of Herbs*, London (Aquarian Press) 1970

— *The Arcana of Symbolism*, London (Aquarian Press) 1970

CROWLEY, ALEISTER *Magick in Theory and Practice*, 3 vols., New York (Castle Books) n.d.

— *The Confessions of Aleister Crowley*, London (Jonathan Cape) 1969

— *The Book of the Law*, Los Angeles (Xeno Publications) 1967

— *The Book of Thoth*, Berkely, Calif. (Shambala Publications) 1969

— *777 Revised*, New York (Samuel Weiser) 1970

FORTUNE, DION *The Secrets of Dr. Taverner*, St. Paul, Minn. (Llewellyn Publications) 1962

— *Psychic Self-Defence*, London (Aquarian Press) 1930

— *The Mystical Qabalah*, London (Ernest Benn) 1935

— *Sane Occultism*, London (Aquarian Press) 1967

— *The Cosmic Doctrine, Cheltenham, Glos. (Helios Books) 1966*

FRAZER, SIR J. G. *The Golden Bough*, London (Macmillan) 1890

GARDNER, DR GERALD B. *Witchcraft Today*, London (Rider) 1954

— *The Meaning of Witchcraft*, London (Aquarian Press) 1959

GARDNER, RICHARD *The Purpose of Love*, London (Rigel Press 1970

— *Evolution through the Tarot, London (Rigel Press) 1970*

GINSBURG, C. D. *The Kabbalah*, London (Routledge & Kegan Paul) 1955

GLASS, JUSTINE *Witchcraft, the Sixth Sense—and Us*, London (Neville Spearman) 1965

GRANT, JOAN *Winged Pharoah*, London (Arthur Barker) 1937

— and KELSEY, DENYS *Many Lifetimes*, London (Gollancz) 1970

GRAVES, ROBERT *The White Goddess*, London (Faber) 1947

GRAY, EDEN *The Tarot Revealed*, New York (Bell) 1960

GRAY, W. G. *Magical Ritual Methods*, Cheltenham, Glos. (Helios Books) 1969

HEYWOOD, ROSALIND *The Sixth Sense*, London (Chatto & Windus) 1959

— *The Infinite Hive*, London (Chatto & Windus) 1964

HUGHES, PENNETHORNE *Witchcraft*, London (Longmans, Green) 1952

JOHNS, JUNE *King of the Witches—the World of Alex Sanders*, London, (Peter Davies) 1969

JUNG, CARL G. *Man and his Symbols*, London (Aldus Books) 1964

KING, FRANCIS *Ritual Magic in England (1887 to the Present Day)* , London (Neville Spearman) 1970

KNIGHT, GARETH *A Practical Guide To Qabalistic Symbolism,*, 2 vols., Cheltenham, Glos. (Helios Books) 1965

KRAMER, HEINRICH and SPRENGER, JAMES *Malleus Maleficarum,* (Cologne 1450), trans. by Montague Summers, Rodker) 1928

LELAND, CHARLES G. *Aradia, the Gospel of the Witches*, New York (Buckland Museum) 1968

LETHBRIDGE, T.C. *Witches: Investigating an Ancient Religion*, London (Routledge & Kegan Paul) 1962

LEVI, ELIPHAS *Transcendental Magic*, London (Rider) 1968

— *The History of Magic*, London (Rider) 1969

— *The Key of the Mysteries*, London (Rider) 1969

LLEWELLYN, MERVYN *Initiation and Magic*, Cheltenham, Glos. (Helios Books) 1964

MAPLE, ERIC *The Dark World of Witches*, London (Robert Hale) 1962

— *The Realms of Ghosts*, London (Robert Hale) 1964

— *The Domain of Devils*, London (Robert Hale) 1964

— *Magic, Medicine and Quackery*, London (Robert Hale) 1968

MATHERS, S.L. MACGREGOR (trans.) *The Greater Key of Solomon*, Chicago (De Laurence) 1914

— (trans.) *The Book of the Sacred Magic of Abra-Melin, the Mage*, Chicago (De Laurence) 1962

— *The Tarot,* New York (Samuel Weiser) 1969

MAYANANDA *The Tarot for Today*, London (Zeus Press) 1963

MULDOON, SYLVAN and CARRINGTON, HEREWARD *The Projection of the Astral Body,* London (Rider) 1968

MURRAY, DR. MARGARET A. *The Witch-Cult in Western Europe*, London (Oxford University Press) 1921

— *The God of the Witches*, Castle Hedingham, Essex (Daimon Press) 1962

— *The Divine King in England*, London (Faber) 1954

OPHIEL *The Art and Practice of Astral Projection*, San Francisco (Peach Publishing Co.) 1961

PAPUS *The Tarot of the Bohemians,* New York (Samuel Weiser) 1958

POWELL, ARTHUR E. *The Astral Body and Other Astral Phenomena*, London (Theosophical Publishing House) 1927

PUSHONG, CARLYLE A. *The Tarot of the Magi*, London (Regency Press) 1967

REGARDIE, ISRAEL *The Golden Dawn*, 4 vols., 3rd ed., Wisconsin (Hazel Hills Corporation) 1970

— *The Middle Pillar*, 2nd ed., St. Paul, Minn. (Llewellyn Publications) 1970

— *The Art and Meaning of Magic*, Cheltenham, Glos. (Helios Books) 1969

ROBBINS, ROSSEL HOPE *The Encyclopaedia of Witchcraft and Demonology*, London (Hamlyn Publishing Group) 1959

SCOT, REGINALD *Discoverie of Witchcraft*, London 1584

STARHAWK *The Spiral Dance*, San Francisco (Harper & Row) 1979

STRACHAN, FRANCOISE *Aquarian Guide to Occult, Mystical, Religious, Magical London and Around*, London (Aquarian Press) 1970

TORRENS, R. G. *The Inner Teachings of the Golden Dawn*, London (Neville Spearman) 1969

TREVOR-ROPER, H. R. *The European Witch-Craze of the 16th and 17th Centuries*, London (Penguin Books) 1969

WAITE, ARTHUR E. *The Pictorial Key to the Tarot*, New York (University Books Inc.) 1960

— *The Book of Black Magic and of Pacts*, Chicago (De Laurence) 1910; revised and reprinted as *The Book of Ceremonial Magic*, New York (University Books Inc.) 1961

WEINSTEIN, MARION *Earth Magic*, Custer, Washington (Phoenix Publishing) 1980

— *Positive Magic*, Custer, Washington (Phoenix Publishing) 1981

WREN, R. C. *Potter's New Encyclopaedia of Botanical Drugs and Preparations*, Rustington, Sussex (Potter & Clark) 1917

Glossary

Akasha, *Akashic Principle*	The spiritual ether; the omnipresent fifth occult element which embraces the other four—earth, air, fire, and water—and from which they stem.
Akashic Records	The traces or 'recordings' left in the Akashic Principle by every event. Advanced occultists acquire the gift of retrieving these events (e.g., details of past incarnations of themselves or others) by 'reading' the Akashic Records.
Alexandrians	Contemporary witches who received their initiation from Alex or Maxine Sanders, either directly or from other Alexandrians, and who in general adhere to their principles.
Ankh	The crux ansata or looped cross (*see* Fig. 6, p. 62), the ancient Egyptian hieroglyph for Life, widely used as a symbol of occultism in general. When combined with a five-petalled rose it is a badge of the Alexandrians (q.v.).
Ankh-ka	The ankh framed by a pair of upraised arms joined together at the shoulders (Fig.7d, p. 75). This, the ancient Egyptian hieroglyph for 'Soul-life', is used as a symbol of the Great Rite (q.v.) or of the soul-mate (q.v.).
Aradia	The commonest Wiccan name for the Goddess.
Arcana, Major *and Minor*	The two parts of the Tarot (q.v.) pack. The Major Arcana (or 'greater secrets') are the twenty-two Trumps Major; the Minor Arcana (or 'lesser secrets') are the fifty-six cards in the four suits.
Astral Body	The psychic 'double' of the physical body, consisting of substance more tenuous than matter, but grosser than mind or spirit. (See also *Etheric*.)
Astral Plane	The level of being and consciousness on which the astral body functions. It covers a broad spectrum, the 'lower astral' corresponding closely to the physical plane, the 'upper astral' approaching the purely mental. (See also *Etheric*.)
Astral Projection	The art of transferring consciousness from the physical to the astral body, so that one perceives and moves

	about in the astral plane while the physical body remains inert.
Athame	The witch's black-handled knife, engraved as shown in Figure 2, page 35. It is a purely ritual tool, unlike the white handled knife (q.v.). Its principle use is in casting and banishing the Circle, for which purpose it is interchangable with the magic sword.
Book of Shadows	The traditional book of rituals, copied out by hand by each new witch after his initiation.
'Burning Time'	A term used by some witches for the period of persecution in the Middle Ages and later. It is in fact a misnomer in England, where witches were customarily hanged, not burned.
Cabala	The ancient Hebrew system of esoteric philosophy centring on the Tree of Life (q.v.). Probably the biggest single influence on the Western occult tradition. (Also spelt Kabbala, Qabala, etc.)
Charge	The traditional words of the Goddess to her followers or 'hidden children', normally declaimed by the High Priestess at every coven Circle. The full text is given in Appendix 2.
Cone of Power	The collective psychic power raised by a coven, visualized as a cone-shaped charged field rising above the Circle.
Coven	A group of witches led by a High Priestess and High Priest and meeting regularly. The traditional membership is thirteen, but in fact it may be anything from four to twenty.
Covenstead	The meeting-place of the coven.
Deosil	Clockwise, in the direction of the sun's movement. 'White' Circles are always cast and banished deosil, in the Northern Hemisphere at least. South of the Equator, where the sun moves anti-clockwise, there are obvious arguments for casting and banishing anti-clockwise. (See also *Widdershins*.)
Drawing Down the Moon	Ritual invocation of the spirit of the Goddess into the body of the High Priestess, by the High Priest.
Element	Earth, air, fire or water—plus spirit which includes them all (see *Akasha*). These are regarded as realms or categories of nature (both material and non-material) and are not to be confused with the physicist's table of elements, which the modern witch of course accepts; nor with the alchemical elements of sulphur, mercury and salt.
Elemental	A primitive non-human entity, of the nature of one of the four elements. The word is also used of a human thought-form which, spontaneously by strong emotion or deliberately by mental effort, is split off from its human originator and acquired temporary independent existence. 'Created elementals' of the latter kind can be given healing work to do; they have also been used maliciously for psychic persecution.
Esbat	A coven meeting, other than one of the eight seasonal festivals. Some covens hold esbats weekly, some monthly at the full moon.
Etheric Body. Plane	A level of being even closer to the physical than is the astral (q.v.). The 'aura' of a person, visible to some sensitives, is associated with the etheric body.
Evocation	The ritual 'calling-forth' of a non-human entity for communication with the caller, whether through a medium or by visible manifestation. (Cf. *Invocation*.)

Fivefold Kiss, *Fivefold Salute*	The witches' ritual salute, with kisses (1) on each foot, (2) on each knee, (3) above the pubic hair, (4) on each breast, and (5) on the lips—really eight kisses in all. It is only used within the Circle, but the words that go with it (*see* pages 14 and 15) are the origin of the universal witches' salutation of greeting or parting: 'Blessed be'.
Gardnerians	Those contemporary witches who stem from the revival movement of the late Dr. Gerald Gardner.
Gnome	A primitive entity of the realm of the earth element.
Golden Dawn	The most important Western occult movement of the late nineteenth and early twentieth centuries, from which much modern ritual (including some Wiccan) derives. Aleister Crowley, Dion Fortune, W. B. Yeats, S. L. MacGregor Mathers, and A. E. Waite were among its best-known leaders.
Great Rite	The rite which is the main feature of third-degree initiation, and which is also laid down for certain festivals. It is sexual in nature, but may be 'actual' (and private to the couples concerned) or symbolic, as the participants wish.
Grimoire	A book of spells and magical procedures. The classic grimoires are mediaeval, the best-known being the *Key of Solomon* (fully, *The Greater Key of Solomon the King*) and *Abra-Melin* (*The Book of the Sacred Magic of Abra-Melin the Mage*)—though tradition says the *Key of Solomon* was compiled by King Solomon himself.
Handfasting	The witches' equivalent of a wedding ceremony.
Hereditaries	Contemporary witches who claim a continuing family practice of witchcraft from the days of the Old Religion.
Hexagram	The six-pointed star (Fig. 1, p. 34) also known as the Seal of Solomon, or (in non-occult contexts) as the star of David. Its two interlaced triangles stand for the occult principle of 'as above, so below'.
High Priest, *High Priestess*	Strictly, any witch who has taken second-degree initiation. More usually, the male and female leaders of a coven.
Inner Planes	Other levels of being and consciousness than the physical, i.e., etheric, astral, mental and spiritual.
Invocation	The ritual 'calling-in' of an entity higher than human, either for communication with the caller through a medium or by visible manifestation, or else to enter into a human body as in Drawing Down the Moon (q.v.). (Cf. *Evocation*. Some authorities apply the term 'evocation' only to evil spirits and 'invocation' only to good.)
Karma	carries from one incarnation to the next—the balance of negative against positive achievement in past lives, which must ultimately be resolved. In the occult view, no one can escape repeated reincarnation, and pass on to a higher level of existence, while his karma is still 'in the red'.
Karnayna	The commonest Wiccan name for the Horned God. Its root is the Gaulish Cernunnos.
Left-Hand Path	The general occult term for 'black' working.
Macrocosm	The great world, the universe. (Cf. *Microcosm*.)
Maiden	An appointment held by one of the women members in many covens. She is virtually the assistant High Priestess.
Manifestation	The appearance to an observer's consciousness of any non-human (or human but discarnate) entity or force. Manifestation may be visible, audible, through a

	medium, or at the most primitive end of the scale by such things as poltergeist phenomena.
Measure	A piece of thread or cord cut to the length of a postulant's body during first-degree initiation. The measure used to be kept by the coven as a guarantee of loyalty, together with hair and nail clippings. Today most covens hand it back to the initiate for the opposite reason, as a mark of trust.
Medium	A pyschically receptive person through whom discarnate entities, whether human or non-human, may communicate with incarnate humans. 'Mental mediums' convey messages orally or by automatic writing; 'physical mediums' produce material phenomena such as table-rapping.
Microcosm	The little world, man. (Cf. *Macrocosm*.)
Pentacle	A disc-shaped talisman; in particular, the metal disc (Fig. 4, p. 47) which represents the earth element among the witch's working tools.
Pentagram	The five-pointed star. With a single point uppermost, it represents a human being, and is also the invoking and banishing symbol for the various elements according to the order and direction in which it is traced. (Fig. 5, p. 49). Inverted, with two points uppermost, it can have Satanist associations; but not necessarily, for its most important 'white' meaning is as a symbol of second-degree initiation (Fig. 7b, p. 75).
Right-Hand Path	The general occult term for 'white' working.
Sabbat	A meeting of one or more covens for one of the eight seasonal festivals.
Salamander	A primitive entity of the realm of the fire element.
Scrying	Concentrating the gaze on a crystal or other object for clairvoyant purposes; the practice of clairvoyance by such methods.
Sephira (pl. *Sephiroth*)	One of the ten spheres of the Tree of Life (q.v.).
Sigil	An occult seal or sign. It should be pronounced with a soft 'g'. Examples are the sigils of Hagiel and of Venus (Figs. 12, 13, p. 159).
Sistrum	A larger equivalent of a child's rattle, used for ritual purposes. It featured in the worship of Isis, who is often shown holding one herself in Egyptian paintings.
Soul-mate	An individual whose destiny is linked with another's through succeeding incarnations.
Sylph	A primitive entity of the realm of the air element.
Tarot	The traditional pack of seventy-eight cards used for divination, but also for other purposes of occult study because of its universal symbolism. It consists of twenty-two Trumps Major (Fool, Magician, High Priestess, Empress, etc.), and four suits (Wands, Swords, Cups and Pentacles) of fourteen cards each (Ace to ten, Page, Knight Queen and King).
Temple	In the Wiccan sense, a covenstead (q.v.) appropriately decorated and furnished and used for no other purpose.
Traditionals	A sect of contemporary witches who, while not necessarily hereditary, claim to be pre-Gardnerian and pre-Alexandrian in their practices. Unlike most other witches, they work robed.
Tree of Life	The Cabalistic diagram of ten interlinked spheres of Sephiroth (singular Sephira) representing the involution of the manifest universe from the Unknowable Ultimate, and its evolution back to its source. It has been called 'the blueprint of the Western occult

	tradition'. (*See* Figs. 8-11, pp. 110-113.)
Undine	A primitive entity of the realm of the water element.
Wicca	The witches' name for their Craft. Traditionally, it comes from an Anglo-Saxon word meaning 'wisdom', though *The Oxford English Dictionary* says the root word *wiccian* (to practice witchcraft) is 'of obscure origin'.
White-Handled Knife	One of the witch's tools, used within the Circle for fashioning other tools. (Cf. *Athame*.)
Widdershins	Anti-clockwise, against the direction of the sun's movement. (Cf. *Deosil*.) Some 'black' practitioners cast their Circles widdershins.
Witches' Ladder	A string of forty beads, or a cord with forty knots, used (like a rosary) for auto-suggestive practices, to avoid the need for conscious counting.
Witches' Rune	The traditional chant of a coven while circling hand in hand to raise power. The full text is given on page 13.